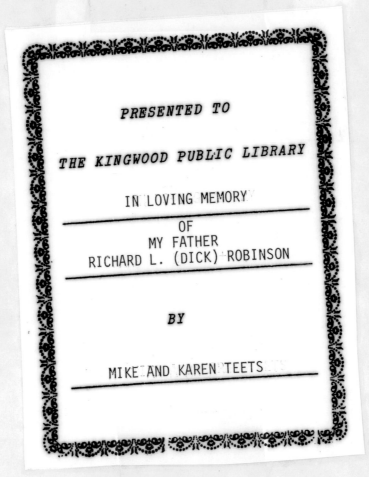

PRESENTED TO

THE KINGWOOD PUBLIC LIBRARY

IN LOVING MEMORY

OF
MY FATHER
RICHARD L. (DICK) ROBINSON

BY

MIKE AND KAREN TEETS

B-25 MITCHELL
THE MAGNIFICENT MEDIUM

by

N. L. AVERY

PHALANX
Publishing Co., Ltd.
1051 Marie Avenue
St. Paul, MN 55118 U.S.A.
612/454-0607

ISBN: 0-9625860-5-6

Library of Congress Catalog Card No: 92-061209

Edited by John W. Lambert

Cover art by John C. Valo

All other drawings by author or North American Aviation

Published by:

Phalanx Publishing Co., Ltd.
1051 Marie Avenue
St. Paul, MN 55118 USA

Printed in the United States of America

The First of 9,889

And the last

4

James Howard Kindelberger

1895 - 1962

John Leland Atwood

1904 -

Under whose leadership North American Aviation Inc. rose from obscurity to one of the giants of aviation, building more military airplanes than any other company.

"Quality cannot be inspected into a product, it must be built into it."

(Sign over assembly bay at North American, Inglewood)

General William C. "Billy" Mitchell

1879 - 1936

U.S. Army

Assistant Chief of the Air Service 1919 - 1925 who sacrificed his career attempting to convince higher authority that the airplane was a potential offensive weapon and that American military aviation should be a separate, independent force, equal to the Army and Navy.

Table of Contents

FOREWARD

The B-25 "Mitchell" was designed to fulfill an Army Air Corps concept developed in the late 1930s and classified as a "medium" bomber. This classification and nomenclature seemed to imply or specify that it would be of intermediate size, range, load capacity, speed, maneuverability and defensive firepower and also that its cost and crew size be medium in the scale of military aircraft. How this concept has survived is not very clear in modern aircraft with electronically directed weapons and fighter - attack combinations. The F-111 alone might today be called a medium bomber in many respects.

As chief engineer at North American Aviation during the design of the B-25, my objectives were to make a sturdy, adaptable design and especially to provide a stable, easy stalling wing profile and generally forgiving flying characteristics. This was, of course, our policy in all designs. However, the B-25 did not offer the opportunity for exceptional drag reduction and really high speed which we were able to incorporate in the P-51 Mustang by exploiting the possibilities in the radiator cooling drag reduction.

The B-25 wing stall characteristics received a great deal of attention, and I selected a wing tip profile that was especially favorable from a stalling point of view. This can be noted today by examining the aileron trailing edge near the tip where the reflex, or reverse camber, can be observed. This paid off in short field landings and takeoffs, as from the deck of an aircraft carrier.

Another aspect of the design worth noting is the break in the wing dihedral at the engine nacelle. This was not intentional, and the original design involved a continuous upsweep or dihedral all the way to the tip. This configuration was easy to fly and made very graceful rudder turns, but was unacceptable from a military point of view. Bombing runs required flat turns - and in order to make them without banking into the turns, the aileron controls had to be applied against the turn, making the pilot's job very difficult in executing an accurate bomb run.

The B-25 was used primarily in the Pacific in the Island campaigns, and the concept that the medium bomber was just a small B-17 or B-29 with the same gun turret protection and target complex underwent major modifications. The targets were more tactical than strategic - including supply ships and beach installations - so some very creative people in the Air Corps, especially "Pappy" Gunn who had operated an airline in the Philippines before the war, took the lead in changing the mission into an attack mode and installed eight forward-firing .50 caliber machine guns which made the plane very effective for attack purposes. These modifications and changes were shortly incorporated at the factory, greatly enhancing its military value. A 75 millimeter cannon was installed in some planes and was used effectively in certain missions.

Norm Avery has put in a tremendous amount of effort in research and compilation of data over a long period, and this book should endure as a journal of record and should be interesting to anyone, military or civilian, who has an interest in the aviation realities of the Great War.

J. Leland Atwood
March 26, 1992

PREFACE and ACKNOWLEDGEMENTS

By the late 1930s the armament factories of America had begun a period of expansion and increased production as the probability of a global conflict appeared ever more likely. Orders for military aircraft, both domestic and export, steadily increased and by the time of the Pearl Harbor attack exceeded production of World War I. North American was not the largest of the nation's aircraft manufacturers but it was one of the busiest. Even after several expansions from the original plant, the floor space became inadequate for the simultaneous production of three types of airplanes. Crowded shops and assembly lines were turning out NA-73 Mustang fighters and Harvard trainers for Britain and AT-6 trainers and B-25 bombers for the Army Air Corps. In the experimental shops the twin engine, high altitude, pressurized XB-28 bomber was taking final form.

Adjacent Mines Field bustled with increasing activity. Douglas, Northrop, North American and the military kept a busy flight line and flight testing from the field was routine. Immediately after the attack on Pearl Harbor the pace rose dramatically and Mines Field was functioning at maximum capacity.

Although the B-25 placed second in the medium bomber competition of 1939, it was built in greater numbers than any other American twin engine bomber and in greater numbers than any other American twin engine combat airplane except the P-38. A total of nearly 10,000 B-25s and an additional 1,340 equivalent units in spare parts were produced by North American over a continuous production period of 48 months.

The service tenure of the Mitchell did not end with cessation of World War II but continued on with the USAF well into the 1950s and in the service of other nations for another decade. Post war surplus sales provided a significant number for civilian buyers and many restored B-25s are airworthy today. By any standard it was an honest product that performed and endured far beyond the expectations of its creators.

The assistance of many individuals and organizations has made it possible to tell part of the story of one of the most outstanding aircraft of World War II and of the company and the people who produced and flew it.

I am deeply indebted to the following whose generosity of time and material made it all come together. Mr. Lee Atwood answered many questions no one else could. Gene Boswell gave enthusiastic support and made possible my access to much company material. Mr. E.W. Virgin wrote informative letters, supplied pages from his log books and provided references to others who flew Old Number 1. Dan Hagedorn at the National Air and Space Museum assisted "above and beyond the call". Fellow 'Bald Eagles' from North American Aviation who well remember those busy wartime years and contributed information are:

Bob Chilton
Roy Ferren
George Bussier
Paul Peterson
Richard Schleicher
W.A. Spivak
Rudy Stolz
Don Kennedy
Ed Stewart
Bill Barker
Paul Brewer

Bill Carr
A.C. "Bud" Snyder
Roland Bliss
Ed Pierce
Jim Dunham
Ed Horkey
E.C. Holton
George Mellinger
Don Rogerson
George Wing
John Young

Photographs and assistance which provided much helpful information were also received from:

Kenn Rust
Gerard Casius
Frank Cook
George Hatcher
Kenneth Sumney
Mrs. A.E. Olson
A.E. Walker
Mike Kusenda
Larry Wilson
LTCR S.J. Bottomley
Phil Marchese
William H. Cather
Kenneth Wilson
Mrs. Lila Fox
James A. Philpott
Robert Johnson
Dave Graham
Robert O'Dell
Douglas Olson
Clarence Becker
Mark Copeland

Bob Davisson
Carl Scholl
Ray Wagner
Frank Hanley
Arnold C. Sayer
John Hooser
Don Holloway
Charles Porter
William Larkins
P.R. Leatherwood
Frank Lary
Bill Ward
Peyton Jacobson
Ole Griffith
Bruce Doyle
Bob Haney
Robert L. Feik
Nico Geldhof
William H. Cather
Howard Naslund

The following organizations were also of assistance:

North American Aviation, Inc./Rockwell International
Canadian Aviation Historical Society
American Aviation Historical Society
National Archives
USAF Museum
National Air & Space Museum
Tailhook Association
San Diego Aerospace Museum
Hayes Aircraft Company
AFSHRC, Maxwell AFB
Naval Ordnance Test Station

Norm Avery

1 B-25 Heritage

The subject of this book, the B-25 Mitchell, was uniquely a product of American ingenuity, business acumen and the native skill of North American Aviation Company employees. And yet, through corporate genealogy it owed something of its ancestry to a Dutch aviation pioneer born on Java in 1890.

Tony Fokker was only four years old when his parents, coffee planters in the East Indies, returned him and his sister to Holland for their formal education. Although a mediocre scholar, the boy showed a distinct aptitude for things mechanical, and while still a teenager was bitten by the aviation bug. Teaching himself to fly, he flung himself into the business of building frail aircraft by the time he was twenty. World War I served as a springboard for his business then located in Germany.

Surviving the defeat of the Kaiser's Germany, and the depression that followed, he nimbly transferred operations to the Netherlands. With an eye toward the foreign market he opened a sales office in New York in 1920. General Billy Mitchell visited the Fokker works in Holland in 1922 on behalf of the fledgling Army Air Service and as a result Fokker received a contract for the rebuilding of one hundred DH-4s and the manufacture of thirty others.

Even at this late date the American aircraft industry was in an embryonic stage, and while Fokker's American efforts were primarily targeted at the commercial market, it was military manufacturing that spurred the Dutch firm. Fokker leased an empty factory in Hasbrouck Heights, New Jersey in 1924 to further his U.S. sales.

Just four years later American investors, tantalized by the potential of aviation, had formed a holding company named North American Aviation. Its initial major acquisitions were Fokker Corporation of America and Berliner-Joyce. In rapid order a labyrinth of transactions intermingled Curtiss Aeroplane, Transcontinental Air Transport, Eastern Air Transport, Douglas Aircraft, Curtiss-Wright, Ford Instrument, Sperry, and ultimately General Motors. The latter became a 40% owner of the burgeoning aviation company while Tony Fokker retained 20%.

Over the next few years companies were spun in and out of the parent, the Fokker name was dropped, and by 1936 Tony Fokker had been bought out and turned his efforts to his Holland based company.

From that point on North American took on a decidedly American look under the initial leadership of a GM executive, Ernest Breech. To manage Eastern Air Transport (later Eastern Air Lines) Captain Eddie Rickenbacker, America's top ace of World War I was brought into the fold as a vice president. (By 1938 NAA divested itself of the airline in compliance with the Air Mail Act of 1934.) Breech also hired three young engineers away from Douglas: James H. "Dutch" Kindelberger, John L. "Lee" Atwood and Stan Smithson.[1]

From its plant in Dundalk, Maryland, then NAAs manufacturing facility, the team designed, tested and won contracts from the Army Air Corps for the O-47 observation plane, (Company designation GA-15) and the BT-9 trainer (NA-16 later modified as the NA-19). But this surge of business only served to show the inadequacy of the Maryland plant and North American looked west.

Kindelberger proposed relocating the company from Maryland to Southern California where weather permits year round flight testing and where a favorable labor market existed. In September North American signed a lease with the City of Los Angeles for twenty acres on the south east corner of Mines Field in Inglewood, now part of Los Angeles International Airport. Construction of the new plant began in early October and was completed in January 1936.

The move from Maryland was made before completion of a Navy contract for floats for Curtiss SOC-1

Fokker customers received more than quality as shown by the burnished panels on the nose and landing gear of this Super Universal. The Universal six passenger transport was the first Fokker airplane designed and built in the United States. (NAA)

Twelve production examples of the Berliner/Joyce XP-16 followed the prototype for the Army Air Corps. This photo from July, 1930 is one of comparatively few from the B/J files. (NAA)

GMAC produced five GA-43 ten passenger commercial transports in 1933. Victims of poor timing, they were ready for sale almost concurrently with a government edict that passenger transports be equipped with two or more engines. NC-13903 was briefly in service with Western Air Lines. (NAA)

airplanes and parts and tooling for these units were shipped to the new plant for completion. About seventy-five employees and their families joined the westward trek. Many were technicians with exceptional skills in sheet metal fabrication and aircraft structure. Some had worked directly for Fokker, their employment continuing on with GMAC, B/J and finally, North American. A few native Californians were soon added to the payroll bringing the total work force to about 150. As Dutch Kindelberger so aptly phrased it,"You were a native Californian as soon as you parked your trailer."

The BT-9 contract represented substantial business but wouldn't last forever. In addition to courting the Air Corps, a sales effort was also directed toward an increasingly favorable foreign market. Though slow at first, foreign sales increased and between 1936 and 1938 export contracts, some for one airplane each, were received from Japan, Holland, Australia, Argentina, Honduras, Sweden and Venezuela. The Air Corps and National Guard ordered 0-47 observation types and the company, which was recovering from the depression in grand style, delivered eighty-two airplanes in 1938.

As the threat of war in Europe increased, the first large orders were received. In 1938 Argentina accepted thirty NA-16-4F trainers and China accepted another thirty-five. Britain placed an order for two hundred Harvards, an unprecedented number. In August the Air Corps accepted sixty BC-1 trainers and O-47 observation types, the highest delivery of aircraft in one month by any

American aircraft company since World War I. The elusive threshold of success had been crossed. From low on the list of aircraft manufacturers in 1936, North American had reached the front ranks.

To understand this rapid rise to success, it is necessary to look beyond the established quality of North American management and its organization and products. The time could not have been better. The years beginning in 1935 were the most advantageous for a new company entering the aircraft business since World War I. Both domestic and foreign military export sales had begun a significant upward trend and although North American had become a prominent supplier of the American military, the company delivered more airplanes to foreign nations than to American markets.[2]

North American's first venture in the twin engine field was the NA-21 "Dragon" bomber of 1937 and later that year design was also begun on the NA-40 twin engine attack bomber. Both were technically successful but neither resulted in a production contract. The third attempt, in response to an Air Corps Circular Proposal of January 1939, defined a twin engine type designed to the medium bomber specification. On the basis of design proposals only, the company received a contract for 184 examples designated B-25.

Denied permission to purchase P-40 fighters from Curtiss, the British Air Ministry approached North American in 1940 with a request that they produce P-40s for the RAF. Kindelberger countered with a proposal to design

NAA first entered the trainer competition in 1935 with the NA-16 for the Army Air Corps. Ordered in quantity, it set the design for its successors, the BT-9, BC-1, AT-6 and SNJ trainers. (NAA)

The basic BT-9 design was carried through on other trainers of which NAA produced over 17,500 examples. (NAA)

NAA's first entry in the twin engine field was the NA-21 Dragon bomber, turbo supercharged for high altitude and equipped with power operated turrets. Never produced, it served as a laboratory aircraft at Wright Field. (NAA)

and produce a completely new fighter incorporating the latest technology and combat requirements. The desperate British agreed, ordered a yet to be designed prototype and 320 examples of an unproven design. Four months later test pilot Vance Breese lifted the sleek NA-73X from the Mines Field runway and the P-51 was born.

The turning point for the American aircraft industry was 16 May 1940 when President Roosevelt, in his national defense message, asked Congress for 50,000 airplanes and an expanded industry capable of producing that number annually. His request was beyond comprehension as the entire aircraft industry was producing about 500 per month at the time. By September America had adequate incentive to speed production. The Battle of Britain presented a clear picture of the future.

A most ambitious plan, initiated by the newly created Office of Procurement Management, provided for the might of the American automotive industry to fabricate parts and assemblies to be supplied to new plants built for and operated by the major aircraft firms. Construction of new factories began on a priority basis. North American's new B-25 plant was constructed at Fairfax Airport at Kansas City, Kansas and the first B-25 was delivered from the new facility just two weeks after the Pearl Harbor

attack. North American's automotive partner in this new arrangement was logically, General Motors, their old affiliate since 1930.

Expansion of the industry and the company progressed steadily. By the time of the Pearl Harbor attack 23,000 employees wore the North American badge, quite an increase from 150 in 1934. Production reached 325 airplanes a month and the American aircraft industry had boosted production to approximately 2,500 airplanes monthly, increasing at a rate of 200 per month.

In an address at the Carnegie Institute of Technology a week before Pearl Harbor, Kindelberger summarized the almost unbelievable accomplishment: "It is hard now to realize that the aircraft industry has had the green light for little more than a year. So much has been accomplished in that time that it seems impossible, looking back, that we have been able to do as much in that period as Germany did in five years...and it is only the beginning."

NOTES TO CHAPTER 1

1. **Brief History of NAA, Inc., Date of Incorporation Through 31 Dec 1934,** North American Aviation, Inc. Pgs. 1-13
2. Oakley, Ralph **North American Aviation, Its Products and People,** American Aviation Historical Society Vol 19, No. 2, Summer, 1974 pgs 134-144

No greater fame could a product bring its maker than the NA-73X brought North American. Designed for the British, unwanted by the U.S. Air Corps, it became the immortal P-51. (NAA)

12

The Curtiss B-2 was placed in production in 1929 and 12 were delivered. The box kite tail and biplane configuration were representative of WW I design. With 90' wing span, two Curtiss Conqueror engines gave a top speed of 130 MPH and a ceiling of 16,140 feet. (NASM 6218 AC)

Fully underhung nacelles, pioneered on the antecedent Fokker XB-8, were used on all subsequent General Aviation Corp. and NAA twin engine airplanes. After the NA-40 this concept was used almost entirely by most other companies. (NAA)

Built by the Martin Aircraft Company to a design by the Engineering Department at Wright Field, the B-10 in several variants became the mainstay of the American bomber force during the early 1930s. (NASM 169368AC)

Bomber Development Between the Wars

The U.S. Army Air Service emerged from World War I with an excellent record, its true capabilities scarcely realized by the brief involvement in Europe. This new fighting force and its civilian industrial base portended a new technology of great potential but along with other services, it fell victim to enthusiastic demobilization dominated by isolationist attitudes. For nearly two decades it struggled through political controversies attempting to achieve recognition as a unified and independent air force, equal in status to the Army and Navy.

Back of this considerable effort was the driving force of Colonel William C. Mitchell, Assistant Chief of the Air Service from 1919 to 1925. His six turbulent years in office earned his distinction among military top brass and War Department officials as the most unpopular and outspoken critic of Air Service direction. His dissidence and frequent intemperate criticism finally led to a charge of insubordination, conviction by courts martial and dismissal from the service in 1925. Mitchell's views were ultimately acknowledged to have been years ahead of his time and before World War II he was posthumously recognized for many of his then discordant opinions, some of which proved prophetically correct.

The years of the Mitchell crusade were not totally in vain for the Air Service. The Air Corps Act of 1926 advanced the service to corps status and in 1933, after seven more years of controversy, hearings and debates, a GHQ air force was established. Considered by most officers as a limited compromise at best, it placed offensive aviation under a unified command. [1]

Military appropriations were lean, all services competed for funds and the Air Service fought a seemingly endless up hill battle. During the first post war decade military aviation was forced to rely on equipment from wartime surplus stocks. A great number of Liberty engines, Curtiss JN-4 trainers and British SE-5s supplied much of the military needs. However economical, it stifled progress of the aircraft and engine industry, seriously delaying the development of modern technology. Strange as it seems, however, appropriations for Air Service research and development for the first three post war fiscal years were higher than for any subsequent time prior to 1936.[2]

Post war aircraft development consisted of little more than advanced World War I design applied to large, boxy, wire braced biplanes of great inherent drag. Typical were the Martin MB-2 of 1921, the huge Barling triplane of 1933 and the big Keystones. The first twin engine aircraft to be classified as a 'medium bomber' was the Curtiss NBS-1 powered by two Liberty engines. Contracted for in 1922, the 100 examples ordered marked the first such procurement of a significant quantity. All lacked offensive capability and their purpose, in step with the times, remained in direct support of ground forces.

By 1927 the post World War I period of military aviation came to a welcome end as surplus stocks of aircraft, engines and other related equipment became exhausted. This was also hastened in part by new developments and engineering and procedural policies.

After the Air Service was advanced to corps status and the Materiel Division was established at Wright Field, conditions became more favorable for the advancement of military aircraft design. This also resulted in part from a brief period of expansion with funding for the procurement of new, experimental models. A bombardment board of eight officers headed by Major Hugh Knerr was formed to make recommendations for changes and procurement of new types of bombardment aircraft and the development and improvement of related equipment.

Early in 1928 the board recommended procurement of the Keystone B-1 and LB-6; the Atlantic LB-2, the Curtiss B-2 and the Huff-Deland bombers. All biplanes, these aircraft appeared to differ little from earlier types but significant improvements were incorporated and capabilities increased by new geared engines of greater power and reliability. By that time developments had also brought about the recognition of tactical bomber concepts and more accurately defined the requirements for attack aircraft and light and heavy bombers.

During the 1920s, years of lean funding and a predominance of horse cavalry thinking, relatively few new airplanes were actually procured and placed in service. This deficiency was severely criticized and by Billy Mitchell in particular. Major Thurman Bane, a pilot with engineering experience and the capable administrator of the Engineering Division at McCook Field, stated the following reasons: [3]

1. Too much time and money spent on projects of questionable value.
2. Hasty decisions when initiating new projects.
3. Time and difficulty in securing experimental airplanes; legal technicalities and associated problems often leading to contract cancellations.
4. Dropping projects of value and starting others of doubtful value.
5. Lack of adequate definition of requirements.
6. Too much work at the Engineering Division at one time; as many as 30 airplanes in work.

7. Inconsistent development program.

8. Very few aircraft manufacturers were considered competent to design and build military aircraft.

The Engineering Division considered the last point the most significant and the reason that design and construction of military aircraft was being accomplished within the service. Under the existing conditions this policy was not conducive to industrial competition. Fortunately, additional aircraft fabricators came into being and established companies made increasing gains in capabilities.

By 1930 the advent of all metal aircraft construction ushered in a new era of aeronautical technology. It was not a new concept, however, as the method was pioneered in steel during World War I by Dr. Hugo Junkers in Germany and later used by Ford on the famous tri-motor. Aluminum alloys were developed to replace the steel and was so utilized that thin, metal skin carried great loads, thus saving a great amount of weight.

Replacing the welded steel tube and fabric covered structure, the thin skins were riveted to the primary frames and ribs. As the structure "loaded" in flight the riveted skins carried tensile and torsional loads. This all metal "stressed skin" design made possible full cantilever wings of great strength, retractable landing gears and the elimination of drag producing external wheels and wire wing bracing. Heavier, more effective armament was more readily installed.

Streamlining became more fact than desire and the airplanes now appearing had top speeds about double that of the earlier biplanes. Although landing speeds rose accordingly, this was held to an acceptable level by the almost universal use of wing flaps. Engine manufacturers were producing ever more reliable, efficient and powerful engines. The potential within grasp was now that of earlier dreams. To make a bad pun - the sky was the limit. Great things had suddenly become possible.

As if to signify a new beginning the Tactical School at Langley Field suggested in 1930 that because of the uncertainty of the meaning of the terms Day - Night - Light - Heavy and Long Range as applied to bombers, that the use of these terms should be discontinued. The Chief of the Air Corps concurred and the decision was made to use the single 'B' as a prefix to a designated numeral.[4]

New specifications for a 'fast day and night bomber' - still hanging on to the vague categorical descriptions - were issued that year. In response to these requirements experimental models were submitted by the Keystone Company (Curtiss Wright), the Stout Metal Aircraft Division of The Ford Motor Company, the Glenn L. Martin Company and the Boeing Aircraft Company. The Keystone and Ford entries were soon after withdrawn from the competition leaving Boeing and Martin to fight it out. Strange as it seems and in spite of the deficiencies and failure to meet requirements, it was Boeing's B-9 that

received the higher rating of merit but Martin's B-10, albeit after considerable rework, won the production contracts.[5]

Designated XB-906, Ford's entry was little more than a "Tin Goose" commercial tri-motor revised to incorporate a bomb bay, provisions for a bombardier and related equipment and a minimal number of guns. Wheel 'pants' failed to offset the landing gear drag although anti-drag rings were fitted to the 500 HP R-1340 engines. Gun handling was clumsy at best and the inspection board devoted little time to the airplane which demonstrated no advancement in design whatsoever.

Keystone's XB-908 was little better. Designed as an all metal, low wing monoplane with retractable landing gears, it was powered by two Curtiss in-line, Conqueror engines. Unimpressed after inspecting the mock up, the review board declined to provide further funding. The Keystone Company ceased operations after completion of their biplane contracts in 1932.

The Boeing XB-901 (B-9) and Martin's XB-907 (B-10) represented notable design advancement and showed considerable promise. The B-10 in several variants was ultimately produced in significant numbers. Three of the entries were designed around an internal bomb bay, finally, after 20 years, getting the high drag pay load out of the slipstream. Boeing's B-9 was the single exception.

Revised procurement policies introduced by that time had a significant bearing on the acquisition of new aircraft for the military. Under those policies new, experimental models could be secured by the government at no immediate cost. Completed airplanes, engines and equipment were furnished by the aircraft industry while the Materiel Division at Wright Field served in an advisory capacity until the completed prototype was delivered for testing. This coordinated effort reduced by as much as one year the time required to ready a prototype for test as compared to the previous policy of contracting for a fully completed experimental airplane.[6]

How far this customer - supplier relationship might be carried is clearly demonstrated by Martin's B-10.

Developed from the advanced commercial "Monomail", the B-9 was characterized by a full cantilever wing, a long, cigar shaped fuselage, retractable landing gear and all metal construction. Crew comforts remained spartan and the pilot, two gunners and bombardier were out in the snow in open cockpits. Powered by two 575 HP Pratt & Whitney engines and anti-drag rings, top speed was 163 MPH at sea level.

The second prototype, powered by two Curtiss V-1570 in-line, liquid cooled Conqueror engines did a bit better at 173 MPH and was the last in-line engine to power an American bomber for over 10 years.

Of the six B-9s delivered the remaining examples mounted Pratt & Whitney R-1860 engines with anti-drag rings. These variants topped out at 188 MPH with a range of 540 miles with one ton of bombs. One example was supercharged and gave outstanding performance at high altitude.

The B-9 was not considered a success and failed to meet Air Corps requirements. It was an economy design from the Monomail, carried the bombs on external racks and was plagued with structural deficiencies and high maintenance costs. After some accidents the Engineering Section at Wright Field recommended that remaining examples be withdrawn from service.

Martin's XB-907 was an outstanding example of the manufacturer supplying the airplane and Wright Field Engineering acting as advisor and more. Martin had preferred to enter the competition with a thin wing biplane, a viewpoint difficult to understand when rapidly changing times made it clear that the type was already obsolete. Further, the design was not accomplished by the Martin engineering department but was done by the Materiel Division beginning in 1929.

Martin wisely acceded to the Materiel Division and proceeded with detail design, submitting the final plans in late 1931. The new airplane was also of all metal construction, full cantilever low wing and retractable landing gears. The internal bomb bay got the pay load out of the slip stream. Except for the bombardier who rode in comparative comfort in the enclosed nose, the other crew members suffered the open cockpits.

Powered by Wright R-1820 engines of 600 HP the 907 prototype had a top speed of 197 MPH, faster than all current pursuits, and a service ceiling of 20,000 feet.

The XB-907 was first flown at the Martin plant in February 1932 and further tested at Wright Field in April. Flight characteristics were far from acceptable resulting in extensive modification as suggested by the Materiel Division, the work including the addition of a top, forward gun turret. With a bit more work the airplane met acceptability requirements.

In November 1932, the Bombardment Board accepted the reworked XB-907 as suitable for procurement and redesignated the airplane B-10. In January, 1933, forty-eight B-10s were ordered with improved crew accommodations by the addition of canopies over the pilot, radioman and rear gunner. The B-10B, powered by 775 HP Wright Cyclones was built in more numbers than

any other variant, 103 being delivered between 1935 and 1936, one of the largest contracts placed since World War I.

Designated Model 139 by Martin, B-10 variants were exported in substantial numbers to Holland, Argentina and Turkey. The long range, Model B-12A, was fitted with auxiliary fuel tanks and used briefly in the Air Mail Service during the temporary and tragic period when the Army carried the air mail after the Roosevelt Administration temporarily canceled commercial mail contracts. The experiences of the longer air mail flights brought to attention the necessity for greater crew comfort and freedom of action, subjects addressed on future bomber designs.

Due to depressed financial conditions at the time and limited appropriations, consideration was given to converting B-10s to attack, observation types and even multi-seat fighters. Such after thoughts have never proven advantageous and in the final analyses the deficiencies, complexities and costs far outweighed any possible savings or benefits.

For all its faults the B-10 served as the mainstay of the American bomber force throughout the mid 1930s, some continuing in service into World War II. The series represented a significant accomplishment at the time and when Glenn Martin received the Collier Trophy in 1932 for the year's most outstanding aeronautical achievement, the Materiel Division felt slighted for no mention of their considerable contribution.

The rapid advance in aircraft design and construction that took place in the early 1930s, combined with the development and production of more powerful engines of great reliability, made clear the practicality and strategic value of a very long range bomber. The bombardment visionaries had long awaited such developments. Envisioned was an aircraft capable of carrying at least a ton of bombs at 200 MPH for a distance of 5,000 miles which would provide the capability of protecting or reinforcing Hawaii, Panama or Alaska from the United States without intermediate refueling stops.

Early in 1934 preliminary design and study contracts were authorized to the Boeing and Martin companies. The Martin effort was later dropped in favor

Replacement for the B-10 was awarded to Douglas for the B-18. A reliable and docile craft, it was an obvious descendant of the venerable DC-3. Built in considerable numbers, some were sold on the export market and saw service well into World War II. (USAF)

of greater funding to the Boeing design, originally designated XBLR-1 and later redesignated XB-15. A subsequent contract was issued in 1934 for further, more advanced design. Construction got underway in 1935 and the first flight was on 15 October, 1937.

The airplane was overweight for the available 1,000 HP Pratt & Whitney R-1830 engines but valuable data could be obtained within the parameters of the capability. It was a big airplane for the time with a wing span of 149 feet and a gross weight of 70,000 pounds.

The XB-15 provided valuable information for future designs and proved the feasibility of a true strategic bomber. Correctly envisioned were the tremendous effects of long range, heavy mass bombing and thus were the future doctrines of air power developed.

While the successful XB-15 program was well under way at Boeing, the Air Corps contracted with the Douglas company in Santa Monica, California for a strategic bomber of even greater size, the XBLR-2, to become labeled by the Army the XB-19. Four Wright R-3350 engines of 2,000 HP powered the 212 foot wing span behemoth at a top speed of 224 MPH. Range was 7,000 miles with an impressive 6,000 pound bomb load.

On 27 June, 1941 the huge bomber first took off from what, in retrospect, seems like a rather diminutive Clover Field near the Santa Monica coast. It is certain that such circumstances would not be authorized today for a first flight of such magnitude. But in those golden days first flights were made from the field where the factory was located. And the employees loved it.

It was the author's good fortune to have witnessed this historic event from the North American factory several miles away. The P-40 chase planes resembled sparrows harassing a hawk.

The single wheel main landing gears on XB-19 mounted such huge tires that to minimize the jolt, friction and drag to get the wheels rolling on touch down, an in flight wheel rotation device was activated on final approach.

Following a successful test program from which more valuable information was obtained, the big bomber spent a number of years as a laboratory airplane.

It was readily apparent in 1934 that the Martin B-10s were rapidly reaching obsolescence and a specification was issued that year for a replacement multi-engine bomber with approximately double the payload and range of the B-10. The designation 'B' for bomber had become standardized but the terms light, medium and heavy continued to be used in a general way. The specification which was technically for a medium bomber, drew considerable response. Bellanca, Douglas, Burnelli, Martin, Boeing and North American all entered the competition.[7]

The Martin entry, Model 146, was an enlarged and advanced B-10, a clean design powered by two Wright R-1820 engines and of greater load and range than its predecessor. Crew accommodations were also improved to some extent. No production contract resulted from the test program at Wright Field.[8]

The Douglas entry, the DB-1, ordered in greater numbers than any of the competitive models, proved a reliable airplane if not representing a great deal of advancement in design. Powered by two Wright R-1820 engines of 930 HP a top speed of 220 MPH was attained with 25,000 foot ceiling and a range of 1,000 miles with over a ton of bombs. The wings, tail and landing gear left no doubt of its DC-3 ancestry.[9]

The fully enclosed interior was well received by air crews who thought it pure luxury compared to the open cockpits of the B-10. No more bulky, uncomfortable flight suits were required with the new airplane. Equipment featured a power operated top turret and automatic flight control.

Although the DB-1 was in an excellent position for a production contract, Douglas declined to deliver the prototype for the price offered by the government. Program delays occurred while differences were being settled, ultimately in favor of Douglas. After the usual testing an Air Corps flight test board accepted the DB-1 on an "as is" basis with recommendations for a number of changes.[10]

The airplane was found satisfactory, if not outstanding, and placed in production as B-18, deliveries beginning in February 1937. Orders were placed in June for 177 B-18As followed in April 1938 by an additional 217. As Britain came ever closer to war, Canada ordered twenty. Following America's entry into World War II 122 B-18Bs were ordered by the Air Corps and equipped with Magnetic Airborne Detector gear for duty in the Atlantic and Caribbean areas. Many B-18s served well into the war as patrol aircraft.

Efforts were made in 1937 to provide better performance than the B-18s which proved to be a reliable, docile bomber but not adequate for projected requirements. A true replacement for the B-10 had not really come forth, the quantities of B-18s contracted notwithstanding.

The Douglas Company had planned to update the B-18 with a variant powered by Wright R-2600 engines but opted instead for an entirely new design bearing no resemblance to the B-18. The new airplane, designated B-23, featured a larger, more streamlined fuselage, Wright R-2600 engines and heavier armament.

Performance was respectable with a top speed of 282 MPH and a range of 1,400 miles with a 4,000 pound bomb load and a service ceiling of 31,600 feet. The first flight took place in July 1939. Only thirty-eight were produced.

Another entry in the February 1937 competition for a twin engine bomber of improved performance was

North American's XB-21 DRAGON. Construction began in January 1936 and the airplane was completed in February 1937.

A large airplane of 40,000 pounds, the XB-21 was powered by two supercharged Pratt & Whitney R-2180 engines which gave a top speed of 220 MPH, a range of 1,950 miles with 2,200 pounds of bombs or 660 miles with a 10,000 pound bomb load. Service ceiling was 25,000 feet.

The DRAGON was plagued by engine problems, was considered underpowered and was nearly lost to fire over metropolitan Los Angeles. The cost was nearly double that of the B-18 and the project was dropped in favor of continued B-18 production and a relatively small number of B-23s.

The XB-21 continued in service for several years as a laboratory airplane.

Boeing's response to the request for a new bomber was the bold approach. Boeing engineers took full advantage of the proposal's failure to specify precisely the number of engines desired to power the proposed airplane. Their new design was based on four Pratt & Whitney R-1690 engines of 750 HP. The most advanced bomber to date, the Model 299 (XB-17) was capable of a 2,500 pound bomb load at over 200 MPH in excess of 2,000 miles.

Soon referred to as the "Flying Fortress", Boeing's new creation thrilled the nation with a 232 mile per hour non stop flight from Seattle to Wright Field at Dayton, Ohio.[11]

During tests and through no fault of the airplane, the prototype crashed in demonstration. Quick to recognize the many merits of the dynamic new bomber, the Air Corps enthusiastically recommended that it be placed in immediate production.

But the B-18 did not die easily. Unfortunately the more generous funding of two years in the future did not exist and the cost of the new Boeing XB-17 was more than double that of the production B-18. To receive more airplanes for given funds the government authorized the purchase of an additional 133 B-18s and 13 YB-17s to be delivered between January and August 1937.[12] This was a classic example of shortsighted procurement but there may have been an unseen advantage to what seemed a mistake at the time. The greater number of B-18s may well have provided more qualified multi-engine pilots, sorely needed when hostilities began.

The depression years had not run out and funds were allocated accordingly. It is also doubtful that more than a few people in the military realized all that the XB-17 portended. In October 1938 the Adjutant General informed the Chief of the Air Corps that four engine bombers were not to be included in procurement from the 1940-1941 funds.[13] This view was soon to change as the YB-17s showed the world what a good bomber was. As Europe edged ever closer to war the requirements for the American military became steadily clearer. The planners wanted another four engine bomber as a back up and as an additional source of supply.

Thus did Consolidated's B-24 come into being when the Air Corps ordered the prototype Model 32. Design began in September 1938. So sure was the Army of success, and they were right, that limited orders were placed before the first flight of the prototype.

In 1937 the Materiel Division investigated the possibilities of a twin engine attack bomber of considerably improved performance over the single engine types then in use, none of which was particularly satisfactory. All had become inadequate because of increased requirements of speed, armament and external stores necessary for effective strikes against mechanized forces.

On the negative side a twin engine design represented a considerable increase in cost and weight, the latter expected to cause some loss of maneuverability and subsequent vulnerability to ground fire. Concerns existed that a two engine type would soon become as overloaded as had the single engine variants. A significant increase in speed was considered essential. Due to the projected higher speeds the bomb load assumed greater importance than forward fire power although the latter remained a significant requirement. To contribute to surprise attack approaches, over-the-wing exhaust tail pipes were favored.[14]

Recognizing the growth capabilities and advantages of the concept, in March 1938, the Air Corps issued Circular Proposal Number 38-385 defining the requirements. Generally specified was a 1,200 pound payload and a 1,200 mile range at speeds well in excess of 200 MPH.[15]

Responses were received from Bell, Boeing-Stearman, Douglas, Martin and North American. Except for the Bell entry powered by two liquid cooled, in line Allison engines, the others utilized air cooled radials. All were of metal construction and incorporated retractable landing gears and internal bomb bays. The Martin and Boeing-Stearman retained the tail dragger configuration.

The competition seemed jinxed from the start, some good airplanes notwithstanding. Although an impressive design, the Bell Model 9 was withdrawn from the competition. The Douglas 7B crashed with fatalities, and somewhat ironically, in North American's parking lot. Changes to the XA-21 took Boeing-Stearman out due to unacceptable speed reduction. North American was on the threshold of success having neared completion of the demonstration program when the NA-40 was lost in a non fatal crash at Wright Field.

Apparently trying for better luck next time the Air Corps canceled the competition and requested new bids without prototypes. New bids were submitted but no winner was declared. For all the effort expended by the Air Corps and participants alike, twin engine attack bombers seemed to be a dead issue. The project did, however, result in considerable success from an unexpected source.

It was the export trade beginning in the mid 1930s that put American aviation on a profitable basis during the Great Depression and advanced the industry before the general expansion of the military in 1938. For all its difficulties American aeronautical technology had made tremendous advances since 1917 and spawned some of the world's outstanding designs, a fact not unnoticed by foreign nations. Numerous nations seemed to want modern military aircraft and the export business soon surpassed domestic sales and carried the industry through some difficult years before the burgeoning demands of World War II placed unbelievable requirements on all aircraft firms.

Although export releases of military equipment were governed by the Neutrality Act, there were actually few difficult restrictions and most were eased considerably by President Roosevelt in the interest of his foreign policies. Japan and Germany, despite their aggressive actions, were authorized generous purchases of American aviation products.

Facing bankruptcy in 1934, Martin suffered heavy losses on three prestigious flying boats for Pan American Airways. The company was saved by a loan from the Reconstruction Finance Corporation without which it could not have continued production of the B-10 for the Army. Military procurement officers had become displeased with the difficulties of dealing with Martin and had the Army not been anxious to receive more than 100 of the new, all metal bombers, it is unlikely that the loan would have been granted. When the time came to replace the B-10 a few years later, Martin's design was passed over in favor of the Douglas B-18.[16]

The B-10 however, represented the greatest advance in bomber design for many years and the merits were well recognized by foreign governments who soon lined up at Martin's door. It was the sales of B-10s through 1936 and 1937 to the governments of Siam, Turkey, Holland, China, Spain and Argentina that saved the company from serious financial troubles. So lucrative were these sales, with better than domestic profit margins, that Martin declared 1937 the best year in the company's history

Douglas was on the export bandwagon in 1936 when several Douglas-Northrop designs were taken up by Japan along with two attack bombers for evaluation by the Imperial Navy. These were followed by the tri-tailed DC-4X, twenty-two DC-3s with license to manufacture, and two flying boats.

The ill fated DB-7B became one of the company's greater successes in early 1939 when a desperate France ordered 105 examples powered by Pratt & Whitney R-1830 engines. Orders were increased and when Germany overran France more than 200 had been delivered. Britain assumed all airplanes remaining on contract labeling the aircraft Havoc I. France had further contracted for but never received 100 DB-7As powered by Wright R-2600 engines. This contract was also assumed by Britain and the airplanes converted to night fighters designated Havoc II. Following these export orders the U.S. Army Air Corps ordered improved DB-7As designated A-20 which became one of the most successful and widely used light bombers of World War II.

The Douglas balance sheet was further improved early in 1940 by an order from Canada for twenty B-18s.

Based in Burbank, California, Lockheed Aircraft Corp. had been a notable commercial firm except for an all metal prototype fighter and military sales of a few of their famous Northrop designed plywood transports. In 1933 the company was delivering the last of the speedy plywood monoplanes and was well underway on the design and construction of the fast, all metal, twin engine Electra transport. Lockheed was not in the best of financial health and the slow, albeit successful progress on the Electra passenger liner rapidly diminished the limited capital.[17]

The company's financial situation was alleviated by Electra sales to Japan where over 100 were built under license, ultimately for military use. A strictly commercial design, these sales were not affected by the Neutrality Act. Limited domestic sales further boosted the small company's resources.

The larger, subsequent Model 14 Super Electra failed to compete with the Douglas DC-3 in the airline transport market and only a limited number were sold to the nation's airlines.

The Douglas 7B prototype was lost during demonstration flights to the French. Not purchased by the U.S. it was bought in large numbers by France and Britain. It was later acquired by the USAAC as the A-20. Seen here is a Vichy French Havoc over North Africa. (L'Armee de l'Air)

Boeing-Stearman's XA-21 was far too slow a design to compete favorably in the attack bomber competition and was carried no further than the single prototype which was purchased by the Army. (NASM #1B-41548)

Lockheed considered a revised design of the Super Electra for the 1938 attack bomber competition but did not develop a prototype for that purpose. The British Purchasing Commission again entered the scene canvassing the American aircraft industry for more airplanes. Lockheed quickly put forth a proposal and mock up for a military variant of the Model 14 to meet British specifications for a coastal reconnaissance type. Favorably impressed, an initial order was placed for 200 examples designated the "Hudson" powered by Wright R-1830 engines of 1,200 HP. Subsequent orders were received from Britain and the U.S. which found extensive use for the Hudsons in anti-submarine and patrol work.

More than 2,000 Hudsons in several variants came off the production line until 1943. It was the export Hudson that brought Lockheed from a small, struggling company into the big time and provided the growth and development for expansion that soon engulfed the industry.

As events transpired it became of little concern to Martin that the XA-22 was not ordered by the Army from the attack bomber competition when in January 1939 the French government ordered 115 examples designated "Maryland" Model 139. Deliveries began in October and with the fall of France all undelivered airplanes were taken over by Britain. These were soon followed by an order for 150 Maryland IIs powered by Pratt & Whitney engines.

The Marylands were followed by the A-30 "Baltimore", a heavier and more powerful bomber with Wright R-2600 engines of 1,600 HP. Nearly 2,500 Baltimores were ordered by Britain under Lend Lease, production continuing until mid-1944.

The Seversky Company of Long Island, New York also entered the export business with a sale of twenty single engine 2Pa-B3s to Japan for use as bomber escorts. This order was followed by sales of another twenty to Siam.[18]

North American's NA-40 fared no better with the Air Corps than the other entries from Martin and Stearman but the company was already established in the export business. Sales of trainers increased considerably throughout 1937 and began a significant escalation when the first large orders were received from Britain in 1938 and from France in 1939. Between 1936 and 1940 North American delivered 1,458 airplanes to foreign purchasers compared to 1,260 to the American military. The volume of the company's exports continued at a substantial rate throughout World War II with Lend Lease deliveries.[19]

As the second decade between the wars drew to an ominous close, the number of American military airplanes purchased by foreign governments exceeded domestic sales. At the end of 1939 export sales constituted sixty per cent of a 680 million dollar backlog comprising some 1,600 airplanes ordered between January 1938 and September 1939. The dollar value of export aircraft rose even more dramatically: from $6,598,515 in 1935 to $196,352,315 in 1940. The expansion of the American aircraft industry during the late 1930s was financed largely by Britain and France.[20]

Martin's Model 139 "Maryland" fared no better than the other contestants in the attack bomber competition of 1938. (NASM #1B-19622)

By late 1938 events in Europe and Asia indicated the near certainty of American involvement in a global conflict. America, inadequately prepared for defense, let alone a major war on distant continents, found it necessary to recognize the prohibitive cost and global effects of isolationism. Time had become perilously short for the alleviation of nearly twenty years of less than adequate preparations. Funding for all services was increased on an unprecedented scale. German and Japanese air forces had been developing to a wartime capability for years and the brief period between 1938 and 1941 was clearly a race against time to close an ever widening lead in superiority.

As the situation in Europe steadily worsened President Roosevelt approved a revised sales policy with Britain and France on March 25, 1940. This policy, with the agreement of the Army Air Corps, provided for the export release of a significant quantity of the latest American aircraft including the P-38, B-24, B-25, and B-26. The recipients in turn, agreed to furnish the U.S with combat performance data, a great advantage to the U.S. at the time. Based on the growing state of the industry and new planned aircraft factories, it was believed that an adequate number of aircraft could come from the American arsenal to supply both foreign and U.S. needs.[21]

The NA-40, North American's entry in the twin engine attack bomber competition of 1938, has remained obscure among the many aircraft produced by the company but was of greater significance to North American's future than history has been kind enough to record. The historical oversight seems justified. Early on the airplane was plagued with problems. It crashed during demonstration tests and was never ordered into production. But its brief and successful test program was not forgotten by the Air Corps and its impact on B-25 development warrants more than passing mention.

The engineering design team headed by Howard Evans, produced an efficient, functional airplane, exceptionally clean by any standards and incorporating excellent features.

The design was based on a crew of five; pilot, co-pilot, bombardier/navigator, radio operator/gunner and gunner. Pilots were placed in tandem under a long, slender canopy, an arrangement that minimized frontal area and permitted a maximum fuselage width of a mere forty-five inches. A "greenhouse" type nose housed the bombardier/ navigator and the radio operator and gunner were positioned aft.

Shoulder mounted wings provided for fully underhung nacelles, a concept first introduced on the Fokker XB-8, followed by the General Aviation YO-27, the XB-21 Dragon and all subsequent twin engine bombers by North American. This feature provided maximum internal nacelle space for the retracted landing gear and accessories resulting in excellent maintenance access. It also minimized disruptive airflow over the wings contributing to aerodynamic efficiency.

Power was initially supplied by two Pratt & Whitney R-1830-S6C3-6 engines of 1,100 HP driving twelve foot diameter, three blade Curtiss electric propellers. Each exhaust collector terminated in a single stack directed upward just aft of the carburetor intake scoops. Total fuel capacity was 476 gallons.

Pratt & Whitney supplied North American with installation drawings and data for their R-1830, R-2180 and R-2800 engines, all of which were approved for the bid. Preliminary designs were prepared based on each type but only the proven R-1830 was selected. It is interesting to speculate on the probable performance of this light airplane had it been equipped with the R-2800 engines. They were far in the future however, and were yet to reach the test stands.[22]

Typical of the period, armament was light, consisting of three .30 cal. flexible guns with 500 rounds

The NA-40, equipped with Pratt and Whitney R-1830 engines. This photograph on the NAA ramp shows the long over-wing exhaust pipes and the square fairing added to the nacelle trailing edge to improve flight characteristics. (NAA)

After being re-equipped with the Wright R-2600-71 engines, the airplane was designated NA-40B. Although not the prototype of the B-25, the shape of the cowlings, vertical tails, underhung nacelles and constant dihedral wing were features carried through the development of the Mitchell. (NAA)

of ammunition for each. One gun was ball mounted in the nose, one in the top turret and another aft, portable between waist and ventral locations. Bays for two fixed .30 cal. guns were designed into each wing between the oil cooler air intake and the landing lights. Wing guns were not installed however, until the airplane was re-equipped with R-2600 engines and designated NA-40B. The airplane was assigned civil registry number X14221.

A considerable portion of North American's business during the 1930s had been the export of military airplanes to foreign nations. This was also considered for the NA-40 and a proposal was prepared for an export version powered by Bristol Pegasus engines.[23]

Company pilot Paul Balfour and test engineer Lyons made the first flight on 29 January 1939 and immediately experienced severe tail shaking which intensified as the speed increased. Various combinations of cowl flap settings, some fixed and others controlled, made some improvement but only resulted in erratic oil and cylinder head temperatures. Subsequently elbows and long tail pipes were fitted to the exhaust stacks and a squared fairing was fitted to the nacelle trailing edge.

Some improvement resulted but the problems remained and were never totally alleviated with the Pratt &Whitney engines. These difficulties and the slow feathering of the Curtiss electric propellers deferred single engine tests indefinitely. As a result, only fourteen flights totaling five hours and twenty minutes were made with the P & W engines. During those tests a top speed of 265 IAS was attained, satisfactory if not spectacular.[24]

Between 28 February and 1 March the P & W engines were replaced by Wright R-2600-A71-3 engines of 1,600 HP and the airplane redesignated NA-40B. The more powerful Wright engines with more streamlined cowlings provided considerable improvement in both performance and appearance. The over-wing exhausts were replaced by collector rings ported out board of the nacelles and the carburetor intake scoops were moved slightly aft.

It was intended to equip the airplane with Hamilton Standard Hydromatic propellers capable of full feathering faster than the Curtiss electrics. The Hamiltons were not available so, to expedite the test schedule, a tank of storage batteries was substituted to assist feathering.[25]

NA-40 PERFORMANCE SUMMARY				
	DESIRED		ACTUAL	
	Spec 98-102		R-1830	R-2600
	Desired	Min		
High speed at 5,000"	280	250	268	287
Operational Speed at 5,000'	240	210	243	261
Range at 5,000' & under 200 MPH	1,200	1,200	1,245	1,176
Landing Speed/MPH			67.5	70
Ser.Ceiling / Ft	25,000	20,000	26,000	25,000
Gross Weight / Lbs			19,500	20,000
Takeoff HP			1,100	1,600
Bomb Load			1,200 lb	1,200 lb

LEADING DIMENSIONS	
Length	47' - 10"
Wing Span	66' - 0"
Root Chord	154"
Root Airfoil	NACA 23017
Tip Chord	67"
Tip Airfoil	NACA 23009
Wing Area	599 Sq Ft
Incidence	Root 3 °
	Tip 1° 30'
Leading Edge Sweep Back	1° 47'
Dihedral	3° 23'

##

ff

On 1 March 1939, Balfour, Lyons and engineer Wheeler flew NA-40B for nearly an hour. Airspeed calibrations and simulated single engine tests were successfully completed and no vibration or overheating problems occurred. The single difficulty was excessive and persistent spark plug fouling on the no. 9 cylinder of each engine, a problem temporarily corrected by fabricating substitute ignition harnesses from friction tape.

On 12 March Balfour, Lyons and Rudy Stolz, North American technical representative, departed Mines Field at Inglewood for Wright Field, Ohio, where demonstration tests for the Air Corps were programmed. Scheduled stops for fuel and inspection were made at Albuquerque, New Mexico and Kansas City, Kansas.

Upon arrival at Wright Field the trial board flights were begun by Major Younger Pitts, temporarily assigned as military test pilot to the NA-40 project. A considerable portion of the programmed tests were completed with satisfactory performance, but due to the slow feathering characteristics of the Curtiss electric propellers, no single engine tests were made with a shut down engine and fully feathered propeller. To simulate shutdown, engines were

totally destroying the airplane. Except for a minor cut on Captain McGuire's head, there were, miraculously, no injuries.

Although the loss of NA-40 was a significant setback to North American, Dutch Kindelberger maintained his usual good customer relations. For each of the lucky officers he purchased a watch, the backs appropriately engraved with a rabbit's foot. [27]

Testing of the NA-40 was not quite complete but the recorded data was adequate proof of a design of excellent capability and potential. North American had failed to win a production contract for either the NA-21 or the NA-40 but the loss was brief. Both played a significant role on behalf of the successor.

By 1938 those responsible for procurement of military aircraft in the United States were seriously influenced by the threatening situation in Europe. The light bombers then in service or in competition were considered unsatisfactory by the Chief of the Air Corps and it was believed that new specifications should be issued requiring a top speed of as high as 345 MPH for

NA-40 front view shows the minimal frontal area achieved by tandem seating of the pilots. (NAA)

alternately idled with the propeller in full high pitch and the airplane trimmed to approximate hands off flight. North American had requested that no dead engine and full feathering test be done until all programmed trial board flights had been completed, and further requested that a company technical representative be aboard for such tests.[26]

On 11 April Pitts taxied NA-40 for takeoff. Stolz was in the co-pilot's seat and Lieutenant Anderson in the aft fuselage. Captain McGuire made a last minute arrival by car and indicated that he wanted to make this flight. Stolz thereby relinquished his position. Shortly after takeoff they approached the field at about 500 feet altitude with one engine shut down and feathered. Proceeding away they turned slightly, losing some altitude. About two miles from the field the airplane struck the ground easily in the first turn of a flat spin. It did not immediately burn.

Stolz joined the fire engine crew enroute to the crash site where all three crew members awaited, safely separated from the crash by a small hill. Fuel soon ignited,

light bombers and in excess of 300 MPH for a heavier twin engine type of capacity between the light and heavy models.

Until this period the category "medium bomber" had little true meaning although the designation had been used since the 1920s. By the 1930s the technology of all metal construction and increasingly powerful and reliable new engines brought abut a wider range of defined capabilities and categories.

Air Corps Proposal No. 39-640 was issued on 11 March 1939 for the design of a medium bomber. Generally specified was a bomb load of 3,000 pounds, a range of 2,000 miles and a top speed in excess of 300 MPH. Specified as a pure bombardment type in support of ground forces, it was to operate at altitudes from 8,000 to 14,000 feet against tactical objectives such as rail yards and harbors.

No liquid cooled engine of adequate power existed or was being developed. The choice of air cooled radials was limited to the Pratt & Whitney R-2800 or the Wright R-

2600 and R-3350 types. Of these only the R-2600 had been tested to known reliability and although the least powerful, presented the least risk. Bidders were free, however, to base their designs on any or all of those engines with choice of supercharger combinations.

A contract for the new medium bomber represented a lucrative proposition for the winning bidder.

The specifications called for considerable advancement in design, technology, productive capacity and a great increase in skilled manpower. More factory space was required than most companies could provide.

Requests for proposals were widely circulated and the response was less than overwhelming. Some companies were pulling out of the Great Depression with

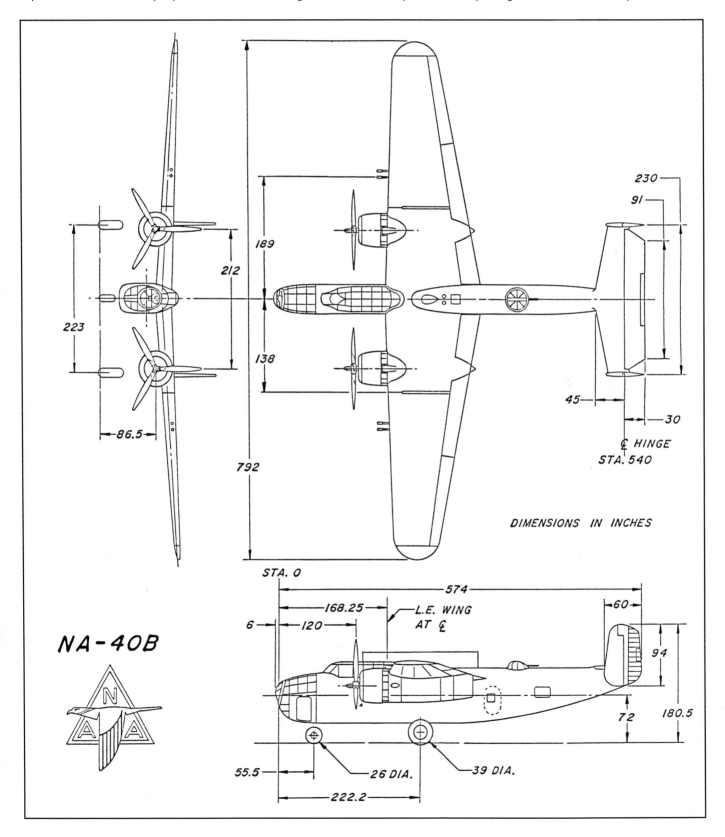

NA-40B

DIMENSIONS IN INCHES

substantial business, both domestic and export, and expressed disappointing enthusiasm for additional work of such magnitude.

Of the few proposals received, the Design Review Board considered four to define acceptable designs in the following order of technical preference: the Martin No. 179 or B-26; the North American NA-62 or B-25; the Douglas B-23 and the Stearman P-23. Of these only the first two received consideration.[28]

Martin's proposal defined a highly esthetic, streamlined airplane and one of the world's most advanced bomber designs. Heavy emphasis was placed on speed which was achieved by a laminar flow airfoil and the 2,000 HP Pratt & Whitney R-2800 engines. Of the four proposals it promised fighter speeds.

On the debit side of the ledger it presented some potentially serious considerations. The comparatively high wing loading and landing speed indicated the need for pilot training beyond the scope of existing programs. Several major components required long development lead time by both Martin and sub contractors. The R-2800 engine was not fully developed and still on the test stands, clouding the project from the start. The B-26 was pushing the state of the art and there were serious doubts that it could be kept on schedule. Nor could the high cost be ignored, nearly 50% more than the estimated cost of a B-25 and about equal in cost to the four engine B-17.[29]

Despite all these problems, the B-26 was clearly an excellent design and with some misgivings and accepted risks, in September 1939 the Air Corps placed an order for 201 examples with a contract value of $15,815,000.

Although not as fast or powerful as the B-26, North American's B-25 was a strong contender. A less dynamic design and more within the state of the art, it indicated virtual promise of success. North American's design team incorporated relatively easy field maintenance and repair features, a major consideration for squadron service. The fuselage section of faired second degree curves was a highly efficient shape and minimized frontal

area. Long lead time and complex developmental components were scrupulously avoided, indicating the probability of adherence to schedules. It promised to be an easy airplane to fly and placed no special requirements on pilot training programs.

The necessity for the development of successful medium bombers was imperative and the advisability of having two competitive sources was well recognized. Hedging all bets, the Air Corps also placed an order with North American for 184 B-25s powered by the proven Wright R-2600 engines. This contract, No. W535-ac-13258, valued at $11,771,000, was approved on 20 September, 1939.[30]

Considerations by the design review board were by no means limited to the technical aspects presented in the proposals. It was of paramount importance that any firm selected to produce these aircraft in quantity could provide the technical competence, manpower and facilities for satisfactory production. Some aircraft plants dated from World War I and were inadequate in both size, equipment and expandability to meet the demands foreseen for the 1940s.

Due to the production of the twin engine Maryland and Baltimore bombers, the Martin factory was considered to be of adequate size and well enough equipped to qualify for a task of the magnitude of the medium bomber program.

North American's plant at Mines Field near Inglewood, California was nearly new and specifically designed for the production of military aircraft. Expandability was designed into the factory and wisely so as expansion continued steadily after initial completion in 1934. Mines Field was of adequate size and in an area where favorable year round weather contributed to the efficiency of flight test.[31]

Events soon proved that the acquisition of both airplanes was one of the outstanding procurement decisions of the years immediately prior to World War II. The initial contracts to Martin and North American for 385 aircraft not only constituted one of the largest orders ever

Martin's Model 179 earned fame as the B-26 Marauder. (USAF #165120))

placed by the Air Corps, but also marked a revolutionary and potentially hazardous procurement policy. Dictated by the growing urgency of the times, these contracts were placed on the basis of bidder's specifications, drawings and performance calculations, no prototypes being required. Previous policy had required manufacturers to produce and test experimental types at their own expense, with no consideration of a production contract until a period of intensive testing had proven the suitability and integrity of the product. It was therefore common for as much as two or three years to elapse between design of an airplane and acceptance of the first production article by the services, a procedure resulting in obsolescence at the time of first delivery.[32]

The effectiveness of this new policy was evident when first deliveries began just seventeen months after contract placement. At the time of the Pearl Harbor attack 130 B-25s and over fifty B-26s had been delivered to the Air Corps. Under previous policy only the beginnings of preparations for production would have been achieved in that time.

It is doubtful, however, that in 1939 any procurement policy would have provided an adequate number of new aircraft in so brief a period without large, skilled and experienced organizations already existing in the aircraft industry. This conveyed an object lesson for all time, effectively demonstrating that the national interest requires the existence of such concerns, capable of rapid design and production in times of emergency, able to train and absorb large numbers of new personnel and form nuclei for expansion of the entire industry.

Design of Martin's Model 179 began in June, 1939 under the direction of project engineer, Peyton Magruder. A highly capable young engineer, Magruder was a graduate of the U.S. Naval Academy and also held a degree in aeronautical engineering. He obtained extensive experience at the Naval Aircraft Factory and on Martin's twin engine B-10s, Marylands and Baltimores.

Initially specified for the Model 179 was an empty weight of 19,250 pounds and a gross weight of 26,625 pounds. In addition to meeting all specified requirements, Magruder placed heavy emphasis on a high speed capability. This he achieved in part by use of a laminar flow wing at zero degrees incidence, a feature which later proved detrimental to other characteristics.

After preparation and rejection of a number of design concepts and combinations, the design team opted for a high mounted wing, single tail, tricycle landing gear and fully underhung nacelles. Pratt & Whitney R-2800 engines of 1,850 HP driving Curtiss electric 4 blade propellers provided power. It was the first U.S. Army airplane to be initially designed for the inclusion of self sealing fuel cells and power turrets.[33]

The selected laminar flow airfoil was not a high lift section but when positioned at 0 degree incidence, provided the desired speed. It also presented some initial risks as it failed to adequately provide for the weight increases certain to occur during production.

Fuselage design was based on heavy, stretch formed aluminum skins flush riveted on four sturdy longerons to create a near tubular structure. The circular cross section resulted in maximum frontal area but provided great internal space for crew comfort, adequate stores and armament. A boat like keel extended along the underside to form the 'backbone' of the structure. The keel also separated the left and right bomb bays. Four bays were provided, two forward and two aft, the forward bay essentially duplicating that on the B-17. The forward bay was deleted effective on the 76th B-26C. Center wing and center fuselage sections were fabricated as a single structure.

Armament consisted of two .30 caliber guns, one socket mounted in the nose and another in ventral position aft of the bomb bay. A power operated turret of two .50 caliber guns was located on the top aft fuselage and a single hand operated .50 caliber gun was mounted in the tail.

On 29 November 1940 the prototype B-26, 40-1361, was first airborne by chief engineer and test pilot, Ken Ebel. A speed of 323 MPH at 14,250 feet was reached. The airplane was clearly an excellent design and was immediately placed in production.

First accepted in April 1942, the B-26B was powered by Pratt & Whitney R-2800-41 or -43 engines providing 2,000 HP. Empty weight of the airplane had risen from 21,375 for the prototype to 22,380 for the B model.[34]

Unforeseen problems soon occurred, most of which resulted from continuing increases in weight by the addition of self sealing fuel tanks, armor plate and additional armament. Crashes began to occur. Takeoff roll was considered too long, landing speed excessive and landing gear and propeller problems took on hazardous proportions. As a result the B-26 was restricted to a limited load until the problems could be corrected.

It was realized at the outset of design that the 602 square foot wing area, the 0 degree incidence and the selected airfoil section did not adequately allow for the increases in weight certain to occur. The hydraulic system utilized flammable fluid which caused extensive seal and 'O' ring failures. These problems were compounded by the need for more advanced pilot training to qualify crews for safe operation of the airplane. No twin engine trainer then in Air Corps inventory was adequate for this task.

The difficulties reached crisis proportions when in April 1941 Wright Field Engineering requested grounding of all B-26s due to a rash of landing gear failures. The B-26 had taken on a bad reputation earning some uncomplimentary names as "Widow Maker", "Flying Prostitute", and "One a Day in Tampa Bay". Review boards seriously considered cancellation of all B-26 contracts as the airplane's reputation continued to deteriorate. Logistics seemed to compound the problems.

A New B-26 plant had been built at Omaha and was staffed and in production with automotive partners including Goodyear, Hudson, Chrysler and dozens of sub-contractors. Thousands of employees at Omaha and Baltimore were effected and the continuing supply of badly needed medium bombers was temporarily in serious doubt.

Propeller problems were isolated and corrected while Martin engineering increased the area of a new tail and produced a new wing of 659 square feet, an increase of 57 square feet from previous models. Wing span rose from 65 feet to 71 feet, changes effective on the last 150 B-26B-10 and subsequent airplanes.

The major problems ironed out, the B-26 went on to become one of the best airplanes of World War II. Initially assigned to the Southwest Pacific, it was replaced in that theater early in the war by B-25s. It became the most widely used medium bomber in the European theater and was used extensively in the Mediterranean and North African campaigns. For reasons unknown the B-26 suffered but .3 of 1 per cent combat losses, the lowest of any World War II combat plane.[35]

The Omaha factory produced 350 unarmed B-26Cs as target tow tugs designated AT-23B. Another 200 were produced less guns and accepted by the navy as JM-1 target tugs. Beginning with 300 F models the wing incidence was increased from zero degrees to 3.5 degrees, which, combined with the previous increase in wing area and span, improved handling characteristics but caused an unwelcome reduction in speed. The G model was last off the production line, a run of 950 being followed by another 57 as TB-26 trainers.[36]

The B-26 was made in lesser numbers than the B-25 due to higher production and maintenance costs and a higher accident rate. A total of 5,157 Marauders were produced when Baltimore ceased production in March, 1945 and the Omaha plant switched to B-29s.

NOTES TO CHAPTER 2

1. Craven, W.F. and Cate, J.L. **The Army Air Forces in World War II**, Chicago, IL The University of Chicago Press, 1953, Vol I, pages 5, 23-43
2. Ibid., page 54
3. Purtee, Dr. Edward O. "The Development of Light & Medium Bombers, Study No. 196, **Historical Section Intelligence (T-2)** AMC Wright Field Dec. 1946, pages 73-77
4. Ibid., page 99
5. Ibid., page 87
6. Ibid., pages 88-89
7. Wagner, Ray, **American Combat Planes**, page 108
8. Ibid., page 109
9. Ibid., page 114
10. Purtee, Study No. 196 Page 102
11. Craven & Cate, Vol. I, page 66
12. Wagner, **American Combat Planes,** page 108
13. Purtee, Study No. 196, pages 100-101
14. Ibid., pages 31-33
15. North American Aviation, Inc., Airframe Contract Record, Internal Document Report 'O' 27 July 1956
16. Biddle, Wayne **Barons of the Sky**, Simon & Schuster, New York, NY 1991, page 235
17. Ibid., page 220
18. Jyoko, Noboru, **The Japanese Severskys**, American Aviation Historical Society, Vol. 30 #3, Pages 214-215
19. North American Aviation, Inc., **Brief History of Operations Immediately Prior To and During World War II**, (Internal Document) pages 17-18
20. Craven and Cate Vol VI, page 191
21. Ibid., page 303
22. NAA Drawings 40-00003 and 40-00025
23. NAA Report No. NA-1099, NA-40 Export, Airplane with Briston Pegasus Engines
24. NAA Flight Test Records, 29 Jan 1939 to 24 Mar 1939
25. NAA Internal Letter 20 Feb 1939 Subj: Feathering of Curtiss Propellers on R-2600 Engines on NA-40 Airplane
26. NAA Internal Letter 24 Mar1939, Manufacturer's Demonstration, NA-40B
27. Letter, Rudy Stolz to Norman Avery, 1973
28. Boyne,Walt, 'Magruder's Marauder', **Wings Magazine**, April/May 1973, Sentry Magazines, New York, NY
29. HQ Army Air Forces Unit Costs of Aircraft and Engines, 1 Aug 1945, Technical Order No. 00-25-30
30. North American Aviation, Inc., Airframe Contract Record, Internal Document Report 'O' 27 Jul 1956
31. North American Aviation, Inc., Brief History of Company Operations Immediately Prior To and During World War II, (Internal Document), page 12
32. Ibid., pages 28-29
33. Purtee, Edward O., Study #196, page 114
34. Wagner, Ray, **American Combat Planes**, pages 121, 130
35. Boyne, Walt, **Wings Magazine**, May, 1973, pages 8-17
36. Wagner, Ray, **American Combat Planes**, page 132

NAA's XB-28 high altitude bomber, powered by two super-charged P & W R-2800 engines, featured remote controlled turrets and carried a 4,000 lb. payload to an altitude of 35,000 feet. First flown in April 1942 it was too late to supersede the B-25 or B-26. It did, however, provide much significant test data incorporated in later long range heavy bombers. (NAA)

③ Design, Flight Testing and Production of the B-25

Lee Atwood, North American vice president and chief engineer, assumed charge of the medium bomber project. A graduate of Hardin-Simmons and the University of Texas, his career began as a stress engineer in the Army Aircraft Branch at Wright Field. Heading west in the depressed early 1930s he joined the Douglas Aircraft Co. and following experience of several airplanes, became chief structures engineer of the DC-1, then being designed.

Modest, reserved and meticulous, Atwood polished his expertise on the BT-9, NA-16, O-47, some export fighters and the NA-21 and NA-40 bombers. Some good NAA designs, both bombers included, had failed to reach production and he resolved that the new medium bomber would be a winner.

Designing a new aircraft involves plenty of second guessing. Concerns and questions abound. Has the customer really set forth all the requirements and are they accurately interpreted? Will the preferred engines be available when needed and will they perform as expected? Will the political situation remain unchanged? These were but a few of the questions facing the design team as they began the proposal.

Time soon proved the wisdom of certain basic ground rules that Atwood established at the outset. Long lead time and complex developmental components would be avoided. The airplane would be produced at competitive cost, reasonably easy to maintain and repair and above all, easy to fly and free of aerodynamic vices.[1]

The 1/9 scale B-25 wind tunnel model ready for testing at California Institute of Technology. (NAA)

Partial B-25 assembly shows the general method of major sub assembly breakdown pioneered by North American. This system was an important factor in simplifying manufacture, maintenance and repair. (NAA)

From the standpoint of fabrication North American's practice of designing sub assemblies that could be efficiently routed to larger or final assemblies was fully implemented. This permitted various parts and assemblies to be prefabricated in many locations, thus minimizing factory time and permitting more people to efficiently work on more parts and reduce airframe cost. Until North American pioneered this technique on the BT-9 it had been common throughout the industry to assemble the fuselage in its fixture, then install the various cables, hydraulic lines, wiring, components and major airframe sections, in many respects an archaic carryover from shipbuilding.

The basic B-25 design bore a number of similarities to the NA-40; the tricycle landing gear, twin vertical tails of almost identical shape, wing area and root airfoil, the same engines and shape of cowlings, constant dihedral and underhung nacelles. These similarities notwithstanding, the NA-40 was not the prototype B-25. The B-25 was a larger airplane of greater speed, range and payload capability. The wing area was some ten square feet larger than the NA-40 wing and the fuselage was six feet longer. Gross weight of the B-25 prototype exceeded 28,000 pounds compared to 20,000 for the NA-40.

Side by side pilot seating made for a wider fuselage and the bombardier's passage to the nose was by a crawl tunnel beneath the flight deck. The wing was lowered from the high position of the NA-40 to a shoulder position permitting a crawl passage above the bomb bay to the aft fuselage.

Although laminar flow airfoils were coming into use, a slower section, NACA 23017, was selected for the wing root, changing to NACA 4409-R at the tip. A slight

28

Dignitaries from NAA and GM in front of the B-25 mockup. Reading from the left: 4th, Al Fisher of Fisher Body; 5th, Ernest Breech, NAA; 7th, Carl J. Hansen, NAA Chief Project Engr.; 8th J.H. Kindelberger, President, NAA; 9th, Fred Fisher, Fisher Body; 10th E.V. Rickenbacker. Others unknown. (NAA)

camber reversal or "reflex", was incorporated at the tip trailing edge which moderated stall characteristics, a feature which contributed significantly to the suitability of the B-25 for the carrier takeoffs of the Doolittle mission against Japan. The root incidence of three degrees remained unchanged throughout production. A hidden fault, the constant wing dihedral, was the only aerodynamic problem, creating a temporary unacceptability to the Air Corps.[2]

North American preferred Pratt & Whitney's R-2800 engines of 2,000 HP, approximately 300 HP more than the Wright R-2600s. The eighteen cylinder P&W was of slightly smaller outside diameter than the Wright which translated into a smaller frontal area and less drag. The heavier P&W engine more than compensated for its extra weight by the greater power. The Pratt & Whitney was the ideal if unproven engine. For the B-25 however, it was not to be. When the Air Corps placed the initial order the proven Wright R-2600 engines were specified.[3]

The fuselage was efficiently designed into four separate and detachable sections; nose, forward, center and aft. Construction was contemporary state of the art comprising formed frames, longerons, stringer and skin, all of riveted assembly. Outside width was held to 56.5 inches, a reasonable minimum for side by side pilot seating and adequate bomb bay volume. The sectional shape of second degree curves provided high aerodynamic efficiency, contours also used on the P-51. This configuration was used in preference to a circular section as high altitude pressurization was not required and frontal area was kept to a minimum.[4]

The navigator's compartment was located directly behind the flight deck and from there a crawl tunnel under the flight deck provided passage to the nose. Crawl space between forward and aft sections was over the bomb bay.

Access hatches were located in the floor of the navigator's compartment and the aft fuselage. An additional escape hatch was provided by the window section directly above the pilots.

Numerous vertical tail configurations were evaluated and the result, be it single or twin tails, will doubtless remain controversial. There seemed to be little to favor either type on medium bombers. Aircraft of the period almost set a fad for multiple tails. The reasons for twin tails on the B-25 are muddied by time but in all probability the arrangement provided a preferred field of fire against attack from the rear.

In retrospect, the defensive armament appears insignificant even for 1939 and when compared to late B-25 variants, almost ineffective. A traditional .30 caliber machine gun was mounted in the nose section and was readily movable to any of three locations. Another .30 cal. flexible gun was mounted in the upper rear fuselage and

Gen. William Knudsen, left, head of the Office of Procurement Management, and General H.H. Arnold on a visit to North American for inspection of the prototype B-25. 'Dutch' Kindelberger at right. (NAA)

a third served as a waist gun with firing positions from each side of the aft fuselage and from the floor.

The .50 caliber tail gun, mounted in a streamlined canopy, had an excellent field of fire. The plexiglass canopy featured clam shell doors which opened sideways to permit traversing of the gun.

To support varied missions the bomb bay was configured to carry a wide range of stores from clusters of twelve 100 pound bombs to varying quantities of 250, 300, 500, 600 and 1,100 pound bombs, combinations of all or a single 2,000 pound bomb.

Pilot visibility was excellent and for whatever value, the wing tips were visible from the cockpit. Visibility downward and to the sides was ideal for the low level attack role, a function not envisioned at the time the airplane was designed.

The proposal, completed in forty days of extended hours and week ends, defined no less than eighty-four separate and viable configurations, each requiring individual analyses and drawings. Numerous fuselage and bomb arrangements and three different wing designs were developed, each concept requiring complete analysis for each engine approved for the bid.

As the final configuration became established the first engineering developmental orders were charged on 12 August 1939 and prior to receipt of the contract some detail engineering and construction orders had been issued to the shop. North American General Order NA-62, authorizing construction of 184 airplanes and one test airframe, was issued on 5 September. The first planning tickets were released to the shop in December.

Upon receipt of the contract work was immediately begun on a 1/9 scale wind tunnel model for testing at the California Institute of Technology. Fabrication then began on the static test airframe and the full scale mock up, complete with instruments, seats, controls and major equipment items. The Air Corps Mock Up Board visited the North American plant on 9 November, 1939 and approved the design with minor changes. The static test airframe was shipped to Wright Field, Ohio on 4 July 1940.[5]

Construction of the first airplane, 40-2165, proceeded concurrently and was in final assembly by early summer of 1940. Various ground and taxi tests progressed with other last minute details. Problems arose with the nose wheel shimmy damper which resulted in nose gear failure during taxi tests. The airplane was repaired and successful re-design of the shimmy damper accomplished. By mid-August the new airplane was ready for flight test.

On 19 August 1940, Vance Breese and company test engineer, Roy Ferren, first flew the new medium bomber. As predicted and intended, it proved to be a docile mount and Breese was apparently satisfied after several flights. Ferren however, reported that in his opinion a severe roll-yaw condition existed.

The flamboyant Breese, always attired in an expensive suit, arrived hastily at flight time, parking his Cadillac convertible on the flight ramp where Ferren waited with engines running. Post flight, Breese reported briefly to management and received his check, supposedly for $5,000 per hop.

Few aircraft companies of the late 1930s could justify a full flight test department and staff of qualified test pilots. Most of North American's products had been single engine trainers, observation craft and except for the NA-21 and NA-40 bombers, the company had no need for multi-engine qualified pilots. It had been convenient to contract one of several prominent, independent test pilots. Among this group were Eddie Allen, Vance Breese, Johnny Cable, D.W. 'Tommy' Tomlinson and the legendary Benny Howard. Tomlinson, of TWA and high altitude research prominence, had tested North American's NA-21 Dragon bomber and Allen had been contracted for the first flight of the NA-16. Neither were approached for the B-25 and Breese was given the nod.[6]

Aside from shimmy damper problems and resulting nose gear failure during taxi tests, the airplane suffered but one threatening emergency. Immediately after take-off and approaching the Pacific Ocean, a fuel line ruptured on the right engine. Raw gasoline quickly ignited with explosive force and although serious, the resulting fire was not the only problem. Control and instrument lines were routed along the forward side of the front wing spar and were accessible from a door in the wing leading edge. The fuel explosion blew the door off, leaving a cavity which became an instant spoiler. The blast passed through control line access holes and into the cockpit with such

Direct front view shows the constant dihedral wing common to a few early examples. (NAA)

During taxi tests a malfunctioning shimmy damper resulted in nose gear failure and minor damage. North American engineers worked with the damper manufacturer and contributed to development of a satisfactory design. (NAA)

force that the windshield was damaged and instrument glass broken.

Still very near Mines Field, Breese made a left turn toward the east dragging low over a local watering hole. With most creditable piloting he made an excellent downwind, wheels up landing on the grass between the runways. Breese and test engineers Roy Ferren and Bill Wheeler made a quick and safe exit. Prompt action by the North American fire department limited the damage and the airplane was soon repaired and back on flight status.[7]

Major Stanley Umstead, Chief of the Air Corps Flight Test Branch at Wright Field, customarily required preliminary flights of all new aircraft for determination of qualitative stability and general handling characteristics. Captain Frank Cook was assigned this task which he also performed for the Martin B-26.

Cook soon discovered a "Dutch roll" characteristic which he considered incompatible with bombing run control with the Norden bomb sight. His report was received by North American with considerable surprise and it seems paradoxical that Breese had not communicated this condition to management. [8]

Considering the importance of the B-25 to the medium bomber program, Major Umstead and Lieutenant George Hatcher flew to North American for a personal appraisal. Wind and gusts accentuated any problems of control. After landing and rolling to a stop on the ramp, Umstead remained silent for a moment, turned to Hatcher and said in effect, " This is the damndest thing I ever tried to fly." In retrospect it seems that he came down too hard on North American but the simplicity of the remedy was yet to be realized. [9]

After a broken fuel line resulted in an explosive fire, Breese quickly turned to a downwind belly landing on the grass between Mines Field runways. No injuries resulted and the airplane was soon repaired. The ungainly 'barn door' vertical tails were the second shape tested on the prototype. (NAA)

L to R: R.H. Rice, NAA chief engineer, Lt. George Hatcher and Major Stanley Umstead of Wright Field. Hatcher and Umstead confirmed Capt. Frank Cook's unfavorable report on B-25 no. 1. (NAA)

That the company had a high priority problem demanding a hasty solution was certainly true. Further analysis indicated that changing the dihedral of the outer wing panels to zero degrees would produce the desired aerodynamic combination.

General Wolfe said to do it, Captain Frank Cook agreed and with typical Kindelberger direction, Dutch told his engineers, "Cut the bull and fix it."

From the engineering and structural standpoints the simplicity of the fix cannot be overemphasized. No change was necessary to the nacelles, center wing section or landing gear, all expensive in engineering and fabrication time. Thus did the B-25 acquire its characteristic gull wing so aptly described by Ed Virgin as the "shot duck look".

This change has been reported to have been made effective on the tenth airplane but no records have been located to confirm this. Of the first ten airplanes the prototype, 40-2165, remained with North American as a test and transport aircraft throughout its existence. Soon after delivery to their first assigned stations numbers 40-2166, 2170, 2173, 2174, and 2176 were briefly returned to North American but no records have been located to explain the reasons. Numbers 40-2168, 2169, 2172, 2173, and 2174 were all damaged in service, probably from use as trainers. The fourth example, 40-2168 may well have been fitted with flat outer wing panels when modified by North American in mid 1943 for use as General Arnold's personal transport.

On 25 February 1941, Ed Virgin and Louis Waite flew the revised B-25 for two hours, discovering that the airplane had emerged from near catastrophe like the proverbial rose. Flight characteristics with the flat outer wing panels were so nearly optimum that the configuration remained unchanged throughout the production of nearly

10,000 examples. Major Donald Stace, resident Air Corps officer at North American, agreed and after an hour flight, he signed the final acceptance.

Apart from the military designation, the new bomber needed a memorable name. It was Lee Atwood who hit on that name.

"Very early in the project several of us were having a bull session in Kindelberger's office and the subject of a name for the new bomber was brought up. I suggested that it be named after General Billy Mitchell but nothing was decided at that time. In a later conversation we settled on MITCHELL."

It became readily apparent to the company that with the prospect of additional large contracts a requirement existed for qualified engineering test pilots within and reporting directly to the engineering organization.

Louis Waite, formerly of Boeing, had been hired as a test pilot and was then organizing an engineering flight test department, directed primarily toward instrumentation. Waite was instructed to locate some well qualified candidates.

Ed Virgin, Air Corps inspector at North American, was a graduate of Randolph and Kelly Fields and had logged considerable time in Norden equipped Martin B-10 and B-12 bombers. He also held an engineering degree and had been serving in a liaison capacity between the Air Corps and North America's engineering department.[10] His qualifications were well known and on 6 February 1941, he became the second of many to wear the NAA test pilot badge. Within a short time Bob Chilton was hired primarily for fighter testing and Joe Barton primarily for bombers, although both men frequently flew both types.

It became obvious to military planners in 1940 that the need for modern aircraft would far exceed the

Major John Griffith (left) of the Air Corps Western District Office and Captain Frank Cook of the Air Corps Flight Test Branch at Wright Field. (NAA)

The first B-25 at Muroc Dry Lake, CA now the site of Edwards Air Force Base. Shown here is the third vertical tail shape. (NAA)

productive capacities of existing manufacturers. Although most were expanding, their combined capabilities would fall far short. North American's Kansas plant was one of several new, government built aircraft assembly plants conceived to alleviate this deficiency. These new facilities resulted from a most ambitious plan, formulated by the newly created Office of Procurement Management, for a program of joint production between the aircraft and automotive industries.

This arrangement utilized the automotive giant of American industry for the fabrication of parts and assemblies for shipment to the new government plants operated by the established aircraft makers. Such a program was not without potential problems of great magnitude. Thousands of new employees were required and the auto industry itself needed considerable training and orientation for a new endeavor and related production methods. Serious concerns prevailed within the aircraft industry that their new automotive partners, with this easy government sponsored indoctrination to aircraft, might well become serious post war competitors. This soon proved an unfounded worry as the automobile makers found little enthusiasm for the low profit margin in the airplane business.

Construction of North American's Kansas plant was approved by the Secretary of War on 16 December 1940 and the formal ground breaking took place at Fairfax Airport on 8 March 1941. The first occupancy by company personnel was 17 April 1942 when a few engineers of the operational nucleus from Inglewood moved into the nearly completed facility.

Kansas City, Kansas, typified the location of the new government installations in the safer American heartland, well away from vulnerable coastal areas. Central United States also had an abundance of available manpower ready and willing to be trained for this new endeavor.

Under the original agreement between North American Aviation, Inc. of Kansas as the prime contractor and the Fisher Body Division of General Motors Corp. (at Memphis, Tennessee) as the major sub-contractor, Fisher was to perform approximately 55% of the total work by value, with North American's portion consisting largely of assembly. The Kansas program was revised however and expanded into a manufacturing as well as an assembly operation. As the war progressed and at the period of peak production, North American was performing 71% of the total effort.

To accelerate the beginning of production at Kansas, North American's Inglewood plant manufactured and supplied the detail parts for the first 100 B-25s built in the new facility. Parts for the first six airplanes were assembled into major sub-assemblies at Inglewood, then shipped to Kansas for final assembly. The detail parts for the next thirty airplanes were sub-assembled at Inglewood, then shipped to Fisher or to Kansas as required. Detail parts for the final sixty-four of the first 100 were shipped unassembled from Inglewood to Fisher or Kansas. Subsequent airplanes were built almost entirely by Fisher and Kansas except for machined parts and occasional spares supplied by Inglewood. Beginning with the 101st

The tail gunners station typical of the first 64 examples constituting the B-25 and B-25A. Plexiglass clam shell doors permitted traversing of the single .50 cal. gun, one of the first departures from the .30 cal. 'peashooters' of the 1930s. (NAA)

Shown here is the 4th type of vertical tail which preceded the final configuration used on all production examples. (NAA)

The cockpit and instrument panel layout was logically arranged and well liked by crews. Various revisions were made on later models but the basic design changed little. (NAA)

Kansas built airplane, B-25D 41-29748,Fisher supplied such items as wing outer panels, fuselage side panels, control surfaces and transparent enclosures.

In February 1942 North American received a contract for 200 B-29 bombers to be constructed at Kansas in addition to the B-25s remaining on order. The B-25 contracts were planned to run out making the plant available exclusively for B-29 production. The B-29 program required a large high bay area which was promptly completed and orders placed for the necessary equipment and tooling. Considerable planning had been accomplished and tooling completed when the B-29 contract was canceled in July 1942 due to the pressing need for more B-25s than originally anticipated. By utilizing the newly expanded facility and additional equipment for continuance of the B-25 program, the production rate was projected to increase from 123 to 217 airplanes per month.

This plan was also changed and an accelerated program was implemented including Fisher to a greater extent and increased the B-25 production rate to 285 airplanes monthly. Production had climbed steadily from July of 1942, reaching a peak in January of 1945 when an incredible 315 B-25s and another 22 in spare parts were delivered. This rate then began declining until August when notice of contract termination was received shortly before the surrender of Japan. From February of 1942, when the first Kansas built B-25 was accepted by the Air Corps, through 14 August 1945 when victory was announced, 6,608 B-25s, (2,290 D models and 4,318 J models) exclusive of spare parts, were delivered from the Kansas plant for an average of 165 airplanes per month during the 40 months of production.

As increasing numbers of aircraft were deployed, new and often unforeseen special requirements frequently arose for various types of missions and weather conditions encountered in the far flung operational theaters. These frequent and sometimes complex design changes presented serious production problems throughout the

Test pilot Vance Breese smiles from the cockpit of prototype B-25, 40-2165. (NAA)

Test engineer Roy Ferren (left) and North American chief test pilot Ed Virgin. (NAA)

Bob Chilton was hired primarily as an engineering test pilot for fighters but flew everything NAA made from the AT-6 through the B-45. He made significant contributions to the P-51 and B-25 airplanes and his impressive log records over 1,700 test flights. (NAA)

Hired primarily as a bomber test pilot, Joe Barton also tested fighters and made notable high speed dive tests in P-51s. A big, jovial and friendly man, his loss in a commercially modified B-25 was deeply felt by all at North American. (NAA)

35

On 3 Jan 1942 employees of North American's Kansas plant gather on a wintry flight ramp to watch their first product and first of 2,290 B-25Ds make its initial flight. Company pilot Paul Balfour at the controls. (NAA)

A small portion of America's productive capacity is evidenced by dozens of B-25s on the Kansas flight ramp. This was a common sight in 1943 and 1944 as many completed aircraft awaited delivery to combat units of the Air Corps. (NAA)

B-25Js near completion at the Kansas plant. At the peak of production almost 10 airplanes per day came off the line. (NAA)

aircraft industry. Special modifications were needed for photo reconnaissance, armament, long range ferry, anti-submarine patrol, winterizing and desert environment, to name a few. Incorporating such changes to a limited number of aircraft on factory assembly lines would have virtually brought the production lines to a standstill.

To meet this urgent need the Air Corps requested the establishment of a number of special modification centers entirely separate from the aircraft manufacturing plants. Such a center was constructed near the North American plant at Fairfax Field, work beginning early in 1942. Airplane modification work was underway before completion of facility construction. Nearly 200 airplanes were modified in temporary facilities until the new center was completed in August. Operations were at peak capacity through 1943 and most of 1944 during which period nearly 4,500 aircraft were modified.

As the modification program was first administered the aircraft were double accepted by the Air Corps, once on leaving the factory and again upon departure from the modification centers. After July of 1944 as the pressure of war diminished, the modification programs were gradually phased out and such work as warranted by future requirements was handled on the factory assembly lines. The aircraft were then delivered under a far less costly single acceptance system.

Following the surrender of Germany, work at the Kansas plant had been progressively reduced. On Tuesday, 14 August 1945 when President Truman announced the end of hostilities with Japan, the future of the Kansas plant and its remaining 7,600 employees, was forever changed. The following morning, plant manager Harold Raynor received the telegram from Wright Field confirming the termination of all work.

At that moment North American Aviation Inc. of Kansas, in which over 59,000 employees had produced 6,608 B-25s and an additional 947 in spare parts, officially ceased to exist. The millions of dollars worth of facilities and equipment which accounted for untold damage to enemy resources, was destined for civilian purposes.

NOTES TO CHAPTER 3

1. Murray, Russ, Rockwell International Corporation, "Lee Atwood, Dean of Aerospace", 1980
2. Letter, Atwood, J.L. to Norman Avery, 24 Mar 1982
3. Ibid., 22 Sep 1982
4. Hansen, C.J. "Design Analysis of the North American B-25 Mitchell" **Aviation Magazine**, March 1945
5. Brief History of North American Aviation, Inc. Date of Incorporation to the end of World War II. NAA Internal Document. p. 28
6. Letter, D.W. Tomlinson to Norman Avery, 11 Jun 1984
7. Letter, Roy Ferren to Norman Avery, 25 Oct 1982
8. Letter, Frank Cook to Norman Avery, 24 Oct 1982, 12 Nov 1982
9. Letter, George Hatcher to Norman Avery, 14 Jan 1983
10. Letter, E.W. Virgin to Norman Avery, 19 Oct 1980

The second B-25, first production line aircraft, 40-2166, during initial flight tests. (NAA)

17th BG officers taking delivery of the first B-25s to McChord Field, Washington. In the background is 40-2170, sixth off the line. (NAA)

4 Production Models and Variants

It is axiomatic that the performance of prototype and early production aircraft exceeds that of subsequent examples. Initial service frequently points up the need for mission changes, addition of armor and armament, structural revisions and increased fuel capacity, all contributing to weight, drag and reduced performance.

The B-25 was no exception. Top speed of the prototype was a respectable 322 MPH but along with other bombers of the period, performance decreased for subsequent variants. The final and heavily armed H and J models gained nearly 8,000 lbs. over the early Mitchells and top speed had dropped to 272 MPH.

B-25, B-25A, B, C & D Models

The first twenty-four airplanes, designated B-25, were lightly armed even by 1940 standards. A complement of three .30 cal. guns and a single .50 cal. tail gun provided for limited defense and virtually no offensive capability. Fuel capacity and corresponding range exceeded that of the B-25A, B and early C models. Self sealing fuel cells were introduced on the B-25A and due to the inherent characteristics of the cell design, fuel capacity was reduced and weight increased. This was not alleviated until the 384th B-25C when additional self sealing cells were added in the outboard wing center section.

Armor protection became effective on the B-25A which made a significant increase in weight and further reduced speed and service ceiling. Performance of the B-25B dropped further by the addition of the top and bottom turrets mounting two .50 cal. guns each. This was partially offset by the deletion of the .50 cal. tail gun.

As the war continued the need for medium bombers increased considerably and the B-25, having proven a most serviceable airplane, was procured in ever increasing quantities. Following the B models a number of contracts were awarded to North American for an additional 1,625

airplanes of more advanced design, designated B-25C, to be produced at Inglewood. Externally the C appeared almost the same as the B but differed considerably by the addition of numerous equipment items, structural changes and revised exhaust systems.

Additional contracts for 2,290 examples designated B-25D were issued almost concurrently to be built at the new plant in Kansas City which was ready to begin production. Incorporation of various equipment items for certain serial number blocks marked the only differences from the C and are described in detail in the summary following.

SUMMARY OF MAJOR TYPE DIFFERENCES

B-25

Engines	Wright R-2600-9
Carburetors	Bendix Stromberg PD-13E-2
Fuel Capacity	2 forward wing tanks, total 484 gal.
	2 rear wing tanks total 432 gal.
	1 droppable bomb bay tank 420 gal.
Armament	3 flexible .30 cal. guns in nose, waist & floor
	1 flexible .50 cal. gun in tail
Armor Protection	None
Weights	Empty 17,258 lbs. Max. 28,557 lbs.
Speed (Max)	322 MPH at 15,000 feet.
Service Ceiling	30,000 feet.
Range	2,000 miles with 3,000 lbs. bombs
Crew	Pilot, Co-pilot, Bombardier, Navigator/Radio, Gunner

First Airplane Accepted February 1941

B-25A photographed at Chanute Field, Illinois in 1941. Typical of early Mitchells are the type 1 insignia, long exhaust pipes and open tail skid. (E.W. Wolak)

SUMMARY OF MAJOR TYPE DIFFERENCES (cont.)

B-25A

Engines	Wright R-2600-9
Carburetors	Bendix Stromberg PD-13E-2
Fuel Capacity	2 forward wing cells total 368 gal.
	2 rear wing cells total 324 gal.
	1 droppable bomb bay tank 420 gal.
	(Wing Cells Self Sealing)
Armament	Same as B-25
Armor Protection	3/8" plate behind pilots and bombardier, under bombardier, bulkhead aft of waist gunner and aft of tail gunner
Weights	Empty 17,870 lbs. Max 27,100 lbs
Speed (Max)	315 MPH at 30,000 feet
Service Ceiling	27,000 feet.
Range	1,350 miles with 3,000 lbs bombs
Crew	Same as B-25

Changes from B-25:
   a. Addition of armor protection
   b. Addition of self sealing fuel cells

The .30 caliber flexible gun stowed at the waist position in the aft fuselage of B-25 and B-25A models. (NAA)

B-25B

Engines	Wright R-2600-9
Carburetors	Bendix Stromberg PD-13E-2
Fuel Capacity	Same as B-25A
Armament	1 .30 cal. gun in nose
	2 .50 cal. guns in top turret
	2 .50 cal. guns in bottom turret
Armor Protection	Same as B-25A except none in tail
Weights	Empty 20,000 lbs. Max 28,460 lbs
Speed (Max)	300 MPH at 15,000 feet
Service Ceiling	23,500 feet.
Range	1,300 miles with 3,000 lb. bombs
Crew	Same as B-25A

Last airplane accepted May 1942

Changes From B-25A
   a. Addition of top & bottom .50 cal Bendix turrets
   b. Removal of tail gun
   c. Removal of armor plate in tail

Below: The top turret, introduced on the B-25B, was carried on all variants. (NAA)

The B-25B differed from preceding models by the addition of top and bottom turrets and the deletion of tail gun. (NAA)

B-25Cs, initially scheduled for delivery to the Netherlands, were fitted with "finger" type exhaust stacks. Effective flame quenchers, these exhaust collectors suffered considerable cracking and few C airplanes reached combat zones without replacement by full collector rings. This new tailskid continued thrugh B-25 production. Contract NA-90 (NAA)

The 200th B-25C shows tail numbers and shortened exhaust stack. The earlier type of insignia and underwing letters, obsoleted in late 1941, still mark this airplane. (NAA)

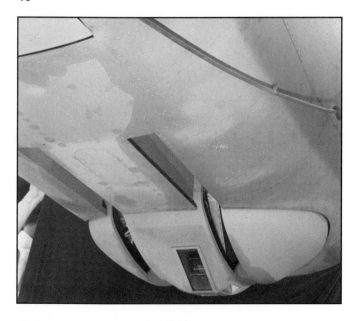
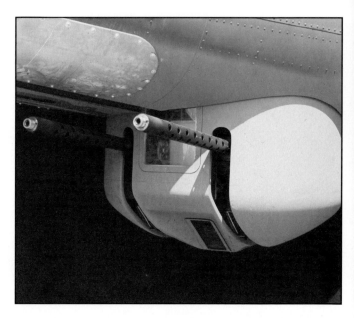

The retractable lower turret common to B-25B, C & D models carried two .50 caliber guns. If lowered too quickly it frequently damaged the retracting micro switch jamming the turret in the down position. The resulting drag and reduced speed on mission return made it less than popular. It also collected mud and was frequently removed in the field. It was deleted on the B-25G and all subsequent B-25s. (NAA)

B-25C

Engines	Wright R-2600-13	
Carburetors	Holley 1685HA	
Fuel	Left Front Wing Cell	184 gal
	Right Front Wing Cell	184
	Left Rear Wing Cell	151
	Right Rear Wing Cell	151
	3 Left Wing Aux Cells	152
	3 Right Wing Aux Cells	152
	Normal	974
	2 Side Waist Ferry Tanks	125
	1 Fixed Bomb Bay Tank	215
	1 Droppable Bomb Bay Tank	335
	1 Fixed Ferry Tank	585
Armament	Same as B-25B	
Armor Protection	Same as B-25B	
Weights	Empty 20,300 lbs. Max 34,000 lbs	
Max. Speed	284 MPH at 15,000 feet	
Range	1,500 miles with 3,000 lbs. bombs	
Crew		

First airplane accepted December 1941
Last airplane accepted May   1943

Major differences from B-25B

a. Holley carburetor replaced Bendix Stromberg carburetor
b. Addition of de-icer and anti-icing systems
c. Addition of Stewart Warner cabin heater in left wing
d. Addition of remote indicating autosyne instruments
e. Revised bomb racks with A-2 electric release
f. Strengthened outer wing structure
g. Changed brake system from low to high pressure
h. Revised tail skid

Changes Effective on B-25C No. 41-12817

a. Increased fuel capacity
b. Added scanning blilster at navigator's compartment

c. Changed turrets to Bendix Amplidyne type
d. Added Carburetor air filter

Effective on B-25C-1 No. 41-13039

a. Added under wing bomb racks
b. Added torpedo rack with electrical and structural requirements

Effective on B-25C-5 No. 42-53332/42-53493

a. Deleted .30 cal nose gun and installed 1 .50 cal flex nose gun and one .50 cal fixed nose gun
b. Installed extensive winterization provisions
c. Installed 'finger' type flame dampening exhaust collector

Effective on B-25C-10 No. 42-32233

a. Installation of AM remote reading compass
b. Installation of additional cabin heating provisions
c. Incorporated improved scanning lens

Effective on B-25C-15 No. 42-32383

a. Replaced exhaust collector ring with Clayton "S" type flame dampening stacks on each individual cylinder
b. Incorporated emergency hydraulic landing gear lowering device

Effective on B-25C-25 No. 42-64702

a. Incorporated "clear vision" windshield
b. Added 215 gallon self sealing bomb bay fuel cell
c. Added 335 gallon metal bomb bay fuel tank on every second airplane

B-25D

Engines	Wright R-2600-13 & Holley 1685 HA carburetors
Fuel	Same as B-25C
Armament	Same as B-25C
Armor Protection	Same as B-25C
Weights	Empty 20,000 lbs. Max 36,500 lbs.

B-25D (cont.)

Speed	284 MPH at 15,000 feet
Service Ceiling	21,200 feet
Range	1,500 miles with 3,000 lbs bombs
Crew	Same as B-25C

Effective on B-25D-1 No. 41-29848
a. Addition of external wing bomb racks
b. Addition of self sealing fuel cells in outboard wing center section
c. Addition of carburetor air filters
d. Change to self sealing oil tanks
e. Provision for torpedo rack installation
f. Addition of scanning blister in navigator's compartment
g. Installation of Bendix Amplidyne turrets
h. Incorporated flame dampening "finger" type exhaust collector through airplane No. 41-30352

Effective on B-25D-5 No. 41-29948
a. Removed .30 cal. gun in nose and added two fixed .50 cal. guns and one flexible .50 gun
b. Installation of improved scanning lens
c. Installation of 585 gal. droppable bomb bay fuel tank on every third airplane through 41-30532

Effective on B-25D-5 No. 41-30057
a. Added provisions for additional cabin heating

Effective on B-25D-10 No. 41-30173
a. Added provisions for winterization
b. Installation of remote reading compass
c. Installation of emergency hydraulic landing gear lowering mechanism
d. Elimination of conduit shielding box

Effective on B-25D-15 No. 41-30353 and subsequent
a. Replaced flame dampening "finger" stack exhaust collector with individual Clayton type "S" stacks to each cylinder

Effective on B-25D-20 No. 41-30533
a. Installation of clear vision windshield
b. Changed from autosyne to AN pressure type oil, manifold and fuel pressure instruments and to type D-14 tachometer
c. Installation of 230 gal. self sealing bomb bay fuel tank
d. Installation of 325 gal. metal bomb bay fuel tank on every other airplane
e. Addition of armor plate behind the co-pilot.

Effective on B-25D-25 No. 42-87138
a. Addition of portable oxygen system

Effective on B-25D-30 No. 42-87453
a. Incorporation of winterization changes
b. Installation of windshield heated air defrosting panel

First B-25D accepted in February 1942
Last B-25D accepted in March 1944

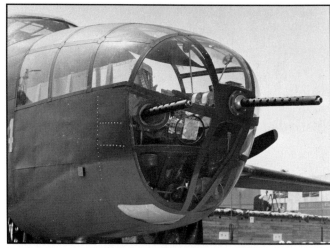

Early B-25Cs carried the same lightweight .30 cal. nose guns as the first B-25s. Effective on the 864th B-25C, 42-53332, the "peashooters" were replaced by 1 flexible and 1 fixed .50 cal. gun. (NAA)

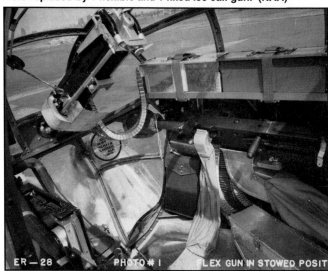

Below: At Kansas City, Kansas, a B-25D makes a pre-flight run up preparatory to initial check flight. This airplane shows the hooded "S" type exhaust stacks which became effective on late B-25Cs and all subsequent models. (NAA)

SINGIN' SAM, B-25D/F-10 of the 18th Combat Mapping Squadron photographed at Espirito Santo, New Hebrides in 1943. (NASM No. 70977 AC)

THE B-25D/F-10s

At the time of America's entry in World War II it had long been known that a significant portion of the earth's surface had never been scientifically charted and that much existing information was dangerously inaccurate. Confronted immediately with operations on a global scale, the need for up to date and accurate charts became imperative.

Aerial reconnaissance and aerial photography are different operations and the science of photographic mapping and charting is yet another, the latter being the process of aerial photography for the express purpose of the compilation and refinement of topographic maps and aeronautical charts.

It was the development in 1942 of the trimetrogon system that made the process relatively straight forward with an extent of coverage and a degree of accuracy unsurpassed until the advent of the U-2 and RS-71 aircraft and subsequent satellite technologies. The trimetrogon mapping system utilized a unit of three synchronized T-5 or K-17 six inch cameras usually mounted in the nose of the airplane. The center camera photographed directly downward and the side cameras at an oblique angle. Coverage was from horizon to horizon and a single airplane flying at 200 MPH could photograph 20,000 square miles in four hours. An especially developed drafting device translated the oblique photographs to precise flat map scale matching the center vertical photograph.

A considerable number of airplanes, both fighters and bombers, were modified for the various requirements of photo reconnaissance and identified with the F designation: P-38/F-4 and F-5; A-20/F-3; P-51/F-6; B-17/F-9;B-24/F-7; B-25/F-10 and B-29/F-13. For aerial mapping and charting the larger bombers were found preferential for crew comfort on long missions.

The B-25/F-10 was found to be an excellent airplane for much of the mapping program. All were new B-25Ds manufactured late in 1942 and early 1943. They were taken directly from final assembly at North American's Kansas City plant to the adjoining modification center where they were modified as photo mappers. For whatever reasons, it was not until 18 August 1943, after several months of service, that the airplanes were officially redesignated F-10.

All armament, armor and bombing equipment was removed, reducing the airplane weight by some 1,000 pounds. Three synchronized cameras were installed in the greenhouse nose which was fitted with a special "bug eyed" chin fairing to house the oblique cameras which protruded slightly beyond the airplane contours. A standard reconnaissance camera was frequently mounted in the aft fuselage and aimed directly downward. The F-10 was crewed by two pilots, navigator, radio operator and photographer.

F-10 of the 91st Photo Mapping Squadron shows the squadron insignia which dates back to 1917. The trimetrogon "bug eye" camera fairings and the F-10 conversions were made at North American's modification center at Kansas City. (Peyton Jacobson)

Accurate navigation and clear weather were obvious requirements for photomapping. The navigator determined precise altitudes and flight paths to correlate with known landmarks. Missions were generally flown as close to 20,000 feet altitude as possible. Missions were frequently as long as ten hours and were not without hazards. An airplane down in the vast, uncharted jungle or mountain wilderness could be lost forever.

F-10s were initially allocated to the 311th Photo Wing and the 1st Photo Charting Group through a number of bases nationwide. From these locations nine squadrons are known to have been equipped with F-10s.

In March 1943 the 3rd Photo Recon Squadron took twelve new F-10s to Alaska and Northwest Canada to provide up to date information for new charts of unmapped wilderness areas. The 3rd departed from Rome, New York where ice tires were fitted. Additional winterization gear was picked up at Camp McCoy, Wisconsin. One flight followed the established Ferry Command route via Great Falls, Edmonton and Whitehorse, one flight continuing on to Fairbanks, Anchorage and the Aleutians. Operating in the far north until June, the squadron returned to Ogden, Utah where the flame quenching "finger" exhaust collectors were replaced with Clayton "S" stacks. The other two flights remained in Canada and operated out of Fort McMurray in Alberta.

The unit returned to Brazil in September where they had previously mapped with F-2s and Lockheed Hudson A-29s late in 1942. This was a brief assignment of one month after which the 3rd departed for duty in India and China. Mapping was begun on the Hump and the air routes to India and the Chengtu area where airfields were being prepared for the forthcoming B-29s.

The 3rd then returned to the U.S. at MacDill Field, Florida where the F-10s were turned in for B-17/F-9s which served as trainers until receipt of new B-29/F-13s.

The 7th and 10th Photo Recon Squadrons provided the necessary training for mapping and charting crews. Operating with F-4, F-5 and F-10 airplanes,

Lt. Ole Griffith, second from right, and his crew of 43-3438 of 91st PM Sq operated in Central and South America. (Ole Griffith)

training was carried out at Will Rogers and Woodward Fields in Oklahoma and MacDill, Savannah and Colorado Springs from January 1942 until May 1944.

In 1944 and 1945 the 11th Tactical Recon Squadron used F-10s and a considerable number of other aircraft in cooperation with maneuvers and training of ground forces. All activity was within the continental United States.

The 18th Combat Mapping Squadron flew F-10s in the summer of 1943 mapping in the South Pacific from bases in New Caledonia and the New Hebrides.

Between 1943 and 1945 F-10s of the 19th Recon Squadron mapped portions of North America before moving on to the Middle East and Africa.

In the European theater the 34th Photo Recon Squadron operated F-10s during 1944. Formerly a Wisconsin National Guard unit, the 34th arrived in England in March and was assigned to the 8th and later to the 10th Photo Group, IXth Air Force. Operations were carried out from French bases from August 1944 until VE Day.

B-25D-1/F-10 No. 41-29886 was one of four F-10s that served in both USAAF and RCAF units as a photo mapper. The Canadian chin fairing is considerably different from the USAAF counterpart. (NASM No. 81-14485)

44

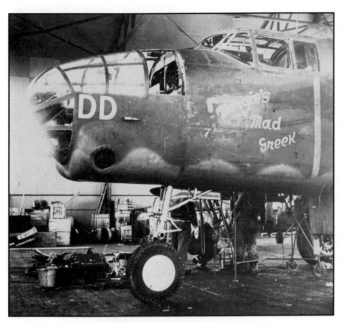

MARGIE'S MAD GREEK, B-25D/F-10 of the 1st Photo Charting Sq flown by Lt. P.A. Chapas, Bradley Field CT. (Edwin S. Root)

CELESTIAL CHARIOT, F-10 of the 3rd Photo Recon Squadron at McDill Field, March, 1944. (Clarence L. Becker)

In 1943 the United States Government negotiated with a number of South and Central American countries for aerial photographing and mapping. Much of this vast area was virtually uncharted and the limited contemporary information notoriously inaccurate. The reasons for this considerable effort are somewhat obscure but are believed to have been a basis for possible operations against German or Japanese coastal intrusions and additional protection of the Panama Canal.

The 91st Photo Mapping Squadron was assigned the greater portion of this area and was equipped with F-10s at Reading Field, Pennsylvania in September 1943. From this station four plane elements were dispatched to Recife and Natal in Brazil; Talara, Peru; Santiago, Chile; British Guiana, the Canal Zone and the Caribbean. Operational headquarters were relocated late in the war from Reading to Buckley Field, Colorado. The 91st

continued the use of the F-10s until general replacement by the B-17/F-9 late in 1945.

Little is known about the 101st Photographic Bombardment Squadron which is known to have flown F-10s in the air defense of the Caribbean in 1944 and 1945. (See Appendix B for -Ds modified as F-10s.)

Flamin Mamie XB-25E

As American aircraft became involved in world wide operations, the icing problem became tactical as well as mechanical. Inflatable leading edge de-icer boots were reasonably effective for removal of moderate ice accumulations but were never noted for effective removal of heavy or rapid build ups.

The Army believed it necessary to develop new methods of combating this problem. Late in 1942 the Air Technical Service Command at Wright Field, Ohio and the National Advisory Committee for Aeronautics with the Air Materiel Command, began a joint developmental program directed toward the study of icing effects and improved methods of anti-icing.

Consideration had been given to the utilization of the heat produced by exhaust gases for a thermal system of ice removal and prevention. The program was therefore directed toward development of exhaust gas to air heat exchangers for thermal anti-icing systems for large aircraft. Preliminary investigations showed that such systems

The outboard side of the right engine showing the heat exchanger installation and duct to the outer wing. The lower ram air duct to the exchanger has not yet been installed. (NAA)

From the cockpit of XB-25E a Northwest Airlines crew chief observes North American engineers Jim Dunham and Ed Pierce in a lighter moment. (NAA)

required great heat and appeared more promising than the use of separate heat sources. This was apparent when it was determined that a 1,000 H.P. engine exhausted adequate heat and that a heat exchanger was capable of 10,000 BTU per hour per pound of exchanger weight.[1]

The requirements for such a unit were especially severe for the state of the art in 1942 and it was questionable that the specifications could be met. Minimal weight was paramount, yet the exchanger needed to be small enough for installation in a crowded nacelle. It also needed to be capable of operating on dynamic pressure without back pressure and resistant to prolonged thermal and vibrational stresses. The N.A.C.A. and the University of California began an investigation with several aircraft and heat exchanger manufacturers to determine the practicality of such a system.

Concurrently, the Ames Aeronautical Laboratory began a series of successful tests with a number of different heat exchangers on a North American O-47, low wing, three place observation aircraft powered by a Wright R-1820 engine. These tests were on the exhaust pipe only, no thermal system being incorporated in the wings or tail. One section of the long tail pipe was removed and replaced by a series of interchangeable exchangers. Results of these tests indicated that the desired product was feasible.

Extensive tests were then programmed to be conducted at the Ice Research Base, a new facility at Wold-Chamberlain Field at Minneapolis, Minnesota. The IRB, operated by Northwest Airlines under contract from the Air Materiel Command, was established to study ice

Left cowl photo gives a view of the integral carburetor and heat exchanger air intakes as differentiated from production B-25 cowls. (NAA)

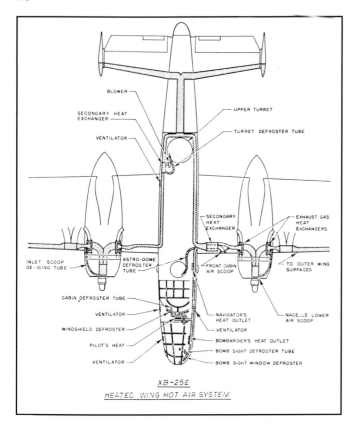

XB-25E
HEATED WING HOT AIR SYSTEM

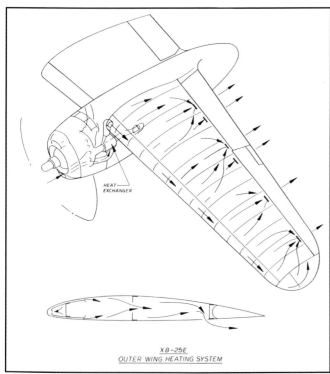

XB-25E
OUTER WING HEATING SYSTEM

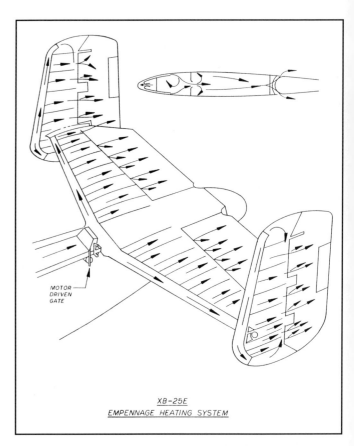

XB-25E
EMPENNAGE HEATING SYSTEM

and frost effects on aircraft and to develop effective methods of coping with the related problems.[2]

The new facility was commanded by Major A.F. Olsen, a NWA pilot recalled to service by the Air Corps. NWA assigned six of their pilots to the project: A.F. Becker, Walter Bullock, A.E. Walker, Marvin Cooney, Dave Brenner, and Richard Barton. The ATSC supplied all aircraft, funding and jurisdiction over testing.[3]

The aircraft modified for the IRB test program included a Boeing B-17F, two Consolidated B-24s, a Douglas XC-53A, an A-26, a Fairchild C-82, a Lockheed 12, a Martin B-26 and a North American XB-25E. All were modified by their respective manufacturers to thermal, heated wing, anti-icing configurations. Separately and at other locations, a Pan American DC-3 and a Navy PBY-5 were flown successfully for many hours with similar systems.

The XB-25E was initially a standard production B-25C-10, 42-32281, powered by Wright R-2600-13 engines. Engineering for the modifications began early in 1943 and work on the airplane was accomplished in the experimental department at North American's Inglewood, California plant. A major portion of the engineering was accomplished by the Power Plant Section where the complex heat exchangers were developed and installation layouts made. From these points the Wing Engineering Group interfaced with the wing modifications and leading edge ducting.

The system utilized by North American comprised four primary exhaust gas to air heat exchangers, two in each nacelle, just forward of the firewall, which provided the heat for anti and de-icing, de-frosting and cabin heat. A secondary exchanger in the inboard wing leading edge was used for cabin heat to insure against possible carbon monoxide contamination.

The only visual difference of XB-25E from standard B-25s was the cowlings. The carburetor air intake duct was faired internally in the top of the cowl and the anti-icing air intake duct similarly configured at the bottom. Each row of cylinders exhausted through a separate exchanger, one ported outboard and one inboard of each nacelle. Ram air from the lower cowl duct was routed under the engine to a split duct, each side leading to a primary exchanger. Air was controlled by gates allowing controlled diversion of heated air to the anti-icing system or out the exhaust. [4]

Major modifications of the wings were required, particularly the internal leading edges. An airfoil shaped barrier, identical in shape but slightly smaller than the inside of the wing skin was fitted inside of the leading edge of the outer wing panels. This barrier extended to the wing tip and allowed about one eighth of an inch gap from the inner surface of the wing skin to form the passage for the hot anti-icing air. This barrier extended aft to about the 15% chord line to a vertical web similar to a spar but of far lighter construction. This member was notched numerous places top and bottom permitting the heated air to move aft within the wing to be ported overboard through holes in the underside. Empennage design was identical. [5]

Design temperatures were sufficiently high that ice on the wing surface was vaporized rather than just melted which would have permitted water to flow aft and freeze on flaps and ailerons.

An instrumentation and monitoring station was installed in the navigator's compartment directly behind the flight deck.

The airplane was completed early in 1944 and first flown on 4 February by test pilot Joe Barton. The first functional flight test of the thermal system was programmed to the 20,000 foot altitude with recorded instrument readings for each 1,000 feet. Barton, co-pilot Talman and test engineers Jim Dunham, Ed Pierce and Don Rogerson took off on 11 February on a southeasterly course from the North American plant. With hot air ducting through the system, Dunham had completed the 9,000 foot entry when flame and smoke entered the monitor area from the right wing.

The heat exchanger dump gates were immediately set to cut off system heat and Barton began the descent for an emergency landing at nearby Los Alamitos Naval Air Station. Rogerson, Pierce and Dunham fought the fire with on board extinguishers until safely on the ground. Inspection revealed charred insulation at a duct joint where temperatures were found to have exceeded calculations. The exchanger by-pass dump gates had failed to function properly preventing complete shut down of heated air. The airplane was inspected, found airworthy, and flown back to the North American plant. [6]

Repairs were completed in late February and the airplane flown to the Ice Research Base in early March, too late in the season for much testing but sufficient icing conditions remained to prove the function and adequacy of the system.

Late in 1944 A.E. Walker flew XB-25E to Cooking Lake, east of Edmonton, Alberta, where an extensive program was conducted to study frost effects on wings. Approximately thirty flights provided significant data and the airplane returned to the IRB at Minneapolis. [7]

XB-25E operating at Lewis Research Center at Cleveland. The dark color on the cowl ring, inboard wing leading edge and left vertical tail is red paint for photographic contrast of ice build up. (NACA via M. Kusenda

The Engineering Division Propeller Laboratory of the ATSC had outlined further tests for developing a means of preventing icing and de-icing propellers. Although it was well known that blade icing reduced efficiency and power, simultaneous icing of the airplane made it impossible to determine the extent. The excellent airframe de-icing system of XB-25E made it an ideal choice for such tests which were conducted in February and March of 1945.

Protection of the propeller blades consisted of rubber heating elements bonded to the blades and heated by electrical energy from hub generators. This proved successful and test results determined with reasonable accuracy that blade icing caused a 15% reduction in efficiency. Further tests were conducted during the winter of 1945/1946 toward development of improved anti-icing systems for cowlings, windshields, turrets, astrodomes and radio masts.

Much of this testing was probably carried out at the Lewis Research Center at Cleveland, Ohio where XB-25E was assigned in July 1944. It was used for continuing ice research until February 1953 when it was returned to the USAF at Wright Field.

The effectiveness of the heated wing system of anti-icing and de-icing was well proven but it was a costly system. Although used to some extent in post war years, cost considerations remained paramount and the inflatable boots continued in general use.

The ultimate destiny of the airplane was the scrap yard but the forward section, complete with nose art, is now with the Confederate Air Force at Midland, Texas.

FLAMIN MAMIE on the ramp at Lewis Research Center. Nose art has been revised and inflatable boots fitted to the tail. Larger propeller blades have been fitted with leading edge heating units and the nose is electrically heated plastic coating. (NACA via M. Kusenda)

The B-25G and the Big Gun

The concept of large caliber airborne cannon was by no means new when it first became known on North American's B-25G in 1942. As early as 1910 Gabriel Voisin in France mounted a 37 mm 1885 Hotchkiss naval cannon on one of his biplanes. In retrospect the flimsy wood and wire structure seems totally inadequate and the degree of success is unknown. [8]

Soon after the World War I Armistice, work was begun to develop a 37 mm gun suitable for mounting on aircraft. Early efforts produced little more than a copy of the French Puteau which was tested in the nose of a Martin MB-2 bomber. The GA-1 bomber, built by Boeing in 1920 to a design by the engineering department at McCook Field, was also fitted with a 37 mm cannon of unknown ancestry. The success of this combination remains a mystery, but the attempt is indicative that intentions existed for making the airplane more than a passive observation machine. This effort was carried further when the Colts Patent Firearms Co. employed John Browning to make design improvements to the gun and he reportedly succeeded in increasing reliability, muzzle velocity and rate of fire. The 1920s were not progressive years for armament design and development as isolationist attitudes prevailed and controlled budgets accordingly. As a result, Browning's work was temporarily shelved. [9]

When aircraft design progressed to all metal construction about 1930 it then became possible to mount heavier and far more effective armament from the devastating .50 caliber machine gun to the 75 mm cannon and further work on the 37 mm gun was resumed. The Vickers-Armstrong Co. in England made a considerably improved gun which was well proven in the Spanish War. In the United States the Ordnance Department resumed work on Browning's developments with sufficient success

The first airborne 75mm cannon was tested on a Douglas B-18 by Army Ordnance Department in 1938. The photograph of the B-18 installation does not show how the blast was deflected from the airframe. (USAF Museum)

that several new attack aircraft were proposed utilizing the gun.

In 1935 and 1936 the twin engine Curtiss XA-14 was designed with a special nose enclosing a single 37 mm gun. Trials at Langley Field were inconclusive due to the almost nonexistent supply of ammunition. The shortage was apparently alleviated as subsequent tests were conducted with the twin engine Bell Model 9 with a similar installation. Results were sufficiently successful that the same gun was designed into Bell's successful P-39 fighter with the gun firing through the propeller hub.

About that time the 37mm gun seems to have been given less consideration in favor of experiments with the 75 mm cannon, initially the tube and breech of the standard French artillery piece.

In 1936 studies were begun on aircraft capable of carrying heavy weapons of great destructive effect and to determine the suitability of a heavily armed airplane for the purpose of airborne destruction of enemy aircraft. These studies concluded that a combat airplane equipped with a modern auto-loading cannon and suitable fire control system was feasible if the military requirement was found to exist.

Tests of the effects of various types of ammunition against aircraft structures was conducted at Aberdeen Proving Ground. These trials showed that a single direct hit by a high explosive 75 mm projectile would bring down an airplane that would not be brought down by hits from a smaller available caliber.

Based on the 75 mm field piece it was estimated that approximately one year would be required to produce a new and lighter weight type of gun if manual loading were permitted, longer if automatic loading were required. Authorization was requested to determine:

a. trajectory effect from a heavy aerial mounted gun

b. practicability of an airborne stereoscopic rangefinder

c. accuracy on towed targets at ranges of from 2,000 to 3,500 yards

d. if a military requirement existed for a combat airplane based on such a weapon system. Should (d) be answered affirmative, the general characteristics of the airplane, gun and fire control system. [10]

In 1938 Captain Horace Quinn of the Army Ordnance Department made a test installation of the 75 mm cannon in the fuselage of a junked Douglas B-18. A good base for ground tests, it proved that modern airframe structures could be made to withstand the effects of heavy blast and recoil.

Quinn subsequently obtained a flyable B-18 for in flight firing tests. Lighter, more efficient gun mounts were developed, five in all, to secure the cannon to the airframe. Sufficient interest resulted from these early trials that an improved cannon was demonstrated at Eglin Field in 1940 and commercial firms were solicited to assist in further development. [11]

These joint efforts produced an aerial cannon of lighter weight and increased punch than the original

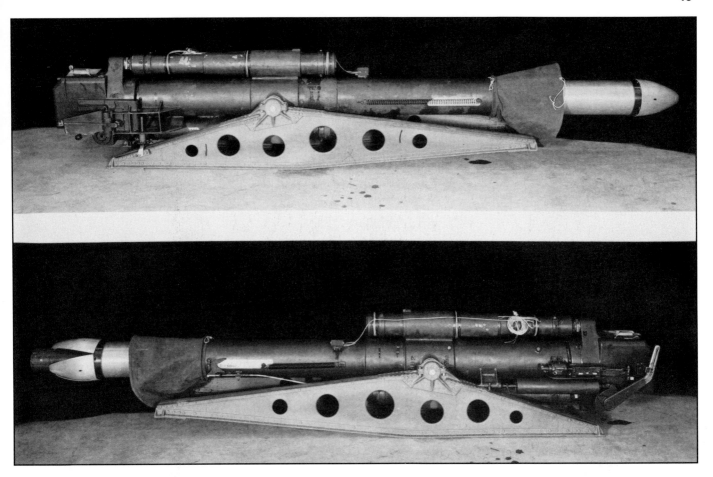

The 75mm artillery gun designated M-4. A lever operated chain drive mechanism opened the breech for loading the first round. The long cylinder at the top rear is a spring actuated oil compensator for regulating variations in oil content in the recoil cylinder due to heat from repeated firings. An aluminum shroud was fitted to the barrel, terminating in a 4 petal protective muzzle cap which opened by the closing of the breech. Neither the cap nor the canvas bag air seal proved satisfactory and were not used on production airplanes. The bag was replaced by a more functional micarta sliding plate which prevented air from coming through the tunnel. (NAA)

French piece. An improved recoil mechanism was adapted to the new gun, designated M-4, and the new combination, flight tested by Captain Quinn, proved that the 75 mm cannon was adaptable to production combat aircraft.

Further evidence of the Army's considerable effort on this project in the years immediately preceding World War II was the development of an automatic feed system for loading the cannon. In March 1942 the twin engine Beech XA-38 was equipped with the auto feed 75 mm gun and referred to as a "Destroyer Type". Flight test results were not considered satisfactory. The airplane had limited forward firing auxiliary armament, sighting left much to be desired, radar was considered necessary and combustion gases from gun firing filled the cockpit. The auto feed gun tipped the scales at 1,800 pounds and it was concluded that better results were likely to be obtained with a manually loaded gun.

By mid 1942 the Army began development work for the production of 75 mm equipped twin engine destroyer aircraft. The third Douglas XA-26 prototype, designated XB-26B, was also equipped with the 75 mm cannon and 500 examples of the B-26B were planned for production. An alternate variant was also considered with a brace of four 37 mm nose guns. Neither were placed into production.

Concurrent with these efforts in mid 1942 was yet another 37 mm gun installation in the Martin A-30 "Baltimore". The successes or failures of this installation are unknown. [12]

Preliminary studies indicated that the North American B-25 could be readily modified into a heavily armed, long range, attack aircraft capable of carrying an effective bomb load. Early in 1942, more than a year before Jack Fox and Captain Paul Gunn pioneered the depot modified strafers in Australia, North American was also given the go ahead for a 75 mm cannon carrying attack bomber. [13]

Called to the office of Ray Rice, North American's chief engineer, structures engineer Richard Schleicher was justly surprised when asked if he had information on the recoil forces of the Army's 75 mm cannon. Nor was it logical that he should have. The Army, Rice explained, intended that the big gun be installed in the B-25 and, if successful, the new variant be placed in production.

Drawings and data from previous experiments were provided to Edgar Schmued of P-51 design prominence and who was in charge of North American's Confidential Design Group. Time as usual, was short. Mid-morning on a Wednesday Schmued explained to

50

In the sand dunes adjacent to the Pacific Ocean, now the edge of Los Angeles Int. Airport, the 75 mm cannon was first tested in a B-25 forward fuselage section. (NAA)

George Wing, one of his designers, that his immediate assignment was a preliminary layout of the cannon installation in the B-25. Schmued further emphasized that the layout would be completed by noon on Saturday of that week.[14]

For a three day effort the assignment was formidable. Wing quickly discovered that the cannon installation project had created enough interest among fellow engineers that continual kibitzing made working difficult if not impossible. Gathering a few drafting tools and a small lap size drawing board he retired to a stall in the men's room where the relative isolation made work

Removal of the nose section shows the ideal location for the 760 pound M-4 cannon in the bombardier's crawl tunnel. (NAA)

Installation and removal of the cannon was relatively simple. (NAA)

possible. Every hour or so an associate would come in and gather sketches from Wing for incorporation in the inboard profile drawing.

Initial consideration indicated that the bomb bay would be the most suitable location for the big gun with a long barrel extending through the bombardier's crawl tunnel and out the nose. Such a location however, would have complicated the bomb bay and made gun loading more difficult. It was therefore decided that the navigator's compartment and crawl tunnel made the best location.

A chain fed loading mechanism was initially decided upon but this method was abandoned in favor of the single hand load system which was used on all production B-25G and H models.

Wing succeeded in completing the design on time but for some unknown reason the package of drawings was not ready for mailing to the Air Corps until mid-afternoon which drew a frown from Schmued. Wing's preliminary work, after Air Corps approval, was turned over to the Armament Engineering Group where production design and flight test participation was accomplished.

The M-4 75 mm aircraft cannon supplied to North American was essentially the French 75 mm tube with vertically traveling breech block instead of the rotating block used by the French. For initial loading the breech was opened manually with a cocking lever. Loading was accomplished by forcing a round into the chamber with sufficient force to unlock the breech block, causing it to rise to the closed or locked position. The gun was then ready to fire.[15]

After firing the counter recoil stroke lowered the breech block and cocked the gun, the fired case was extracted and the breech block was locked open (lower position) ready for loading of the next round.

Conceptual design had shown that the gun needed fourteen feet of space including the recoil travel. The B-

25 fuselage proved a natural. The crawl tunnel to the nose accommodated the barrel, and the navigator's compartment, just aft of the flight deck, provided adequate space for the breech, recoil stroke, working space for the gunner and an ammunition rack.

This location, however, positioned the muzzle well aft of the front of the airplane necessitating a shorter nose or much longer and heavier barrel. A new nose section, 26 inches shorter than the original, was selected as the shortest possible from an aerodynamic standpoint. Even this change left the gun muzzle slightly aft of the forward contour.

Effects of the heavy muzzle blast on the nose were of unknown magnitude and no precedent existed for determination of the required structural reinforcement. Actual firing tests were necessary. A complete forward fuselage section with cannon was trucked to a concealed area in the sand dunes by the Pacific Ocean west of Mines Field where firing tests could be conducted. Using varying propellant charges, non-explosive projectiles were fired into the dunes. The structure was progressively strengthened until resistant to prolonged firing of rounds loaded to 115% of normal charges.

B-25C-1, 41-13296, was modified as XB-25G. Initial test flights were made by company test pilot Ed Virgin and test engineer Paul Brewer and accompanied by other flight test and armament engineers on subsequent flights. The first two flights on 22 October 1942 were for procedure, function and cannon loading with dummy rounds. Stall characteristics were normal and diving to 340 MPH indicated revealed no problems.

The B-25 featured a type N-3B optical gun sight with a type A-1 combination gun/bomb sight head mounted on the left side of the cockpit cowl. This combination unit provided sighting of cannon and nose guns and for minimum altitude bombing. The sight reflector was adjustable by a calibrated knob from a gun sight position parallel to the aircraft flight path to a bombing position varying from 1° to 15° below the flight path. A rheostat regulated the light intensity of the reticle image on the reflector. (NAA)

Directly abaove the breech on the left side of the airplane a rack was installed for 21 rounds of 75 mm ammunition. On production airplanes the rack was protected by armor plate on three sides. (NAA)

A loading tray aft of the breech provided increased safety and precise alignment for loading the heavy rounds into the chamber. The tray and cannoneer's seat hinged upward to provide access to the forward hatch. (NAA)

On October 23 over the Pacific Ocean, Virgin, Brewer and Colonel Quinn began the first in-flight firing tests. Initial rounds were loaded to 50% and 75% of normal propellant and the crew reported the moment of firing to be a heavy jolt, neither severe or frightening. The projectile was clearly visible very briefly after firing.

These "short" rounds occasionally produced an unexpected and spectacular phenomenon. Due to incomplete combustion of the propellant within the barrel, unburned powder frequently ignited in a fire ball ahead of the airplane. This was usually followed by a sharp, secondary shock, an effect not experienced with full propellant charges. [16]

As firing tests continued the muzzle cover was refitted with a stronger spring but it failed to operate properly with propellant charges exceeding 75% and it was thereby deleted. On subsequent flights full charge loads produced no problems and preliminary testing was considered complete.

Other armament was limited to two .50 caliber nose guns and two in the top aft turret.

On 31 October XB-25G was flown to Kansas City for installation of bomb controls, then returned to Inglewood for additional tests. On 22 November after ten hours flight time, it was flown to Eglin Field, Florida for further testing by the Air Corps. Following this program the Air Corps placed an order for 400 examples to be supplied without lower turrets. [17]

In addition to the 400 B-25G-5 and -10 airplanes in mid 1943, the NAA modificaton center at Kansas City modified five B-25Cs nos. 42-32384/42-32388 and fifty-eight B-25C-20 and -25 with solid nose, two nose guns and 75 mm cannon, all redesignated B-25G. Some of the latter grup were done by the Republic mod center at Evansville, Indiana but the arrangements between the two are unknown. The converted B-25C-20/-25s are: 42-64531, 64558, 64561, 64563, 64569, 64579/64582,64584/64587,64649, 64654, 64668, 64670/64675, 64692, 64693, 64696/64707, 64753/64772,74779,64780.

Preparatory to the anticipated invasion of Japan the Hawaiian Air Depot replaced the cannon with the 8 gun nose on an unknown number of B-25Gs. Wing launching studs for 5 inch HVAR rockets were also added.

B-25G

Engine	Wright R-2600-13
Carburetors	Holley 1685 HA
Fuel	Same as B-25C
Armament	75mm cannon and 21 rounds ammunition
	2 .50 cal fixed guns in nose 400 rds/gun
	2 .50 cal guns in top turret 400 rds/gun
	2 .50 cal guns in lower turret 350 rds/gun
Armor Protection	3/8" behind pilots
	Forward of instrument panel,
	Forward of cannoneer's station,
	Bulkhead aft of turrets,
	Around 75 mm ammunition rack,
	Plate below windshield
	External flak plate on left side only
Weights	Empty 19,200 lbs. Max 35,000 lbs.
Speed	Max 280 MPH at 15,000 feet
Service Ceiling	24,300 feet
Range	1,560 miles with 3,000 lbs. bombs
Crew	Pilot, co-pilot, navigator/cannoneer, 2 gunners

Major Differences from B-25C/D

a. Greenhouse nose replaced by shorter solid nose
b. Two fixed .50 cal. nose guns
c. 75mm cannon in crawl tunnel
Note: Lower turret deleted effective on B-25G No. 42-65001
First B-25G accepted in May 1943
Last B-25G accepted in August 1943

A B-25G undergoing tests conducted at the AAF Tactical Center at Orlando FL. (USAF)

B-25H

Although the B-25G was less successful in combat operations than expected, North American received a follow on order for 1,000 cannon carrying attack strafers, designated B-25H.

Principal differences from the G models were the lighter weight 75 mm cannon, four nose guns instead of two, two guns at waist stations, two in a tail turret, top turret moved forward to the navigator's station, the addition of four forward fuselage blister gun packs and elimination of provisions for a co-pilot.

Some controversy arose over the exclusion of co-pilot provisions. In 1943 General James Doolittle had questioned the need for a second pilot in B-25 and B-26 aircraft. The use of a single pilot, he believed, would permit a narrower fuselage so that visibility to the right and rear would be vastly improved for formation flying. There was also a precedent in the Douglas A-20 and the British used the single pilot system almost entirely, even on the huge four engine Lancaster. Reasons for a co-pilot had been for reduction of fatigue on long flights and as a safety factor in combat should the pilot be wounded or killed.[18]

A general description of the B-25H had been circulated to all commands for comments and anticipated allocations. Early in September subsequent dispatches were sent out informing that the blister gun packs were being deleted from the left side to make space for cabin heating equipment and that provisions for a co-pilot were also being eliminated.

The only partially negative response was from General George Kenney, commanding the Fifth Air Force in the Southwest Pacific. Kenney stated in no uncertain terms that he wanted the second pilot for long, over water missions under hazardous conditions. He also made it abundantly clear that he needed two more fuselage blister guns a helluva lot more than cabin heaters.

Fully understanding the requirements, General Arnold replied to Kenney's objections in considerable detail:

With reference to the B-25H, the first 300 airplanes will have four .50 caliber guns in the nose plus the 75 mm cannon and two .50 caliber guns on the right side of the fuselage. After the 300th H all subsequent airplanes will have two additional blister guns on the left side of the fuselage, making a total of eight fixed forward firing guns in addition to the cannon.

As regards the cabin heater, we were unsuccessful in getting all other theaters to concur in removing it and it will, of necessity, remain in as a production item. At present, modification centers are unusually busy, but we will arrange for an Air Service Command depot to remove the heaters from your airplanes.

Regarding the elimination of the co-pilot from B-25H, this airplane was designed for tactical use principally as an attack bomber. Other bombardment airplanes with a similar mission are flown by one

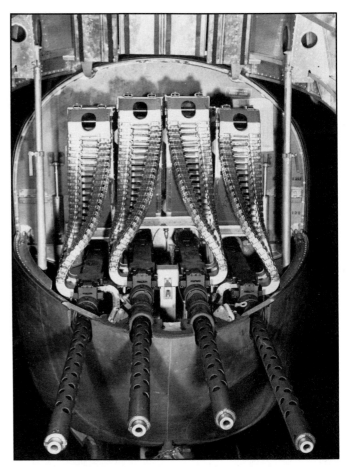

The B-25H nose section structure was little changed from the B-25G except for the accommodation for 4 guns. (NAA)

pilot and operations flown by one pilot were considered in planning for the B-25H.

Before building the airplane without co-pilot provision, the advantages and disadvantages were carefully weighed. The elimination of the co-pilot was strongly indicated for the following reasons:

1. The new armament added a great deal of weight in the nose. Any possible reduction of weight forward of the C.G. was mandatory. A saving of over 300 pounds was possible through elimination of the co-pilot's seat, armor plate and controls.

2. The airplane's improved defensive armament, consisting of waist guns and tail turret, compelled the shifting forward of the upper turret to maintain proper balance. Moving the upper turret forward to the former navigator's compartment not only solved the balance problem but provided better turret location. However, with this installation and the addition of the cannon ammunition and loading provisions in this compartment, no space remained for the navigator. It was possible to provide a jump seat and a navigator's table at the co-pilot's position. Placed here, the navigator would be well positioned to function as navigator on low altitude missions and to assist the pilot in any possible way as well as acting as cannoneer.

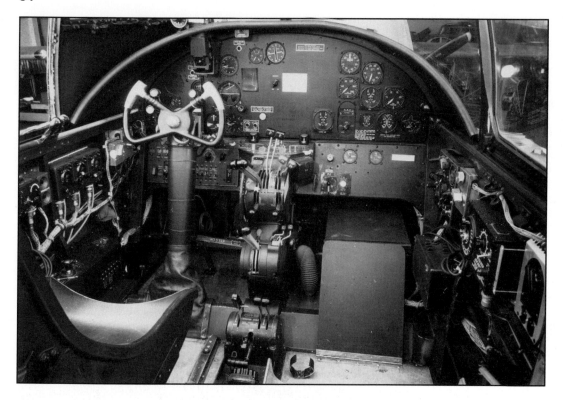

Notable from previous B-25 furnishings and equipment, the B-25H was devoid of provisions for a co-pilot. A simple seat was installed on the right side for the navigator/cannoneer, and a chart board (not shown) was mounted under the right window. A radio and foot rest were located under the right side of the instrument panel. (NAA)

The type A-1 pilot bomb sight was mounted on the base for the N-3B gun sight and was used for minimum altitude bombing. When set at a 0° reading the reflector glass is at 45° to the aircraft flight path for use as a gun sight. The adjustment knob rotated the reflector toward vertical moving the sighting angle downward to stops provided for pre-determined bomb sight angles. A rheostat provided variations in light on the reflector plate. Ring and bead sights were also mounted on the B-25H. (NAA)

3. Since, in this airplane the co-pilot does the bombing, it was necessary to locate all bombing equipment in the cockpit. Also the radio compass was removed from the former navigator's compartment and placed in the cockpit. These installations made the elimination of the co-pilot's provisions unavoidable.

4. Because of the attack nature of the airplane, it was important to give the pilot more armor protection. To have provided a co-pilot's position with more than normal armor was out of the question from the weight standpoint.

5. If possible to eliminate the co-pilot, the consequent elimination of trained personnel would be of considerable value.

6. A test was conducted at Eglin Field to determine the need for a co-pilot in the B-25H. The conclusions reached as a result of the test were that the airplane could be handled satisfactorily in combat without a co-pilot; that it could be flown in all positions of close V formation and close echelon formation day or night; that evasive action could be taken; that landings and takeoffs day or night could be accomplished satisfactorily and that cannon and machine guns could be fired efficiently. The test report recommended elimination of the co-pilot from the cannon bearing B-25s. The single adverse comment resulting from this test was to the effect that pilot fatigue is greatly increased by single pilot operation especially when flying formation.

7. A cable was sent 13 February 1943 to all theaters scheduled to receive B-25 airplanes. In

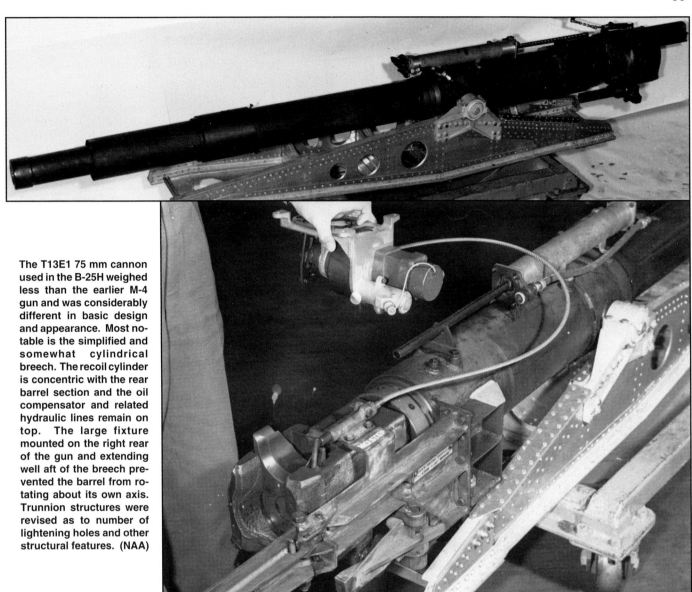

The T13E1 75 mm cannon used in the B-25H weighed less than the earlier M-4 gun and was considerably different in basic design and appearance. Most notable is the simplified and somewhat cylindrical breech. The recoil cylinder is concentric with the rear barrel section and the oil compensator and related hydraulic lines remain on top. The large fixture mounted on the right rear of the gun and extending well aft of the breech prevented the barrel from rotating about its own axis. Trunnion structures were revised as to number of lightening holes and other structural features. (NAA)

this was set out the plan for making B-25Hs and the airplane's proposed features were outlined, including the fact that there would be but one pilot. Theaters were asked to submit their recommendations for allocations of these airplanes. In direct reply to this cable all theaters queried sent replies giving their percentage requirements for the cannon bearing B-25. In none of these replies was an objection raised to the elimination of the co-pilot.

Decision to proceed with production was made after consideration of the above projects.

Wright Field states that to provide for co-pilots in B-25Hs would now mean a great deal of work with consequent delay and no assurance that the result would be satisfactory. Kits could be made up and shipped to the field, although this too would take time and the same problems would be encountered there.

My people have felt that an influence in the demand for co-pilots is the fact that the B-25s have always had co-pilots. The B-25H differs in many respects from earlier B-25s and it is believed that the airplane should be tried as built. [19]

And so it was.

B-25C-10, 42-32372, was modified as the prototype B-25H and appropriately named "Mortimer II" after its famous Fifth Air Force field modified strafer predecessor. (See Part V.) For test purposes the airplane was fitted with a two gun nose and M-4 cannon as used on the B-25G. The revised and lighter weight T13E1 cannon was not available for the prototype.[20]

All co-pilot equipment was deleted and a small jump seat and chartboard were installed in the right side of the flight deck for the navigator/cannoneer.

The top turret was relocated from the aft fuselage forward to the navigator's compartment where stowage racks for 21 rounds of 75 mm ammunition, case ejection

56

A shell case deflector was installed back of the 75 mm gun. Ejection from the recoiling cannon propelled the empty case back against the deflector which directed the case down a chute and overboard. After an ejected shell hit another aircraft the casings were stowed. (NAA)

and other necessary cannon equipment was installed. The lower turret and scanning lenses were removed. Two .50 cal. guns were added at the aft waist stations.

Two .50 caliber guns were mounted in an armor protected, hydraulic electric Bell M-7 tail turret. To accommodate the gunner, a subtle airframe change deepened the aft fuselage which raised the tail seven inches above the fuselage reference line than on previous models.

Waist station guns were fed from ammunition boxes just aft of the armor plate bulkhead. Fired cases were ejected into canvas bags. (NAA)

Phosphor bronze blast arrestors were designed to deflect muzzle blast upwards and down to reduce effects on the fuselage. They were factory installed on certain B-25H and B-25J airplanes. (NAA)

Bombing and torpedo equipment remained unchanged although numerous changes of components and locations were made regarding radio, electrical and hydraulic components.

"Mortimer II" was powered by Wright R-2600-20 engines equipped with Bendix Stromberg PR48A1 carburetors and American Bosch SF14LU-10 magnetos. Two-speed centrifugal superchargers provided a low blower ratio of 7.06 to 1 and a high ratio of 10.06 to 1. To provide added cooling due to the greater power of the

Increased spacing between the guns on the B-25H resulted in separate blisters. Ejection chute and port for expended case links is clearly shown. (NAA)

The twin gun M-7 Bell tail turret provided an excellent field of fire. Picture at the right (looking down and aft) shows gun controls and protective armor plate. (NAA)

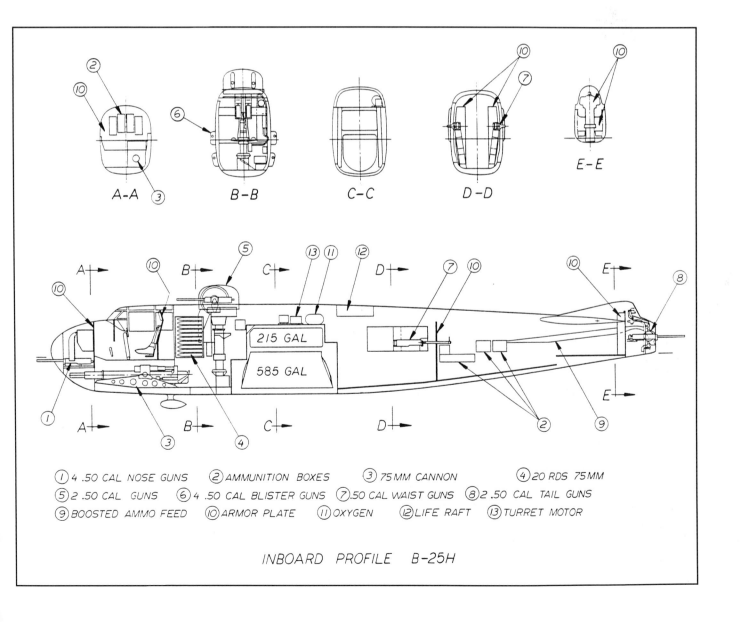

A-A   B-B   C-C   D-D   E-E

215 GAL

585 GAL

① 4 .50 CAL NOSE GUNS   ② AMMUNITION BOXES   ③ 75 MM CANNON   ④ 20 RDS 75 MM
⑤ 2 .50 CAL GUNS   ⑥ 4 .50 CAL BLISTER GUNS   ⑦ .50 CAL WAIST GUNS   ⑧ 2 .50 CAL TAIL GUNS
⑨ BOOSTED AMMO FEED   ⑩ ARMOR PLATE   ⑪ OXYGEN   ⑫ LIFE RAFT   ⑬ TURRET MOTOR

INBOARD PROFILE   B-25H

Production B-25H No. 1, 43-4105, nearing completion on the North American ramp. Typical of the first 300 examples, blister guns were installed on the right side only. (NAA)

Dash 20 over the Dash 13 engines, the internal diameter of the cowl nose ring was increased to thirty-eight inches from thirty-six inches on previous models.

The prototype was first flown on 15 May 1943 by North American pilots Ed Virgin and Gus Pitcairn who continued test flights with Joe Barton, Bob Chilton and Major Tom Gerrity of 3rd Attack Group prominence.[21]

Final design, tooling and fabrication of production examples progressed concurrently with the modification and testing of the prototype. The Dash 20 engines of the test airplane gave way to the more generally used Dash 13 types. The first B-25H off the line, 43-4105, was flown on 31 July 1943 by Bob Chilton and deliveries to the Air Corps began in August.

The first allocation of B-25H models went to the 498th Squadron, 345th Bomb Group of the Fifth Air Force.

B-25H
Engines	Wright R-2600-13
Carburetors	Holley 1685 HA
Fuel	Same as B-25C
Armament	75 mm cannon and 21 rounds ammunition
	4 .50 cal. nose guns 400 rds/gun

The 301st B-25H, 43-4405 also mounts the left blister guns which were added beginning with this airplane. Firing tests have been extensive as evidenced by the blast effects on the flak and blast plates. (NAA)

As the 1,000th and last B-25H and final Inglewood B-25 neared completion in July 1944, employees covered the airplane within and outside with dollar bills. All money was removed and donated to the Army-Navy relief fund. NAA President, "Dutch" Kindelberger, arranged for paint and brushes that employees could autograph this historic Mitchell. Known as "Old Bones", 43-5104 arrived in India on 30 November for assignment to the X Air Force, 12th BG. This unusual photograph shows all but four of the North American production test pilots with the last of 1,000. Front row L to R: Ted Terry, George Ornstein, Abelardo Rodriguez, Roger Ruud, Leon Indart, Wilcox 'Tex' Wild, Dick Chapin. Back row L to R: Spencer Jennings, Harlan Sharman, George Annis, Jack Bryan, Paul Torrance, Paul Franklin, Bob Marriot, and Paul Balfour. (NAA)

	2 .50 cal blister guns on right side of forward fuselage 400 rds/gun
	2 .50 cal. guns top turret 400 rds/gun
	2 .50 cal. guns at waist station 200 rds/gun
	2 .50 cal. guns tail turret 600 rds/gun
Armor Protection	Same as B-25G except for addition of 3/8" plate aft of tail gunner
Weights	Empty 19,600 lbs. Max 35,000 lbs.
Speed	Max 275 MPH at 13,000 feet
Service Ceiling	23,800 feet
Range	1,350 miles with 3,000 lbs. bombs
Crew	Pilot, navigator/cannoneer, engineer/gunner, radio operator/gunner, tail gunner

Major Differences From B-25G
a. Eliminated provisions for co-pilot
b. 4 nose guns instead of 2
c. Lighter weight 75mm cannon
d. Top turret moved forward to navigator's compartment
e. Installation of Bell electro-hydraulic tail turret
f. Aft fuselage deepened to accommodate tail gunner

Effective on B-25H-5 No. 43-4535
a. Deleted provisions for carrying 2,000 lb. bomb

B-25-H

Reynolds Brown

Effective on B-25H-5 No. 43-4405
   a. Addition of 2 .50 cal. blister guns on left forward fuselage
   b. Addition of gun sight aim pointing camera
   c. Installation of electric bomb controls

Effective on B-25H-10 No. 43-4705
   a. Re-arrangement of pilot's instruments
   b. Increased size of life raft compartment
   c. Revision of brake system control cable

First B-25H accepted August 1943
Last B-25H accepted July 1944

Super Strafer Project NA-98X

In early 1944 there was more going on at North American's California plant than pushing B-25Hs and P-51Ds out the back door. At the behest of the Wright Field Engineering Department, North American submitted a proposal for an improved B-25 attack bomber, providing the fire power of a fully armed B-25J with eight gun nose and with substantially improved performance.[22]

With the NA-98X North American may have been bidding to some extent against the heavily armed Douglas A-26B. There was logic in the plan which was not without support at Wright Field as the cost of the up rated Mitchell was substantially less than the A-26B. The ability of North American aside, it still would have been quite a gamble against the established engineering talent and productive capacity of the Douglas firm, regardless of Wright Field interest.[23]

The proposal defined three optional configurations; a medium bomber and two strafer bombers, all powered by the Pratt & Whitney R-2800-51 engines and Bendix Stromberg carburetors.

Armament improvements included a computing gun sight and a new North American designed low drag canopy for the top turret. A compensating sight was fitted to the tail turret guns and illuminated reflector optical sights were used on the waist guns.

Controls were revised to reduce stick forces and the wing tips were changed from the rounded production configuration to a square shape like the P-51, total wing span remaining unchanged at 67 feet, 6.7 inches. This change permitted the outboard end of the aileron to be extended twelve inches, increasing the area of each aileron by 1.4 square feet. To further increase aerodynamic efficiency, the ailerons were internally balanced by a canvas seal which enclosed the air space between the aileron leading edge and the wing rear spar.

Common to production B-25s, 1,624 gallons of fuel and seventy-five gallons of oil were provided. Twenty one gallons of anti-detonate mixture provided water injection at war emergency power for fifteen minutes.

The eight gun nose strafer was manned by the same five man crew as the production B-25H consisting of pilot, navigator, waist gunner/radio operator, engineer/gunner and tail gunner. Carrying the following maximum useful load, the airplane gross weight was 34,822 pounds.

    5 crew and parachutes
    8 .50 caliber nose guns and 3,200 rounds ammunition
    2 .50 caliber turret guns and 800 rounds ammunition
    2 .50 caliber tail turret guns and 1,200 rounds ammunition
    2 .50 caliber waist guns and 400 rounds ammunition
    974 gallons fuel-wing self sealing cells
    75 gallons oil
    42 gallons anti-detonate injection fuel
    Four 500 pound bombs

The twelve gun nose strafer was identical in crew complement, fuel, stores and armament except for the addition of four fixed .50 caliber forward fuselage blister guns and 400 rounds of ammunition each. A heavy airplane, it grossed out at 35,522 pounds.

As a third alternate the airplane could be equipped as a medium bomber, basically an up-rated J model with bombardier's plexiglass nose compartment and the same crew complement as the B-25J consisting of pilot, co-pilot, bombardier, navigator, engineer-gunner, waist gunner/radio operator, tail gunner. Including the following maximum load, the airplane gross weight was 33,930 pounds.

    6 crew and parachutes
    2 .50 caliber fixed nose guns and 600 rounds ammunition
    1 .50 caliber flexible nose gun and 300 rounds ammunition
    2 .50 caliber tail turret guns and 1,200 rounds ammunition
    2 .50 caliber top turret guns and 800 rounds ammunition
    2 .50 caliber waist guns and 400 rounds ammunition
    974 gallons of fuel, wing self sealing cells
    75 gallons oil
    42 gallons anti-detonate injection fluid
    Four 500 pound bombs

Designated company project NA-98X, the 302nd B-25H, 43-4406, was modified as the super strafer prototype under M.C.R. B-508. The major change was re-equipping the airplane from the R-2600 Wright engines to the Pratt & Whitney R-2800-51 engines with Stromberg carburetors and water injection. Visual differences were the propeller spinners, high speed inlet cowlings and square wing tips. The upper cowl was identical to that used on the Douglas A-26.

This is a B-25? A rare photo of the NA-98X power package shows the high speed inlet cowl and spinner. (NAA)

Equipped with Pratt & Whitney R-2800-51 engines and designated NA-98X, the B-25 Super Strafer prototype nears completion on the North American flight ramp. (NAA)

Calculations based on a gross weight of 34,000 pounds indicated a top speed of 300 MPH at military power and a rate of climb of 1,800 feet per minute at sea level. Predicted high speed at war emergency power was 325 MPH.

The additional power and reduced frontal area of the Pratt & Whitney engines did not promise as great a net gain over the Wright engines as might have been expected. For production airplanes it was required that wing structure be increased to provide an allowable indicated diving speed of at least 400 MPH for strafing missions. This would have added at least 400 pounds which, combined with the heavier R-2800 engines, would have increased the airplane gross weight by nearly 1,500 pounds.

Except for the removal of the fuselage blister gun packs the standard B-25H armament including the 75 mm cannon was retained on the NA-98X test aircraft.

The increased weight and power of the R-2800 engines, combined with increased aileron area and reduced stick forces, was capable of inducing higher resultant forces than on production B-25s. It was known that at high maneuvering speeds this combination could cause excessive bending moments in the wings. Failure in leading edge torsion had been known to occur on B-25s under extreme conditions and increased strength was achieved on NA-98X by increasing the rivet size for attaching the leading edge skins. Test data required from this airplane could be safely obtained within restricted parameters with no other structural reinforcement. Maximum speed was therefore restricted to 340 IAS and a normal acceleration of 2.67g.

North American test pilot Joe Barton made the initial flight on 31 March and reported higher speed and acceleration, reduced vibration and a marked increase in

Performance of NA-98X with Pratt & Whitney R-2800-51 Engines
All Power Settings 2,700 RPM

	Military Low Blower	Military Hi Blower	War Emerg. Low Blower	War Emerg Hi Blower
Hi Speed at Sea Level	307		328	
Hi Speed at Crit. Alt.	324	330	333	346.5
Crit. Alt	4,350	15,150	550	12,600
Man Press. in. Hg.	50.8	47	58	51
BHP	1,935	1,550	2,245	1,790
R.O. Climb at Crit. Alt.	2.,140	1,450	2,500	1,855

Comparative Engine Performance of R-2600-13 and R-2800-51 Engines

ENGINE	RPM	ALT	POWER	BHP
R-2800-51	2,700	S L	Mil	2,000
R-2600-13	2,600	S L	Mil	1,700
R-2800-51	2,700	7,000	Mil	1,700
R-2800-13	2,400	6,700	Mil	1,500
R-2800-51	2,700	15,000	Mil	1,550
R-2600-13	2,400	13,000	Mil	1,350

The squared wing tips and longer ailerons are clearly shown in this flight photo of NA-98X. (NAA)

roll rate. Performance clearly indicated what the B-25 could have been and should have been from conception had the R-2800 engines been made available to North American at the beginning of the B-25 program.

The airplane was also flown by chief test pilot Ed Virgin, army pilots Major Otto McIver, Captains Fountain and McFadden and Squadron Leader Hartford of the RAF, indicating possible British interest in the NA-98X.[24]

At a gross weight of 29,000 pounds no buffeting or instability occurred in a 350 MPH dive with cowl flaps open. A single engine pulling forty-two inches manifold pressure at 2,400 RPM maintained altitude at 195 MPH indicated and an easy climb at 160 MPH at a gross weight of 30,000 pounds; fifty-two inches manifold pressure at 2,700 RPM provided a takeoff run of 1,470 feet to clear a fifty foot obstacle. War emergency power brought NA-98X to 10,000 feet altitude in 4.9 minutes and in 5.3 minutes at military power. Climbing time to 15,000 feet on war emergency power was 8.2 minutes and at military power, 8.9 minutes.[25]

The Flight Test Branch of the Air Corps at Wright Field assigned Major Perry Ritchie and First Lieutenant Winton Wey to conduct a series of tests. An experienced military pilot, Ritchie held an engineering degree, had completed a two year assignment at the Engineering Aircraft Laboratory and two years as a test pilot. He was regarded as highly competent but considered to be a bit "spectacular".

Soon after beginning his assigned test program, Ritchie lost little time in expressing his pleasure with the airplane. Following completion of each day's tests he concluded with a high speed, low level pass over the company flight ramp, followed by a steep spiral pull up. North American pilots and structural engineers emphasized that the airplane was under specified red line restrictions for good cause. Their advice remained unheeded.[26]

On Monday, 24 April 1944 military personnel at the anti-aircraft battery west of Mines Field interrupted a ball game to watch another high speed, low level pass by NA-98X. Approaching from the west Ritchie dropped low over the ocean at wave top height, rose quickly to clear the sand dunes and dropped low again as the B-25 roared over the AA battery. Reaching the flight line and North American's final assembly area, he pulled up in the usual climbing spiral, wing tips vaporizing. At an altitude of about 200 feet both outer wing panels separated, knocking the entire tail assembly off. The airplane rolled slightly, rose another 300 feet, headed northeasterly and crashed east of Aviation Boulevard under the Mines Field approach. The wreckage was widely scattered but did not burn. Both crewmen were killed instantly.

The flight ramp and the camouflage netting above were strewn with debris. Inspection of the wreckage disclosed that the outer panels had separated at the landing light cutouts. The right panel was recovered intact from the netting. A deep buckle on the top surface extended from the leading edge tip to the inboard edge of the aileron. The buckle itself was believed not to have caused the failure but may have alarmed the pilot so that his reaction was destructive. It was generally concluded however, that the airplane was simply flown beyond its structural limitations.[27]

Many outstanding aircraft have been victims of circumstance and North American's NA-98X is a classic example. Its tragic and unnecessary crash after only three weeks of testing precluded the possibility of a production contract, historically common even when the airplane is found not to have been at fault and meets or even exceeds requirements.

In April of 1944 the need for an attack airplane like the NA-98X was valid. The war was far from over. Victory in Europe was more than a year in the future and Japan remained a formidable enemy against whose forces the B-25 had proved remarkably effective. The single example was destined to obscurity, but had it been produced in quantity would have been a more outstanding airplane than its famous predecessors.

B-25J

In mid 1943 North American's Kansas plant began the transition from B-25D to production of the heavily armed B-25J medium bomber. Built in greater numbers than any other variant, the J was the final B-25 configuration. Both models were briefly produced concurrently as the D was phasing out, the first J being accepted in December 1943 and the final D in March 1944.

Aft of the nose attach bulkhead at station 70 the J is essentially identical in airframe and armament to the B-25H attack bomber. Major differences were the use of the bombardier nose as used on the D and the addition of the bombardier and co-pilot to the crew. Numerous equipment changes were made throughout production and are defined in the summary of major type differences.

A standard factory produced eight gun nose was adaptable to all B-25s but is most commonly photographed on and associated with the B-25J. So configured with fourteen forward firing guns, the J was a most formidable strafer with nearly double the firepower of the Fifth Air Force field modified strafers.

The final suitability report by the Air Technical Section, U.S. Army, described the operational characteristics of the B-25J compared to the B-25D. It was found preferential to the B-25D for increased firepower, improved bomb run stability and superior to all other similar aircraft for armament, speed, performance at altitude, stability of bombing platform, visibility and night flying and short field characteristics. Sea level speed was 261 MPH at 2,600 RPM and 42 inches manifold pressure. With low blower at 4,000 feet speed was 271 MPH and high blower at 11,000

B-25Js were initially fitted with 1 flexible and 1 fixed .50 cal. gun in the nose. (NAA)

feet gave 274 MPH. Single engine speed at 7,000 feet, 2,100 RPM and 31 inches manifold pressure was 160 MPH.

The airplane was stated to be superior to the B-26 in side visibility, speed at military power from sea level to service ceiling and better performance at 17,000 feet. Performance at 18,000 feet was equivalent to the B-26F at 12,000 feet.

In the spring of 1944 the B-25Js first reached the Pacific. Built in greater numbers than any othr B-25 variant, some were produced as medium bombers and many others were fitted with the factory produced 8 gun nose for use as strafers. (NAA)

Hinged panels of the 8 gun nose provided easy access to all guns and for replenishment of ammunition. After the war this nose section, sans guns, was widely used for military transport B-25s and found ready use for housing avionics equipment or baggage.

By the end of the war a total of 4,318 B-25Js had been produced plus an additional seventy-two incomplete but flyable airplanes representing a production average of 175 per month during twenty-five months of production.

B-25J Summary of Major Differences

Engines	Wright R-2600-13
Carburetors	Holley 1685 HA
Fuel	Same as B-25C
Armament	1 .50 cal. fixed gun in nose
	300 rds
	1 .50 cal flexible gun in nose
	300 rds
	4 .50 cal. fixed blister gun packs,
	2 on each side of forward fuselage
	400 rds/gun
	2 .50 cal. guns top turret
	400 rds/gun
	2 .50 cal. flexible waist guns
	250 rds/gun
	2 . 50 cal. guns tail turret
	600 rds/gun
Armor Protection	3/8" plate behind both pilots
	3/8" plate forward of instrument panel
	External flak plates for both pilots
	Plate below windshield
	Behind top turret in bomb bay crawl space
	Plate at rear of waist gunner
	Plate behind tail turret on both sides
Weights	Empty 19,500 lbs. Max. 35,000 lbs.
Speed	Max 272MPH at 13,000 feet
Service Ceiling	24,200 feet

Range	1,350 miles with 3,000 lbs. bombs
Crew	Pilot, co-pilot, bombardier/gunner, engineer/gunner, waist gunner, tail gunner (No bombardier on strafer variant)

Major Differences From B-25D
a. Blister gun packs on forward fuselage
b. Top turret moved forward to navigator's compartment
c. Addition of waist guns
d. Addition of tail turret
e. Deeper aft fuselage same as B-25H
f. Bombardier and bomb bay controls in pilot's station
g. All electric bomb racks and bomb bay doors
h. Revisions to pilot's instrument panel
i. 50,000 BTU Surface Combustion heater at waist gun station
j. Provision for three 1,000 lb. bombs instead of 2
k. Provision for two 1,600 lb. armor piercing bombs
l. Provision for six 325 lb. depth charges on wing racks

Effective on B-25J-1 No. 43-4019
a. Deleted provision for 2,000 lb. bomb

Effective on B-25J-5 No. 43-27793
a. Revised brake system control cable
b. N-3C gun sight replaced N-3B sight and A-1 bombing head
c. Installed de-icing windshield panels
d. Installed gun blast arrestors on top turret guns and side fuselage blister guns.

Effective on B-25J-10 No. 43-35995
a. Installed mounting lugs and controls for wing bombs
b. Electric bomb racks
c. Removed heaters at waist gun stations

Effective on B-25J-15 No. 44-28711
a. Installed N-8A optical gun sights on waist guns
b. Added provisions for ring and bead sights for nose guns

Effective on B-25J-20 No. 44-29111
a. Revised cabin heating system with 50,000 BTU/hour heater
b. Added second fixed .50 cal. gun in nose
c. Incorporated hydraulic emergency brake system
d. Added armor protection in floor for bombardier
e. Changed to Holley 1685 RB carburetor on airplane 44-29340
f. Reinforced top turret canopy
g. Relocated flexible nose gun 4 inches higher

Effective on B-25J-25 No. 44-29911
a. Provided for carburetor heat rise
b. New type armored seats for both pilots
c. Reduced elevator control friction
d. Added armor plate deflectors for top turret guns on 44-30111
e. Increased strength of leading edge wing structure. Outer wing panel attach bolts increased from 5/16 inch diameter to 3/8 inch
f. Added provisions for wing bomb rack mounted chemical tank effective on 44-30309/31110

Produced by North American in 1943, the factory 8 gun nose was readily adaptable to all B-25s but was used almost entirely on the B-25J. So equipped, the 'J' represented the ultimate in destructive capability of any World War II strafer, mounting 14 forward firing .50s. (NAA)

Effective on B-25J-30

a. Stainless steel "S" type exhaust stacks replaced the enameled 1020 steel stacks on cylinders numbers 1,7 and 9. Effective on No. 44-30911

b. Made provisions for wing bomb rack mounted chemical tank effective on No. 44-31111

c. Made provisions for type C-6 electric bomb hoist effective on 44-31311

d. Incorporated provisions in the wings for T-64 zero length rocket launchers effective on No. 44-31338

e. Installed K-10 computing gun sight and M-8A gun mount on tail turret effective on No. 44-31491

f. Incorporated glide bombing provisions effective on No. 44-86692

g. Installed N-9B bombsight effective on No. 44-86793

h. Re-routed rudder control cables effective on No. 44-86799

Effective on B-25J-35 No. 44-86892

a. Added provisions for aerial mines
First B-25J accepted Dec 1943
Last B-25J accepted Aug 1945

US Navy/ Marine Corps PBJs

When America entered the war in December 1941 the Army Air Forces held a virtual monopoly on long range, land based, multi-engine aircraft. The Navy, generally responsible for anti-submarine defense, found their inventory lacking in both surface vessels and suitable airplanes to cope with the ever increasing menace of German submarine action. The Atlantic U-boat crisis emphasized that effective anti-submarine action required more multi engine types than current production for the Navy could supply and that modern land based bombers with high speeds, firepower and bomb load were best suited for the job. [28]

Early in 1942 Admiral King expressed to General Arnold that naval operations as sea patrols, protection of coastal shipping and convoy escort could not be performed by seaplanes in winter weather conditions from northern bases.

To provide the required equipment as soon as possible, Admiral King requested the transfer to the Navy from Army allocations of 400 long range B-24 Liberators and 900 B-25 Mitchells with the hope that of these numbers 200 B-24s and 400 B-25s could be received by the Navy no later than 1 July 1943. [29]

King's request could not have been made at a less propitious time. The sudden demand for aircraft by the accelerated expansion of Army units and Lend Lease allocations to Britain absorbed all current production.

So, it is not surprising that Navy procurement efforts were met with considerable resistance from the AAF which was itself, less than prepared to combat the U-boats. The need was acute but neither service had adequate anti-submarine training and modern search gear was lacking in both development and availability of existing equipment. Arnold countered that any diversions of his badly needed airplanes would have a serious delaying effect on future Army operations and he considered it a better plan to expand the Army's anti-submarine capability instead of creating another and somewhat duplicated force in the Navy. He readily recognized, however, the great impact of submarine action on the supply lines to Britain and the expansion of American forces in Europe. He proposed that the bombers be retained by the AAF and anti-submarine aircraft be deployed in accord with previously established Joint Action Operations. [30]

Because of immediate pre-war expansion, the AAF was better equipped and experienced in general bombardment with the result that the immediate need for anti-submarine action early in 1942 fell mainly on the AAF. The Anti-Submarine Command was created in October 1942 and operated with the Navy until it was phased out in the summer of 1943. [31]

Admiral King's efforts to obtain Army bombers was partially rewarded in August 1942 when the Navy received the first of fifty-two B-24s delivered throughout the remainder of the year. Under the terms of an inter-service agreement approved by the President, the Navy was to receive 1,520 long range heavy and medium bombers in 1942 and an additional 3,810 in 1943. Due to the urgency of Britain's survival these allocations were

After arriving in San Diego in August, 1944 enroute to overseas assignment, Marine Squadron VMB-612 received a PBJ-1D prototype equipped with zero length rocket launchers, forward fuselage blister gun packs and APS-3 night search radar. This equipment was installed by the Consolidated Vultee Modification Center at Elizabeth, New Jersey and the remainder of VMB-612 airplanes were similarly equipped after reaching Oahu. (NAA)

clouded by a later policy, also approved by the President, that maximum aid to Britain would proceed even at the expense of deliveries to American forces.[32]

The Navy's belated acquisition of B-25s was the culmination of involved events brought about by the cancellation by the Navy of the Boeing Sea Ranger flying boat. In June 1940 the Navy placed an order with Boeing for the XPBB-1 Sea Ranger. Powered by Wright R-3350 Cyclone engines and fitted with the wing later used on the B-29, the XPBB-1 was the largest twin engine flying boat. Original plans called for procurement of 500 examples from a large, new plant at Renton, Washington.

It is generally accepted that the Battle of Midway changed the Navy's view of procurement of flying boats in the quantities previously considered. Although the XPBB-1 test program proved a satisfactory product, the big boat joined the category of what might have been.

Late in 1941 North American Aviation, Inc. agreed to participate in the manufacture of the B-29 Superfortress. Boeing's facilities were inadequate for this extensive work in addition to the B-17 program, necessitating that other plants and manufacturers be brought into the B-29 program. North American's part of the project was to be handled at the Kansas City B-25 plant where a new B-29 assembly

area was added to make the facility adequate for production of both aircraft.

On 7 February 1942 the Army contracted with North American for 200 B-29s, an order subsequently increased to 300. The B-29 contract was to run concurrently with the B-25D production line which was just beginning to roll. After the B-25D contracts were completed and the assembly line phased out, the entire Kansas plant was programmed for B-29 production.

When the Navy shelved the PBB-1 flying boat project the new Boeing plant at Renton became available for B-29s. As a result all work on North American's Kansas City B-29 project was terminated on 31 July, 1942. At that time the AAF decided that the increasing requirements for B-25s made it desirable for North American's Kansas plant to utilize all its expanded facilities for continuing Mitchell production. The new high bay B-29 assembly building became the final assembly shops for B-25s. Combined with the B-25G and H models coming off the Inglewood line, the Kansas built B-25D and concurrent J models made it possible to supply all allocations including those for the Navy.

So it was that the Navy waited until early 1943 for the initial delivery of 706 B-25s, designated PBJ(P for patrol, B for bomber, and J for North American, the manufacturer). The B-25B was designated PBJ-1 and the PBJ-1C, PBJ-1D, PBJ-1H and PBJ-1J corresponded to their respective AAF counterparts. All PBJs were assigned to the Marine Corps for patrol and anti-submarine duties but as the war progressed the versatile Mitchell was also used as a medium bomber and as an attack aircraft adapted for carrying torpedos and radar directed rockets.

VMB-413, commissioned 1 March 1943 was the first of sixteen USMC squadrons equipped with PBJs and VMB-423, 433, and 443 were commissioned on 15 September followed by VMB-611, 612, and 613 on 10 October. These seven squadrons were the only PBJ units to served in combat. They were soon followed by VMB-614, 621, 622, 623, 624, 453, 463, 473 and 483. All were commissioned at Cherry Point, North Carolina.[33]

VMB-413, 423, 433, 443 and 611 operated in the Central and South Pacific and VMB-612 and 613 operated in the Central Pacific. All spent a brief training period in Hawaii where the airplanes were equipped and painted dark midnight blue.

VMB-413 initially trained on the East Coast then headed west, arriving at North Island, San Diego, California on 3 December 1943. In January 1944 the unit departed for Espiritu Santo via Hawaii for an additional training period. Moving to Stirling in the Treasuries the squadron, commanded by Lieutenant Colonel Andrew Galatian, began its combat experience with daylight strikes against Kavieng and Rabaul. The squadron then began perfecting the art of night heckling weary enemy troops. Night operations soon earned VMB-413 the name of the "Flying Nightmares" which it surely was to the sleepless Japanese under continual attack. Following daylight raids by other units, the Mitchells of 413 commenced their dark assaults, each aircraft following the previous attacker by just enough time to keep the enemy continually off balance.

In July VMB-413 was based at Munda, relocating at Emirau in mid October for operations against New Ireland and New Britain until the end of the war.

VMB-423, "The Sea Horse Marines", arrived at Espiritu Santo in April 1944. In June the squadron moved to the Green Islands and was soon at work on submarine patrol, depth charging, attacking barges and night heckling. In January 1945 the base of operations was transferred to Emirau where the squadron, in company with VMB-413, 433 and 443 worked over the Solomons and Bismarcks until the surrender of Japan.

VMB-433 trained at El Centro, California and departed for the Pacific late in May 1944. The squadron arrived at Ewa on 1 June and the Green Islands in mid July. In August operations were begun from Emirau where the unit remained until war's end.

VMB-443 initially trained at Boca Chica, Florida and then moved on to El Centro, California. The squadron departed San Diego for Emirau, arriving in mid August, 1944. Participating in the neutralization of the Bismarcks 443 relocated in the Philippines and teamed up with 413, 423 and 433 until the end of the war.

The instrument panels of the night search PBJs were modified to fit the retractable radome scope of the APS-3 search system (scope missing). The APS-3 was a 3 centimeter airborne radar system designed for locating surface vessels, aircraft and for bombing approaches. It was capable of locating ground targets at 70 miles, ships at from 40 to 50 miles, aircraft at 5 to 8 miles and a surfaced submarine at 15 miles. (NAA)

VMB-611 arrived at Emirau in December, 1944 where the unit began strikes against Tobera and Vanakanau and night heckling missions. The base of operations was transferred to Zamboanga, P.I. on 30 March 1945 and they finished the war in that area.

VMB-613 trained at Boca Chica, Florida and Newport, Arkansas, arriving at Kwajalein in mid December, 1944 and ended the war operating in the Marshalls.

VMB-612, commanded by Lieutenant Colonel Jack Cram, first trained on the east coast and in February 1944, was selected for torpedo launching and radar directed night operations. After additional training the squadron flew to San Diego in August enroute to assignment in the Pacific.

At San Diego a PBJ-1D of VMB-612 was received equipped with Loran and APS-3 radar search gear, underwing zero length launchers for five inch HVAR

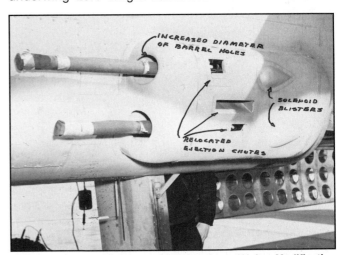

Fuselage blister gun packs by the Consolidated Vultee Modification Center are almost identical in shape and location to those fitted on the Fifth Air Force strafers early in 1943. (NAA)

Tested on a PBJ-1H in April 1945 by the Naval Ordnance Test Station at China Lake, California, the 11.75 inch 'Tiny Tim' rocket packed the heaviest punch of any airborne weapon of World War II. Black and white striping indicates dummy rounds. (Naval Weapons Center via E.C. Holton, NAA)

Utilization of both fuselage and wing launchers provided heavy strike power per mission. Outboard of the Tiny Tim launcher are the attaching studs for four 5 inch HVAR rockers. (Naval Weapons Center via E.C. Holton, NAA)

rockets, and blister gun packs attached to both sides of the fuselage. The radar equipment was characterized by a long, ungainly nose radome. Directly in line aft was the display screen at the top of the instrument panel. This equipment was installed on the Squadron's other airplanes when the unit arrived in Hawaii where training began for night attacks using the new search gear. Accurate range information was determined by flying at a precise altitude coordinated with rocket ballistics, weight corrections, wind drift and speed.

Arriving at Saipan late in October 1944 the squadron underwent intensive training before commencing radar directed night strikes against shipping around the Bonin and Volcano Islands. This action continued until April 1945 when the unit was relocated on Iwo Jima. As Allied forces forged ever closer to Japan, and Okinawa was secured, VMB-612 transferred operations to that island. Radar directed night attacks were made against Japanese shipping along the Southern Kyushu coast. Between 10 April and the move to Okinawa VMB-612 flew 251 missions and claimed hits on over fifty vessels with five probable sinkings. During the first half of August thirty-one missions were flown with claims of damage to twenty ships.

Missions were frequently of long duration, which, combined with usual stormy weather conditions, made navigation critical. Night operations required less defensive armament which permitted weight reduction on some airplanes by removal of top turrets and fuselage blister gun packs, allowing a greater fuel load with as much as a 400 mile reserve after a ten hour mission.[34]

Performance in night attack earned VMB-612 the distinction of being the single operational unit assigned to carry the new 11.75 inch "Tiny Tim" rocket against the Japanese. Tiny Tim was one of several rockets developed under a joint program begun in 1943 between the Naval Ordnance Test Station (NOTS) at Inyokern, California and the California Institute of Technology to develop operational rockets adaptable to Navy fleet service aircraft. Twenty-nine airplanes and six manufacturers were assigned to the test pool.[35]

It was late in 1944 when NOTS equipped PBJ-1H, 43-4835, Buaer 89002, to carry the 11.75 inch rocket. The North American company designed a special launcher to mount one of the rockets on each side of the fuselage above the bomb bay doors. Launch was by free fall and ignition actuated by lanyard. After launch the bomb bay doors could be opened for conventional bomb drops. Wing rocket launching studs were also fitted.[36]

Considered combat ready by mid 1945, Tiny Tims and launchers were shipped to Iwo Jima where a number of PBJs of VMB-612 were fitted with the new equipment. In addition to regular combat missions, training with Tiny Tims was carried on during the first half of July. By the 16th of the month a total of twenty-seven of the rockets were fired in experimental tests and training which comprised the entire quantity allotted for the purpose. Firing at 1,000 yards range and 500 feet altitude resulted in minor damage to the aircraft from rocket and target fragments. The range was then increased to 1,350 yards and the elevation raised to 700 feet.

No combat missions were flown with the new weapon until the 11th and 13th of August, dates between the dropping of the atomic bombs and the Japanese acceptance of the surrender terms.

All VMB squadrons increased the fire power of their earlier PBJ-1C and D airplanes. Depot fabricated tail turrets similar to the factory types on the H and J models provided aft protection and the addition of nose guns and forward fuselage blister packs similar to the Fifth, Seventh and Thirteenth Air Force strafers made attacks more effective.

Many missions flown by the VMB squadrons were under hazardous conditions which were made even more so by abundant tropical thunderstorms. The cost was high in both men and airplanes.

VMB-614 was commissioned with PBJ-1C/D airplanes for low level bombing and the unit underwent torpedo training at Boca Chica, Florida. In July 1944 the squadron was equipped with PBJ-1H airplanes with APG-23 search gear for operations from Midway Island. Due to the considerable weight of the radio and search equipment the bomb load was reduced with a corresponding reduction in mission effectiveness. The PBJ-1H was not too popular and the cannon flash tended to blind the pilot at the moment of pull-out. In November the squadron was re-equipped with the PBJ-1J with eight gun nose for low altitude bombing and strafing missions. (See Appendices C through F.)

By 1944 it had become frequent practice to load fighter aircraft aboard carrier decks for transport to combat areas where they were unloaded by crane. This procedure was straight forward enough unless complications arose at the destination during the voyage.

Catapult launching seemed the best solution to this potential problem and a number of land based Army P-39, P-40 and P-47 aircraft were carrier transported and catapult launched. Single examples of the P-51D and a PBJ-1H were modified for both carrier landing and catapult launching trials at sea.

Modification and testing of the P-51D was based on the possible need for long range fighter protection of the B-29s on the programmed raids against Japan. In November, 1944 the nearest American base suitable for B-29 deployment was on Guam, well beyond fighter reach. Although the sea trials were successful, no other P-51 was equipped for carrier launch and recovery.

PBJ-1H, 43-4700, Buaer 35277, was structurally modified for catapult launch and arrest retrieval by North American's modification center at Kansas City and the gear was installed by the Navy at the Naval Air Materiel Center (NAMC) at Philadelphia. Following required ground tests, the airplane was approved for sea trials by the Carrier Suitability Test Unit at NAMC along with the P-51D and the Navy's new Grumman F7F-1. The Navy was also interested in the tailhook action on tricycle gear aircraft in off center landing modes

Drop sequence of simultaneous launch of fuselage mounted Tiny Tims shows the stable fall of the rockets. Second frame: curve of ignition lanyard is visible. Frame 3 ignition has occurred. 4th frame: near rocket has moved approximately two feet ahead of the left. (Naval Weapons Center via E.C. Holton, NAA)

70

On 15 November 1944 flying P-51D, 44-14017, Lieutenant Robert Elder departed Norfolk, Virginia, making rendezvous with CV-38, Shangri La. His first landing was excellent with minimal cable runout and this was followed by three more required take offs and landings, all satisfactory. Due to the late hour and the pressure of qualifying three new airplanes in one day, the P-51 catapult trials were canceled as all catapult tests at the Philadelphia Navy Yard had been satisfactory.

Not until 1600 hours did Lieutenant Lane flying the F7F-1 make the required landings and takeoffs before returning to Norfolk.

Approaching the carrier in the PBJ-1H, Lieutenant Commander Bottomley inadvertently actuated the oil dilution switch instead of the arresting hook. Correcting immediately, the dilution switch stuck, thinning the oil dangerously. The engine was cut and the propeller feathered for the return to Norfolk for repairs and a change of oil. [38]

Time was running out when Bottomley returned for a second approach. The carrier was available for one day only and it was a simple case of "make it or forget it". The approach was on and the landing excellent with an arresting cable runout of 120 feet. The PBJ was then available for deck handling tests and inspection by Buaer personnel and North American technical representatives and engineers. For easier handling the PBJ main landing gear had been modified so that the wheels could turn sideways to a limited degree.

At a gross weight of 27,000 pounds the PBJ was taxied to the catapult position and launched. Dropping in a bit hard on the second landing the arresting cable was engaged about twenty feet off center as intended. Inspection revealed that the main landing gear door had blown off shortly after takeoff, the arresting hook dash pot was damaged and the left main tire also showed some damage. The PBJ was again positioned on the catapult and launched for the flight back to Norfolk. [39]

So ended the brief sea trials of the single B-25 equipped for carrier operations. Neither the PBJ or the P-51 were produced so equipped although both performed well during tests. American gains in the Pacific in 1945 negated the necessity for such variants.

Notes to Chapter 4

1. Pitt, Paul A., Utilization of Exhaust Heat Exchanger Installations, **Aero Digest Magazine**, 1 Mar 1945
2. Ingells, Staff Sgt. Douglas J. "They Wage War on the Icing Menace", **The Pegasus**, Fairchild Engine and Airplane Corp. Jul 1945
3. Letter, A.E. Walker to NLA 5 Jan 1967
4. North American Aviation, Inc., "Supplementary Instructions for the XB-25E With Heated Wing Installation" Internal Document Report No. NA-8073, 24 Feb 1944

PBJ-1H 43-4700 was the single B-25 adapted for carrier trials. On 15 November 1944 LCDR Bottomley made the first landings and catapult takeoff from CV-38, Shangri La 90 miles east of Norfolk, Virginia. (NAA)

This excellent photo shows the moment of touch down and the arresting cable engaging the tail hook. (NAA)

5. Letter, William Barker to Norman Avery, March 1975
6. Letters, Edgar Pierce to Norman Avery, 1975
7. Letter, A. E. Walker to Norman Avery, 5 Jan 1975
8. Woodman, Harry, **Early Aircraft Armament**, "The Airplane and the Gun up to 1918", Smith Institution Press, Washington, D.C.
9. Purtee, Dr. Edward G. "The Development of Light & Medium Bombers Historical Section Intelligence (T-2) Air Materiel Command Wright Field 1946", Study No. 196, page 16
10. Letter, Plans Division, USAAC to Commandant Air Corps Tacatical School Maxwell Field, Alabama, Test of 75 mm gun and mount on B-18 airplane, 30 Apr 1940
11. "Flying the Big Gun", **Popular Science Magazine**, Feb 1944, pages 105-108
12. Purtee, Study No. 196, page 57
13. Letter, R.L. Schleicher to Norman Avery, 6 Jun 1984
14. Letter, George Wing, to Norman Avery, 6 Jun 1989
15. Letter, P.F. Peterson to Norman Avery, Oct 1989
16. Letter, E.W. Virgin to Norman Avery, May 1989
17. NAA Inc. Flight Data Record Card B-25 No. 41-13296
18. Purtee, Study No. 196, page 119
19. Reply, General H.H. Arnold to General George Kenney, Sep 1943, "The Fifth Air Force in the Huon Peninsula Campaign", Jan-Oct 1943. **USAF Historical Study No. 113**, AFSHRC, Maxwell Air Force Base, Alabama pages 267-269
20. North American Aviation, Inc. "Design Description of Prototype B-25H 'Mortimer II', Internal Report No. NA-5707
21. North American Aviation, Inc. Flight Data Record, B-25C, No. 42-32372
22. North American Aviation, Inc., Proposal - Pratt & Whitney R-2800 Powered B-25 Strafer Bomber, 17 Mar 1944
23. Letter, Frank Cook to Norman Avery

24. North American Aviation, Inc., Flight Data Record Card, B-25H-5, No. 43-4406
25. USAAC Flight Test Engineering Branch, Flight Test of NA B-25H Airplane No. 43-4406 With R-2800 Engines, Memo Report No. ENG-47-1751-A, 9 May 1944
26. Letter, E.W. Virgin to Norman Avery, 8 May 1989
27. Army Air Forces Materiel Command, Engineering Division Memorandum Report, No. ENG-51-4263-49, 17 May 1944, Subject: NAA Model B-25H No. 43-4406 With P&W R-2800 Engines Accident Investigation
28. Craven, W.F. and Cate, J.L., **The Army Air Forces in World War II,** Chicago, IL, The University of Chicago Press, 1953, Vol I, pages 522, 538, 539
29. Ferguson, **The Anti-Submarine Command,** USAF Historical Study No. 107, Note No. 40, King to Arnold, AFSHRC Maxwell AFB, Alabama, 15 Jan 1942 and 5 Mar 1942
30. Craven and Cate, Vol VI, page 404
31. Ibid., Vol I, pages 519 and 540
32. Ibid., Vol I, page 247
33. Sherrod, Robert, **History of Marine Corps Aviation in World War II**, San Rafael, California
34. Action Reports, USMC Bombing Squadrons Nos. 413 and 612
35. Action Report, USMC Bombing Squadron VMB 612 12/13 August 1945, Summary of VMB 612 Combat Operations 14 Sep 1945
36. Status of Aircraft Assigned to Experimental And Developmental Projects, Naval Ordnance Test Station, Inyokern, California as of 23 Jul 1945
37. Bottomley, LCDR Syd, The Hook, Winter, 1978, pages 6-8
38. Letter, LCDR Bottomley to NLA, 6 Mar 1988
39. North American Aviation, Inc. Internal Field Service Department Letter, Joe Schaffer to John Casey, Subject: Carrier Tests P-51D No. 44-14017 and PBJ (B-25H No. 43-4700) 16 Nov 1944.

PBJ of VMB-413, "The Flying Nightmares", on the maintenance stand in the Southwest Pacific. (NAA)

This twin .50 cal. gimbel mount on a B-25D is a product of North American's modification center at Kansas City. However functional, it was never produced. (NAA)

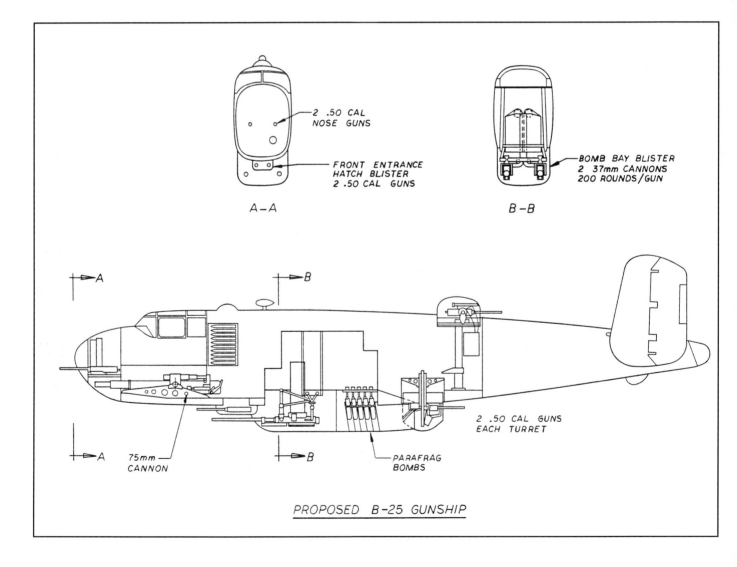

2 .50 CAL NOSE GUNS

FRONT ENTRANCE HATCH BLISTER 2 .50 CAL GUNS

A-A

BOMB BAY BLISTER 2 37mm CANNONS 200 ROUNDS/GUN

B-B

2 .50 CAL GUNS EACH TURRET

75mm CANNON

PARAFRAG BOMBS

PROPOSED B-25 GUNSHIP

PART III

5 Experimental Armaments

Among the many armaments tested on the B-25 the airborne flame thrower was probably the most unusual. It was tested with unknown results in 1944 and considering that Allied forces were becoming ever more victorious at the time, it could not have been a desperation measure, however dangerous and bizarre. The test pilots can be assumed to have been adventurous volunteers.

B-25C, 42-32732 was fitted with a special bomb bay rack to carry the 1,570 pound unit. Structural additions were installed on the fuselage at station 290 and to the bomb bay doors. Tank capacity was 210 gallons and the entire unit could be dropped in case of emergency.

It is not clear how the unit was to be deployed. It was suspended from a standard D-7 bomb shackle and extended well below the airplane. The reinforced bomb bay doors provided mounting bases for sway braces. The recommended test altitude was 15,000 feet, airplane on autopilot and both pilots positioned behind the seats. Another airplane flying nearby warned the launching crew if the airplane caught fire, in which case bail out was the ordered procedure.

Following the development in 1942/43 of the Fifth Air Force B-25C/D strafers mounting eight forward firing .50 caliber guns, Major Paul Gunn developed an experimental installation of three guns to the underside of the fuselage between the bomb bay and the forward access hatch. Due to feed belt problems and blast effects on adjacent structure, the concept proved difficult and the project was abandoned as impractical.

Probably a follow on to Gunn's efforts, North American developed a module containing two .50 caliber guns and 225 rounds of ammunition for each. Designated "Hatch Guns", the unit fit into the forward access hatch and was secured in place by the same pins that secured the hatch door.

Servicing of guns and replenishment of ammunition was easily done from within the airplane. Blast was resisted by sheets of stainless steel over 1/8 inch thick sponge rubber. Total unit weight was 325 pounds.

Tests of the Hatch Gun unit proved mechanically successful but it was never ordered into production. Unless the unit was installed after crew boarding, it was necessary to enter the airplane from the aft hatch, then crawl over the bomb bay to the flight deck. Additional blast resistant structural modifications were also required. The forthcoming B-25H had all the firepower needed without the inconveniences.

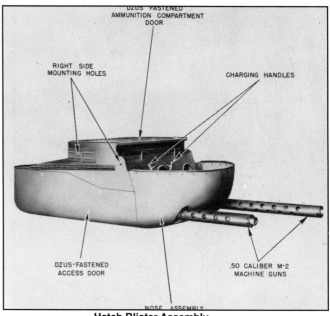

Hatch Blister Assembly

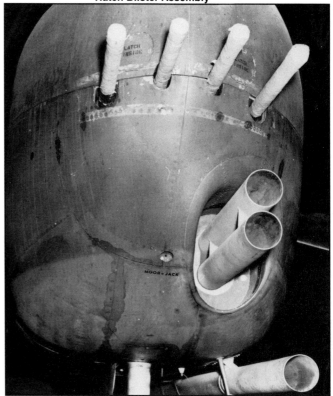

Five inch diameter "Center Jet" rockets were tested but never developed on this B-25H after removal of the 75 mm cannon. The rocket powered projectile was launched from a simple and easily mounted light weight tube. Trajectory was relatively high making accuracy mediocre. (USAF)

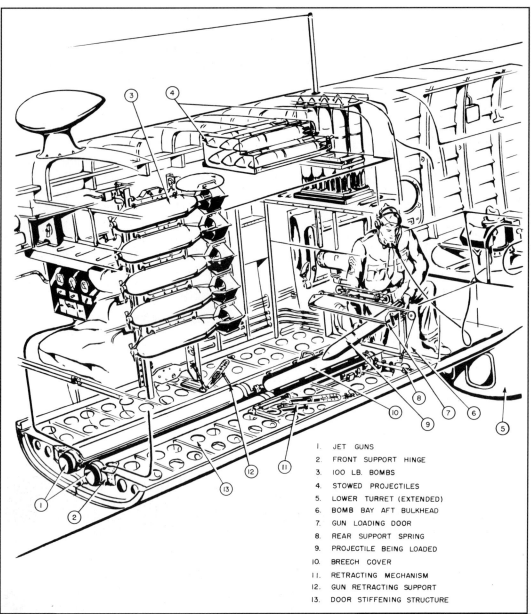

1. JET GUNS
2. FRONT SUPPORT HINGE
3. 100 LB. BOMBS
4. STOWED PROJECTILES
5. LOWER TURRET (EXTENDED)
6. BOMB BAY AFT BULKHEAD
7. GUN LOADING DOOR
8. REAR SUPPORT SPRING
9. PROJECTILE BEING LOADED
10. BREECH COVER
11. RETRACTING MECHANISM
12. GUN RETRACTING SUPPORT
13. DOOR STIFFENING STRUCTURE

In December 1942, two months after the B-25G first carried the 75 mm cannon aloft, the Engineering Division of the Air Force Materiel Center directed that two M9 37mm cannons be adapted to a bomb bay installation on the B-25. Response to this direction stated that the success of the project depended entirely on the blast effects on the aircraft structure as determined by preliminary tests. Blast from the high velocity 37mm round was known to be extremely severe and considerable experience had been obtained with a similar installation on a Douglas A-20.

The concept was considered impractical on the A-20 due to extensive blast damage to the fuselage structure and the costs of structural revisions capable of withstanding it. It appears in retrospect a questionable decision to continue the experiment on another aircraft. However, the Engineering Division of the Materiel Center considered the B-25 fuselage to be the maximum in rigidity and strength of contemporary airplanes and on that basis justified further tests.

North American prepared a brief proposal of a most formidable attack aircraft, preceding by over a year the first flight of the heavily armed B-25H. Armament consisted of two fixed .50 caliber guns in the nose, a 75 mm cannon in the crawl tunnel, two fixed .50 caliber guns

As late as 1944 forward fuselage gun packs were still being tested as evidenced by this unique concept of blast deflection. Insignificant improvement was noted as compared to the production B-25H/J gun packs and no production of this type was made. (NAA)

in the hatch gun module and twin .50 caliber guns in both aft turrets. A standard bombardier nose without cannon was also defined in the proposal.

Two 37 mm cannons were housed in a deep fairing under the bomb bay between the hatch guns and the bottom turret. Designed in three sections, the "bathtub" housing consisted of a forward section attached to the fuselage structure and a center section of two doors hinged from the longerons. The aft section, containing a parafrag bay, was secured to the aft fuselage structure and blended into the bottom turret. The 37 mm cannons were subassembled as a module and provided with quick release pins for easy installation and removal with a standard bomb hoist.

The airplane, so configured with twenty-one rounds of 75 mm, 200 rounds of 37 mm and 1,600 rounds of .50 caliber ammunition and 974 gallons of fuel had a calculated range of 1,900 miles and a top speed of 284 MPH. Gross weight was 34,600 pounds.

B-25C, 41-12800, was received by North American on 12 February 1943 for use as the test aircraft. A ground test fixture positioned the 37 mm guns sixteen inches under the fuselage, a location determined as the maximum aerodynamic distance from the fuselage.

One round of the high velocity ammunition shattered the adjacent airframe along with any hope of success. Structural damage was of such severity that necessary revisions to the airframe made the concept impractical. It was therefore recommended that any future 37 mm installations in the B-25 be made in the crawl tunnel like the 75 mm gun.

A crawl tunnel installation was subsequently accomplished on a B-25H at the Kansas City Division. The 37 mm gun was not adaptable to that location in the B-25 as it was necessary to load the ammunition through a port in the flight deck just behind the pilot, a location providing minimum and inefficient space for the gunner and stowage of ammunition .

Firing test over the Missouri River provided results less favorable than anticipated. Excessive smoke filled the airplane, few rounds were expended and the concept abandoned. The production installation of the 75 mm gun in the B-25H was considered far more effective.

In 1945 the Naval Ordnance Test Station at China Lake, California conducted a joint program with the Harvey Machine Company for development of an automatic launcher for a five inch diameter spin stabilized rocket. The projectile was fitted with fins to provide stabilizing spin as it passed through a short, simple launching tube.[1]

It was desired that the system be capable of firing a salvo of five or six rounds at 0.3 second intervals and to be reloadable in flight either mechanically or manually, depending on the configuration of the specific aircraft equipped to carry the system.

One concept utilized a stationary barrel and blast deflector with either vertical or horizontal magazines and a motor driven breech and loading mechanism. The concept tested consisted of a motor driven, rotating drum with five rocket chambers which rotated to align with a single launching tube through the aircraft nose. A deflector tube ported the blast downward out of the airplane at the aft end of the nose section. Some difficulty was encountered in determining the optimum launch tube length for best projectile stability.[2]

Ground and aerial firing tests failed to prove the concept effective enough to order it into production.

Rotating drum magazine developed by Harvey Machine Company carried five spin stabilized rockets. It was a compact unit, 2 drums easily fitting in a standard factory B-25 eight gun nose, one on either side of center, providing a 10 round capacity. (U.S. Navy Photo)

The rocket blast, ported overboard directly under the airplane, was more than adequate to stir up a cloud of dust from the dry California lake bed. (U.S. Navy Photo)

PBJ-1J 44-30980, Navy 35849 was selected as a test aircraft for much of the rocket testing conducted by the Navy in the vast test range northeast of Los Angeles. A spin stabilized rocket is shown at the moment of firing, the projectile having just cleared the launch tube. (U.S. Navy Photo)

A low level firing test shows the high rate of fire. The next to the last rocket shows a slight pitch up, not yet having stabilized. (U.S. Navy Photo)

Notes to Chapter 5

1. Letter, Naval Weapons Center Fleet Service Rocket Tests, 3 Dec 1974
2. Internal letter, Naval Ordnance Test Station to Steering Committee. Subject: Automatic Launcher For 5.0 inch/14 GASR For PBJ Nose Installation 17 May 1945

⑥ Bombs and Stores

After the remarkable success of Japanese torpedo bombers at Pearl Harbor and against the British capital ships Prince of Wales and Repulse, the Air Corps directed that first line aircraft capable of carrying torpedoes be equipped to do so. This was immediately done on Martin's B-26 Marauder and within days after Pearl Harbor, design was well underway to similarly equip the B-25.

In October 1942, General Arnold ordered the Army Air Force to take immediate action to develop a glide torpedo, specifying a launch speed in excess of 250 MPH. If that requirement could not be met with a modified Navy torpedo then a new design would be made. Obviously stepping over the line into the Navy's established jurisdiction, the word TORPEDO was dropped and the project designated HYDROBOMB.

The scheme of attaching wings and tail to bombs and torpedoes enabling them to be launched at greater and thereby safer distances from the target, dates back to Britain in 1939. The concept was proposed as a possible means of improving the success of attacks on German naval units and reducing the loss of men and airplanes. A launch speed of 200 MPH was desirable but far from attainable with the aircraft then in RAF inventory. British experiments continued until early 1943 when the program was canceled following persistent problems with directional control and stability. By that time experimental work on glide weapons was underway in the U.S. with relatively high priority which could well have influenced the British decision to cancel their efforts.

The early British experiments sparked an interest in General Arnold, Chief of the Air Corps, and early in 1941 he directed General Oliver Echols of the Materiel Division at Wright Field to organize a project to develop an effective winged bomb. Echols initiated the project in February and requested information from Britain regarding their experiments. Cooperation was minimal as the U.S. was not yet a belligerent against Germany which presented possible international complications. Arnold then directed that a test and development program get underway without further assistance from Britain.

As a result of this direction a joint advisory committee for Army-Navy development of glide weapons was formed, designating the Navy as authority over torpedoes and the Army over bombs.

The Glide Bomb, designated GB-1, was mechanically a simple high wing glider based on a 2,000 pound bomb fitted with a relatively streamlined nose and twin booms supporting tail surfaces and a twelve foot span wing. The "airframe" components were produced by the

In mid December 1941 design was begun to adapt the B-25 to carry the standard marine torpedo. The proposal was submitted and approved in March 1942 and the first 5 sets of racks were delivered and installed 11 days later. Delivery of the first production racks began in July. An apparently simple engineering and fabrication job, the project finally involved 120 new or revised drawings, 210 new parts and assemblies and 180 new tools and fixtures. First tested on B-25B 40-2274, no adverse characteristics resulted although air speed at normal cruise was reduced by 14 MPH. (NAA Report NA-5211, 31 Dec 1942)

Aeronca Aircraft Company and the Hammond Instrument Company supplied the gyros. Controls were pre-set.

Tests of the pre-set type were conducted in 1941 at Muroc (Dry Lake) Bombing Range and at Tonopah, Nevada. Radio controlled variants were concurrently tested at Eglin Field. Although directing that extensive

The MK-13 glide torpedo was fitted with the same airframe as the glide bomb except for longer booms to position the tail aft of the propeller. (USAF Museum)

GB-13 glide bomb with Ratron Marine Contrast Seeker in nose. (NASM #4A-16875)

The 330 gallon auxiliary bomb bay fuel tank was used for long range ferry flights. (NAA)

Wing mounts were provided for the 4.5 inch M8 rocket tube bundle which could be jettisoned in case of emergency. Drag reduced airspeed by 7 mph. (NAA)

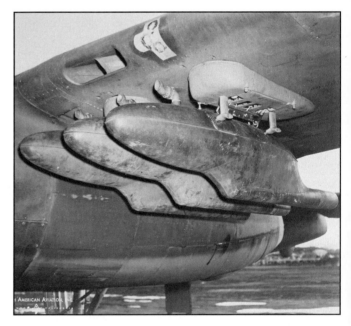

"Hey Joe, don'tcha' think we're running a bit rich?" Smoke dispensers were carried on the standard wing bomb rack (above). Smoke found limited use screening troops on beachheads. (NAA)

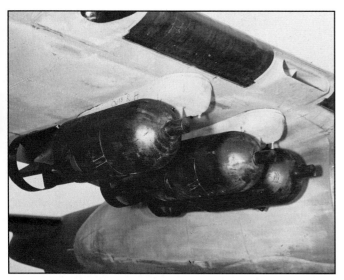

Three 300 pound depth charges were carried under each wing (left) on the NAA designed wing bomb rack equipped with standard B-7 bomb shackle, or four 500 pounders in the bomb bay (right). (NAA)

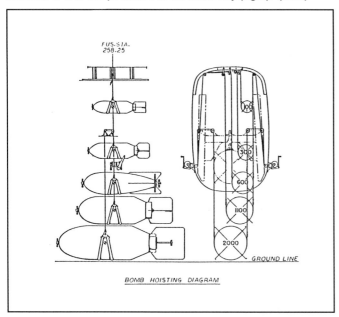

BOMB HOISTING DIAGRAM

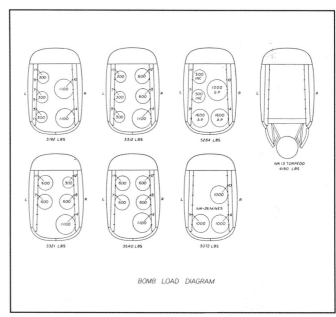

BOMB LOAD DIAGRAM

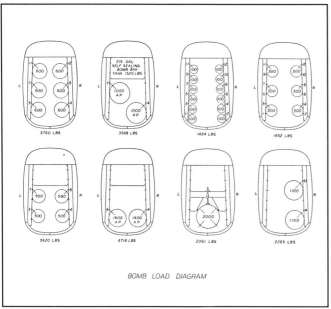

BOMB LOAD DIAGRAM

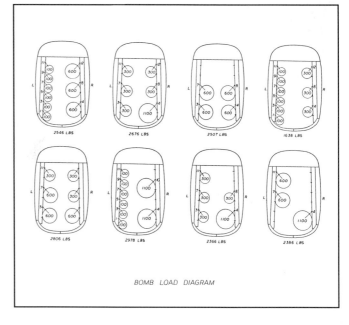

BOMB LOAD DIAGRAM

In 1944 the Air Technical Service Command at Wright Field tested the Fixed Assist Take Off unit on a B-25 (upper left and right). Initial trials began in 1940 and although ultimately successful, the innovation is not known to have been used tactically in World War II. The unit was designed and manufactured by Aero Jet Corp. (USAF Museum)

testing be done with controllable glide bombs, Arnold assigned higher priority to the simpler pre-set types.

Not until May 1944 was the glide bomb tried in combat. The single mission by 41st Bomb Wing B-17s against Cologne did not produce particularly effective results and further GB missions were not recommended.

Subsequent variants up to and including GB-13 were launched from B-25s and were tested with flares, radar homing devices, infra-red, TV, radio control and Ratron Marine Contrast Seeker. Tests were not without some hazards, moments of apprehension and a few laughs. On one occasion at Eglin Field a GB homed in on the control tower but fortunately the destructive, if non explosive, device went on by to be recovered without damage to life or property.

It appears that by 1942 greater attention may have been given to the hydrobomb than the glide bomb although the latter underwent development and testing almost throughout the duration of the war. The glide torpedo had some enthusiastic supporters, Colonel George Younger and General Barney Giles in particular, who visualized their use against heavily defended objectives like Rabaul, Lae and Truk with reduced casualties.

The first test example, designated GT-1, was an MK-13 torpedo fitted with the same wings and tail as the glide bomb but in all probability the tail booms were a bit longer to correctly position the tail for the longer weapon. Controls were pre-set and a paravane fired explosive bolts which separated the airframe when the torpedo was at the correct altitude above the water for normal launch. Drop tests were conducted at Eglin Field between 20 August and 11 October 1943.

During December 1943 final drop test were made with both dummy and live torpedoes. Satisfied that the system was viable, the First Provisional Glide Torpedo Squadron was formed and trained for a month on deployment tactics. In March, 1944, eighteen B-25 crews were organized at Hunter Field, Georgia where they took delivery of the following B-25J-1 airplanes modified as required for the torpedoes:

43-3905: 3906; 3907; 3955; 3957; 3959
3963; 3971; 3973; 3975; 3976; 3977
3978; 3979; 3980; 3981; 3982; 3983

The aircraft departed for McClellan Field at Sacramento, thence to Fairfield-Suisun (now Travis AFB). They departed 1 May for Hickam Field, Hawaii for assignment with the Seventh Bomber Command Training Detachment.

The units were subsequently assigned to the 41BG and on 31 July 1945 took the glide torpedo into action for the first time. Taking off from Kadena Airfield, Okinawa, the new weapons were launched against naval and shipping targets in Sasebo Harbor, Kyushu. Hazy conditions and smoke from fires previous to the attack made observation difficult. A possible hit was made on a CV and another ship hit and set afire. One miss hit shore installations in the main harbor and torpedo nets may have been effective to an unknown extent. Although heavy anti-aircraft fire was encountered there were no casualties.

Shipping in Nagasaki Harbor was the objective of the second glide torpedo mission by nine B-25s of the 41st on 1 August. Three AKs and seven other unidentified vessels came under assault. Because of clouds and the distance from the breakaway point, results could not be determined. Three torpedoes struck the water short of the harbor mouth, one spun in, and five made a normal glide path toward the target. Due to the poor visibility no hits were observed and no enemy losses sustained. No anti-aircraft fire was encountered and all B-25s returned safely with no casualties.

Torpedoes were released from distances as far as twelve miles from the objective and breakaway was made immediately thereafter. As a result, accurate observations by the attacking aircraft were difficult if not impossible. It was concluded that on future glide torpedo missions it would be necessary to have a photo reconnaissance or other observation airplane accompany the B-25s.

No other glide torpedo missions are known to have been made.

PART IV

7 The Dutch Connection

During the late 1930s the Dutch Government began a significant modernization of their aging air force, primarily for defense of the Netherlands East Indies. Several American aircraft firms were contacted as potential suppliers of fighters, transports, trainers and modern bombers to replace their obsolete Martin model 139 and 166 airplanes. Initial attempts to purchase Lockheed model 37 Ventura bombers failed when purchase authority was not received from the U.S. government.

The Netherlands Purchasing Commission (NPC) then turned to North American Aviation whose twin engine experience was limited to two bomber prototypes and the new B-25 which had been in production only four months. Although the B-25s were going to the rapidly expanding U.S. Army Air Corps, the Dutch succeeded in obtaining export release and purchase authorization. On 30 June, 1941 contract 71311/NA was signed with North American for 162 B-25C airplanes, company designation, NA-90. With this sale the Dutch had the distinction as the only purchaser of B-25s outside the U.S. The airplanes were paid for in cash by the Netherlands, then a government in exile in London.

Terms of the contract specified delivery beginning with twenty-five airplanes in November 1942; fifty in December, eighty in January 1943, and the final seven in February. Deliveries were to phase in immediately after completion and delivery to the U.S. of all 184 B-25, B-25A, B-25B and all 863 B-25C airplanes of contract AC16070 by the end of October, 1942.

It could appear unusual that the U.S. Government authorized this sale when the USAAC was accepting all the B-25s as they came off the assembly line. It also took place as Japan threatened expansion into southeast Asia and the Netherlands East Indies under threat of an oil embargo being considered by the American government. The Dutch purchase, along with sales to other nations, continued under a revised foreign sales policy of 1940 which provided technical benefits to the USAAC. Foreign deliveries continued on this basis until the Lend Lease program in 1941.

After the attack on Pearl Harbor, however, immediate changes were made in all aircraft allocations including the Dutch B-25s. Although many were ultimately received by the Netherlands East Indies Air Force, the accounting of allocations, assignments and re-assignments constitutes a series of involved transactions between the United States, The Netherlands, Britain and Australia.

Almost immediately after contracting with North American, Captain te Roller of the NPC requested an

In June 1941 Captain E.J.G. teRoller of the Netherlands Purchasing Commission (right) negotiated the Dutch purchase of 162 B-25Cs. He is shown here in a rare photograph with test pilot Louis Wait (left) and NAA representative Harold Raynor. Lt. Col. TeRoller later commanded NEI 18 Squadron and was lost in June 1944 on a mission in the East Indies. (NAA)

accelerated delivery schedule, assistance in ferrying the airplanes to the East Indies, numerous equipment items and that quality control of the Dutch airplanes be performed on the assembly line by North American inspectors.

In July 1941 General Spaatz notified the NPC that three B-25s would be released to the Dutch in September for training purposes. He also stipulated that specifications governing their airplanes not be in the metric system or in any other way delay production of B-25s for the U.S. In a letter of 11 August Spaatz advised Captain te Roller that an accelerated delivery schedule had been approved: forty-two airplanes to be delivered from March through September; thirty-six during October and November; seventy-two during December 1942 and January 1943 and the final twelve airplanes in February. Approval of this schedule, however, was subject to change depending on conditions that could exist in early 1942, prophetic thoughts indeed.

82

Airplanes with tail numbers and foreign insignia were a rare sight on North American's Inglewood flight ramp. This photo shows American, Dutch and British. In all probability the American insignia on 41-12525 has been painted over in preparation for a Russian red star. The triangular black and orange Dutch insignia on N5-126 was superseded by a reproduction of the Dutch flag. (NAA)

Complications soon arose regarding Dutch acquisition of drift meters, auto pilots, radios and S-1 bomb sights in lieu of the restricted Norden sight. Procurement of numerous other items also became a logistical and supply problem. Spaatz reiterated that the original specifications upon which the NPC obtained their export release did not include bomb sights and many other items regularly installed in combat ready airplanes, and therefore recommended that such items be obtained from other sources.

The NPC approached the Lend Lease Administration (LLA) for resolution of the equipment problems. The LLA suggested the Dutch use the British Mark XIV sight to be produced in the U.S. or the Sperry sight which had been released to the British. Negotiations were apparently unsuccessful.

The NPC again requested faster delivery of their Mitchells. This was denied but due to the seriousness of the situation and the urgency of the Dutch request, the American government concluded that augmenting Dutch strength in the East Indies was in the best American interests. As a result the decision was reversed and on 21 January an emergency allocation of sixty B-25s was approved for delivery to NEIAF units at Archerfield, Australia and Bangalore, India. These airplanes were to be diverted from U.S. deliveries and would be replaced later by an equal number from the NA-90 contract. Ten were scheduled for delivery in January 1943; forty-three in February and seven in March.

After the unsuccessful efforts by the Dutch government to procure bomb sights, it is ironic that the sixty airplanes of the emergency allocation were delivered equipped with the Norden sights. The Sperry sights were unavailable and the B-25 was produced to accommodate the Norden. As a result the time and effort to refit the airplanes for the Sperry sight would have caused unacceptable delays in deliveries. Understandably, this decision was made at the highest levels of the U.S. government.

On 28 January 1942, the U.S. Ferry Command was ordered to arrange for ferrying the sixty B-25s by any means at its disposal to destinations specified by the NEI government who would pay all costs. To avoid complications, General Olds of the Ferry Command contracted with Consolidated Aircraft Corporation on 6 February for crews to ferry eight airplanes in February; sixteen in March and from fifteen to thirty-two per month thereafter to complete delivery.

An interesting aside to the ferry arrangements was the involvement of British Overseas Airways Corporation. In February Major te Roller met in Montreal with Captain Thomas of the Ferry Command and Air Vice Marshal Sir Frederick Bowhill of the Royal Air Force. Following this meeting arrangements were made for RAF crews to ferry twenty Dutch B-25s from West Palm Beach, Florida to Australia via Africa and an additional ten via the South Pacific route from Hamilton Field near San Francisco.

General Olds reported that AVM Bowhill had, on several occasions, offered RAF crews for ferrying American aircraft to overseas destinations. The reasons are somewhat obscure but the RAF probably found this an easy means of transporting personnel to new stations while gaining experience in the bargain. The British offer was readily accepted as the cost of Consolidated crews was exorbitant due to the complex logistics of returning them to the U.S.

Consolidated however, ferried a limited number of the Dutch Mitchells. Four of the B-25s departed via the South Pacific route from Hamilton Field, California in early March 1942 escorted by Jack Fox, North American Aviation technical representative assigned to the NEIAF in Australia. At Hamilton Field Fox met with Lieutenants Leegstra and

Hoogeveen, NEI representatives, for acceptance of the airplanes following arrival from Long Beach where they were processed for overseas shipment.

During March five of the airplanes arrived at Bangalore and twelve at Archerfield near Brisbane. The Royal Australian Air Force and the U.S. Air Force in Australia concurred that the Archerfield twelve should form the nucleus of the new NEIAF squadron as the airplanes became available. Ten of these were deployed from Darwin against the Philippines in mid April for an operation known as the Royce Mission. (See Part V, Battle Line in the Pacific.) It was then agreed that the next eighteen to arrive would go to the NEIAF, but that too was changed with the capitulation of the East Indies on 9 March and the U.S. ceased to recognize the NEIAF as a combatant power.

Early in April General Van Oyen and General Brett, respective commanders of Dutch and American air forces in Australia, agreed that eighteen of the B-25s on order should equip one complete Dutch squadron. This was deferred due to the seriousness of the tactical situation in Northern Australia resulting in twelve of the airplanes being diverted to the USAAC upon arrival. The U.S. then agreed to credit the Dutch government accordingly or replace the airplanes in Australia or the U.S. depending on availability and preference of the Netherlands government.

Of considerable concern to the staff of the newly organized Allied Air Forces in Australia was the part the evacuated Dutch personnel and equipment would play in the organization. Of equal concern was the distribution of the airplanes then on order and paid for in cash by the NEI government. On 10 March approximately 500 expected airplanes had not been delivered, the last scheduled to arrive in Australia in December. Of this number, 129 were B-25s plus an additional thirty-four then enroute from the U.S. It was then decided that those enroute via the

Atlantic would be held in India, but lacking adequate knowledge of the status of Dutch equipment and personnel, the staff then directed that the Dutch aircraft then on order be delivered to Australia. NEI forces would receive as many as they could use and the RAAF and the USAAF would use the remainder.

Being short of badly needed medium bombers General Kenney, commanding the Fifth Air Force, made an unsuccessful attempt to acquire five B-25s from NEI 18 Squadron which were being used for training and anti-submarine work. He proposed trading eighteen weary A-20s for the B-25s which the Dutch understandably refused due to the condition of the A-20s and their lack of range for operations from Darwin against Indonesia.

Following the fall of Java the NEI crews of the five Bangalore airplanes, N5-139, 143, 144, 145, and 148, were isolated in India. The RAF, the Netherlands Navy and the USAAF all maneuvered to get the B-25s. Resolution was made by the Dutch government in London in the allocation of two to the RAF and three to the USAAF. The Dutch Navy wanted all five for photo reconnaissance operations with the RAF but the Dutch crews refused to fly the unarmed airplanes. The Mitchells were later converted in Karachi for photo recon work. The Dutch crews tested the airplanes, checked out the RAF crews, then joined 18 Squadron in Australia. Two of the B-25s were assigned RAF numbers MA 956 and 957, the others retaining NEI numbers N5-144, 145 and 148. All were actually assigned to the RAF for 681 PR Squadron at Alipore and Calcutta.

These airplanes were of considerable value at the time as little was known of Japanese movements in Burma and considerable aerial reconnaissance was required.

Continual controversies over allocations and reassignments of the NEI Mitchells had unavoidably created administrative confusion. There were documented assumptions that the B-25s delivered to the NEIAF were

N5-128 (41-12935) was the first N numbered airplane when B-25s were first received by the Dutch in late August 1942. The airplane remained in service until February 1945. (NAA)

part of the 162 NA-90 airplanes which were paid for in cash by the Dutch government. This was not so. All were Lend Lease.

Delivery of the emergency allocation of the sixty Lend Lease B-25s began on 6 February. All however, did not reach the Dutch forces. One crashed, a total loss, and two others were seriously damaged. Accountability was clarified on 28 March 1942, in a letter from the Air Staff to the Air Forces Materiel Command stating that the NPC had also requested changes relative to a portion of their airplanes.

The disposition of the remaining fifty-seven was as follows:

1. Eighteen to Australia for the Dutch, thirteen arrived and five enroute.

2. Twenty-four to Australia for allocation by General Mac Arthur. Of those five were enroute and nineteen were in the U.S. awaiting ferry to Australia.

3. Six to the USAAC for delivery to Brazil or to replace other airplanes that may have been used for the same purpose.

4. Five enroute to India for assignment to the Air Forces commander there.

5. Four were held at the modification center operated by the Chicago and Southern Airlines at Memphis, Tennessee pending a decision to send them to Australia or to an operational training unit of the AAF.

The NPC had not relinquished rights to the ultimate deliveries of the initial - and paid for - 162 B-25s. The eighteen airplanes in (1.) were charged to the Dutch account and the remaining 144 were to be delivered according to previously established schedules except for forty-four airplanes to be delivered at the rate of thirteen in January, thirteen in February and eighteen in March, 1943.

It was therefore directed that:

a. In addition to those B-25s that reached Australia that nineteen more be ferried there as soon as possible by crews from Consolidated or the RAF.

b. Considering a total of forty-two B-25s in Australia, action is to be taken to ensure adequate supplies and spare parts to keep the airplanes combat ready. Since some spares are enroute, exact quantities to be determined in conjunction with the NPC.

c. The five Dutch airplanes in India will be placed under the control of the Commanding General, U.S. Forces in India.

d. The NPC will make the necessary financial arrangements with Consolidated and the RAF for ferrying. Delivery of the remaining 144 B-25s due the NPC will be made as soon as possible.

e. The following summary kept the emergency allocation of the sixty Dutch B-25s in order:

Charge the NPC with eighteen airplanes to Australia plus one airplane which crashed in Africa.	*19*
Charge the U.S. temporarily with the two airplanes damaged at West Palm Beach to be repaired at Dutch expense.	*2*
B-25s to Australia	*24*
B-25s in lieu of others delivered to Brazil	*6*
B-25s to India	*5*
In U.S. pending decision of Chiefs of Staff	*4*
Total	*60*

Not until August 1942 did 18 Squadron finally receive their promised and long awaited B-25s, all delivered new from the North American factory. On 21 August 1942 Major te Roller wired the AAF Materiel Command the status of the B-25 deliveries to the Dutch as follows: Airplanes No. 41-12445,468,495,507,508, and 509 were ferried from West Palm Beach and 41-12468 crashed in Africa. Numbers 41-12493 and 510 were damaged at West Palm Beach. The following twenty-four airplanes departed from Hamilton Field beginning in April: 41-12437, 438, 439, 442, 443, 444, 455, 462, 464, 466, 470, 472, 476, 478, 481, 494, 496, 497, 498, 499, 501, 502, 511, and 514.

This wire was followed on 8 September by a letter to the Materiel Command requesting concurrence of the disposition of the Dutch airplanes. (See Appendix H)

Following the loss of the East Indies the NIEAF was organized under RAAF control. Personnel from both air forces were assigned to NEIAF 18 Squadron and ultimately equipped with B-25s. No. 18 Squadron began operations from McDonald airstrip in January 1943 and transferred to Batchelor Field south of Darwin in May. Primary assignments were the interdiction of the resources of the East Indies from the Japanese by photo reconnaissance, attacks against Japanese airfields, troop

The Royal Netherlands Military Flying School at Jackson Field, Jackson, Mississippi, was equipped with 15 B-25Cs, 5 B-25Ds and 10 B-25Gs. The first class graduated in September, 1942 and operations ceased in early February, 1944. (NAA)

concentrations and harbors, sea patrols for warning against possible fleet movements against Australia and attack against shipping in the Indonesian area.

Crews were a mix a both air forces; all pilots and observer/bombardiers were Dutch, most aerial gunners were RAAF and radio operators comprised both. After trained crews began arriving with new B-25s from the school at Jackson, the RAAF flying contingent decreased somewhat. Ground crews however, remained predominantly Australian with Dutch senior mechanics.

In early 1945 three missions of three aircraft each, stripped of most armament for maximum range fuel, flew successful leaflet raids to Java. The Japanese were caught by surprise and the B-25s, although minimally armed, managed to shoot things up a bit. All aircraft were marked with very large Dutch flag insignia for the morale of the POW camps they overflew.

In May 1944, Lieutenant Colonel te Roller took command of eighteen Squadron and his B-25s continued attacks against ground installations and Japanese shipping. By then the unit began receiving the first of the B-25J models to replace the weary Ds, some of which were converted to transports. Delivery of the Js continued until August 1945 and during that time sixty airplanes were received. The NEIAF Mitchells had maintained a steady level of sorties. Numerous NEIAF B-25Js were converted to strafers by replacement of the greenhouse by the eight gun strafer nose received directly from North American.

The combat role of the B-25s did not end with the cessation of hostilities with Japan. As the war drew to a close in August, Indonesian Nationalists proclaimed independence from the Netherlands. Following relinquishment of control by the RAAF, the NEIAF began independent operations and action against Indonesia continued into 1947 with the reliable B-25s in a major role. By year's end Dutch sovereignty over the East Indies was terminated at which time forty-one B-25s were on strength.

The first "police action" by the Netherlands government against Indonesia at Java and Sumatra took place between 21 July and 4 August 1947. During the second police action between 19 December 1948 and 8 January 1949, the B-25s of 18 Squadron flew 529 sorties. The Republic of Indonesia became officially independent on 27 December 1949 and in March 1950 the transfer of bases and equipment began. The Indonesian Air Force expressed little interest in the acquisition of B-25s and only three examples were taken over by the IAF.

In the post war period several other Dutch units flew B-25s:
>16 Squadron was formed 1 November 1946 with 9 B-25Js in both strafer and medium bomber configurations. The squadron operated from Palembang until merging into 18 Squadron on 1 August 1948.
>OOS (Overgang-Opleidings School) Conversion school at Biak operated from mid 1946 until August, 1948 retraining former POWs and new pilots from Holland. The original inventory of twelve B-25s was reduced to five when the unit was disbanded.

B-25C of the Royal Netherlands Military Flying School was photographed at Ottawa, Canada on 31 June 1943. (Robert T. O'Dell)

>PVA (Photo Verkennings Afdeling) PRU unit, was formed on 1 January 1947 with five B-25s, two P-51s and one P-40N. It merged into 18 Squadron 1 August 1948.
>19 Squadron was formed in 1944 as NEI No. 1 Transport Squadron and in August, 1945 was equipped with C-47s and about twelve B-25s converted to transports. It was redesignated 20 Squadron and operated until December 1947.

In the post war years the NEIAF's greatest problem was a shortage of personnel. Many of the new people had signed on in Holland to train for the fight against Japan. They were to be trained in Australia but immediately after the Japanese surrender, Australia failed to cooperate due to local political conditions and labor union attitudes against Dutch colonialism. Training programs were conducted with repatriated ex POWs as cadre but many volunteers were then returning to Holland.

ROYAL NETHERLANDS MILITARY FLYING SCHOOL

Following the surrender of Dutch forces on 9 March 1942, approximately 900 military personnel were evacuated from the Netherlands East Indies to Australia. About half were air force, the majority being students. Within the organization was an adequate number of instructors to complete student training but available facilities did not exist in Australia. The few airfields were sorely needed by combat units and training of Australian crews.

To alleviate the problem and take maximum advantage of well qualified personnel, General Van Oyen went to the U.S. in mid April to establish a training program for Dutch students then in Australia. The project was approved by the War Department and preliminary details were soon worked out by Colonel Weijerman of the Netherlands legation and the Flying Training Command of the AAF.

The AAF agreed to supply a training base with accommodations for 1,000 personnel including ninety Dutch instructors from Australia. Establishment of the RNMFS at Jackson, Mississippi relieved congestion at Australian air fields, leaving those bases to combat units and the heavy maintenance required. On 17 April the

A B-25 of the RNMFS and another B-25 escorted HRH Princess Juliana to Surinam from Miami in a KLM Lockheed. (G.J. Casius)

B-25C M 351 42-32485 was taken on strength 7 April 1943 and was in the Personnel & Equipment Pool in September 1944. The airplane operated as a photo recon FB-25 in 1947/48. (G.J. Casius)

N5-158 41-30589 carried General Spoor, CG of the RNEI Army, to Holland in July 1946. Photograph at Valkenburg Airfield. (G.J. Casius)

Dutch personnel in Australia began departing from Melbourne.

Although deliveries of B-25s to the Dutch had ceased after the surrender, it was agreed between the U.S. Government and the NPC that delivery of the remainder of B-25s on the NEI contract would resume when the Dutch in training at Jackson would be combat ready. The first contingent was expected to be ready in October.

The first class graduated in September 1942 and the training of Dutch crews continued until 8 February 1944 at which time the airplanes reverted back to the USAAF. The terms of the return is not clear but some kind of reverse lend lease was probably implemented.

In addition to the B-25s listed in the table of RNMFS airplanes, the following B-25Ds were ferried to Australia in 1944 by returning graduates of the school:

B-25D-30	43-3421	became N5-185
	-3422	187
	-3423	181
	-3424	
	-3425	
	-3426	
	-3427	193
	-3607	194
	-3613	195
B-25D-35	-3620	
	-3623	197
	-3624	198
	-3625	199
	-3626	200
	-3765	
	-3766	201
	-3767	202
	-3768	203
	-3769	204
	-3770	205
	-3791	207
	-3830	
	-3832	
	-3833	208
	-3834	210
	-3835	209
	-3836	211
	-3867	
	-3868	
	-3869	

Ten B-25Gs were on loan from the USAAF to the RNMFS. Eight are known to be 42-65000, 65005, 65011, 65037, 65045, 65063, 65064, 65102.

Royal Air Force 320 Squadron was formed in June 1940 from personnel of the Royal Dutch Naval Air Service* who reached England after the invasion of the Netherlands. Operating with miscellaneous British aircraft the squadron performed anti-submarine, convoy escort and air-sea rescue duty. These operations were expanded to include attacks on shipping on the Norwegian coast.

In March 1943 the squadron received B-25 Mark II and III Mitchells and began operations in Europe against gun emplacements, railway yards, bridges, troops and other tactical targets. Moving to Belgium in October 1944 the unit continued tactical missions until VE Day. It was disbanded in August 1945. (Mitchells of 320 Squadron are listed in Appendix J.)

* Marine Luchtvaart Dienst
(Naval Aviation Service)

B-25B of 320 Squadron, Royal Netherlands Navy. (NAA)

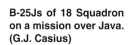

B-25Js of 18 Squadron
on a mission over Java.
(G.J. Casius)

88

Lashed aboard Hornet's deck, engines and turrets covered, the Tokyo bound B-25s ride out some stormy weather enroute to the task force rendezvous north of Midway Island, April 1942. (NAA)

8 Doolittle'sTokyo Raiders

The attack on the Japanese cities of Tokyo, Kobe and Nagoya in April 1942 was conceived for the most part as a retaliatory move against Japan in the interest of bolstering American morale and inflicting as much tactical damage to the enemy as possible. The disaster at Pearl Harbor had been the worst defeat in American history and throughout the early months of 1942 every theater of operations reported discouraging news.

On 18 April the war was suddenly brought to the Japanese doorstep and the first good news in months emblazoned the headlines as the American press went wild. Sixteen North American B-25 Mitchell bombers and eighty men commanded by Lieutenant Colonel James Doolittle had struck Japan with a hit and run attack. Overnight America had her first heroes of World War II who had struck an offensive blow and the B-25 became almost as famous.

Plans for such an operation took form almost by coincidence. The means of execution, if not the plan itself, may well be credited to the creative minds of General Arnold and Captain Francis Low, a submariner on Admiral King's staff. Conferring with the British regarding operations in North Africa, Admiral King, Chief of Naval Operations, suggested that both fighters and bombers be transported on the decks of aircraft carriers to be unloaded by crane at North African harbors. Alarmed by the vulnerability of the aircraft, Arnold considered the possibility of carrier transportation with allowance for adequate deck space that the airplanes could take off under their own power. This would eliminate dependence on harbor facilities at a time when conditions could deteriorate to serious disadvantage.

While Arnold and his staff addressed the problem, Captain Low, concurrently and apart from Arnold's people, was struck by the idea of army bombers taking off from the Navy's carriers. Should this be possible could the carriers take the bombers near enough Japan that they could strike Tokyo and then proceed on to China? What better target of quick revenge than the industrial centers of Japan. A submariner, Low was out of his element but took the idea to Captain Duncan, Admiral King's air officer.

After a thorough study Duncan concluded that the concept was technically feasible and on King's orders presented his analyses to Arnold. After reviewing Duncan's work Arnold sent for his new special projects officer and famed aviator, Lieutenant Colonel Jimmy Doolittle who quickly confirmed Duncan's estimates.

A "Tokyo Project" was quickly and secretly formed, Duncan and Doolittle being assigned project responsibility

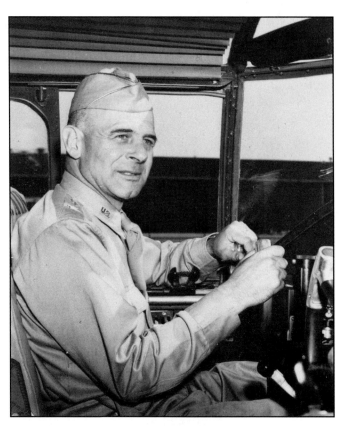

Shortly after the raid against Japan, Brig. Gen. Jimmy Doolittle visited the North American plant and addressed the justly proud employees. (NAA)

for their respective services. The carrier Hornet, commanded by Captain Marc Mitscher, was chosen as the legendary Shangri La from which President Roosevelt claimed the B-25s had secretly flown.

Logistics and complex problems abounded. As the B-25s could not be recovered by the carriers, a land based destination was an obvious requirement. Earlier plans had considered arranging for operational bases in China and with the cooperation of Chiang Kai-Shek, the bombers could land on prearranged fields in eastern China. From there they could continue on to Burma to serve in General Stilwell's command. Absolute secrecy was paramount. Even Chiang was given but minimal details and with considerable reluctance he agreed. Fields were subsequently prepared at Kian, Yushan, Lishui and Kweilin, the latter some 1,900 miles southwest of Tokyo.[1]

Doolittle preferred a takeoff point 450 miles east of Tokyo with 550 miles as the acceptable maximum. The mission therefore required bombers capable of short takeoff run, a range of 2,400 miles and, if worthwhile

On the Eglin Field ramp Doolittle's B-25Bs were fitted with bogus tail guns. The long exhaust pipes and hydraulic tail skids typify the early variants. (NAA)

damage were to be inflicted, must carry a minimum 2,000 pound bomb load.

Two aircraft in the inventory were of potential capability; Martin's B-26 Marauder and North American's B-25 Mitchell. Both had been designed to the same procurement specification and both were being delivered to squadrons. The choice quickly became clear. The more powerful and faster B-26 was lacking in range and due to a higher takeoff speed, would not have sufficient run to lift from Hornet's deck. The B-25 had the range and calculations showed a takeoff capability with deck to spare. A run of 450 feet was established, leaving space on the aft deck for sixteen closely packed B-25s.

The 17th Bomb Group comprised of the 34th, 37th, and 95th squadrons and the 89th Reconnaissance Squadron (then attached to the 17th) were the only units then equipped with the new B-25s. Stationed at Pendleton, Oregon, the 17th was scheduled for transfer to Columbia, South Carolina in February. From this unit came the aircraft and volunteer crews who knew only that they had volunteered for a secret and dangerous mission against heavy odds.

Moving to Eglin Field, Florida, training began under Doolittle's second in command, Major John Hilger, assisted by Lieutenant Henry Miller, borrowed from the Navy to instruct the crews in short takeoff techniques. They soon discovered that with a reasonable headwind a 450 foot run would get a B-25 safely airborne. But Doolittle was cautious and arranged for two B-25s piloted by Lieutenants Fitzgerald and McCarthy to make carrier takeoffs at sea under simulated mission conditions. In company with Captain Duncan they steamed from Norfolk, Virginia well beyond sight of land. Their successful takeoffs from Hornet left no doubt that the B-25 had the right stuff. [2]

Doolittle, meanwhile, had been involved with top mission planners selecting targets and alternates and details of modifications to the airplanes. Arriving at Eglin Field on 3 March 1942 he met the crews for the first time. Opportunity was again given should anyone choose to back out, but none did.

Modification to increase fuel capacity was accomplished by Mid Continent Airlines at Minneapolis, Minnesota. Mitchells of the 17th BG began arriving by twos and threes on 10 February and the final airplane departed on 28 February. Three shifts of mechanics worked around the clock under extremely tight security. [3]

Bombing the Japanese objectives was planned for 1,000 foot altitude, well below the effectiveness of the Norden bomb sight. These units were removed, reducing weight and eliminating any possibility of the highly secret device falling to the Japanese. A simple, inexpensive hand held sight was substituted and functioned perfectly.

The low attack altitude also negated requirements for the lower turret. Mechanically problematical anyway, its removal reduced aircraft weight by 450 pounds and provided space for a fifty gallon fuel tank. Two more fuel tanks of 160 and 230 gallons were placed in the crawlway over the bomb bay and in the top of the bay leaving space for four 500 pound demolition bombs and a cluster of incendiaries. Normal fuel capacity of the B-25B plus the amount in the auxiliary tanks increased to 1,150 gallons. Fifty gallons was required for engine run up and takeoff. Lean cruise calculations showed that 170 MPH indicated could be maintained at a consumption rate of eighty gallons per hour, providing a theoretical range of 2,250 miles, marginal but possible.

B-25Bs were not factory equipped with tail guns, relying on the aft dorsal turret of two .50 caliber guns. To discourage fighter attack from the rear fake tail guns made of wood and painted black were installed. Small arms ammunition consisted of approximately 800 rounds of .50 caliber in the proportion of one tracer, two armor piercing and three incendiary and about the same in .30 caliber.[4]

Although North American informed Doolittle that the use of de-icer boots on wings and tail would cause a slight drop in air speed, the decision was nonetheless made to fit the airplanes with that equipment as well as propeller de-icing. The decision was based on the possibility of unpredictable weather should any of the airplanes find it necessary to land in Russia.

Concurrent with planning for the Tokyo raid, North American and the Wright Aeronautical Corporation jointly conducted a series of tests on B-25Cs as factory equipped with Holley carburetors to determine simplified long range cruise conditions for ferry flights. These tests were primarily for the benefit of Consolidated crews contracted for ferrying B-25s to Australia. As the Tokyo mission plans progressed these tests increased in importance and the Flight Test Branch at Wright Field requested that as part of mission preparations the 17th BG conduct a parallel program with specific B-25Bs assigned to the project, airplanes equipped with Bendix carburetors on the production line. An indicated air speed of 170 was desired and much of the testing was based on that figure.[5]

A B-25B (with Bendix carburetor) weighing 31,500 pounds consumed eighty-five gallons of fuel per hour at sea level at twenty-nine inches of manifold pressure at 1,475 RPM. Following the mission one of the pilots reported that after bomb release and reducing power to twenty-five inches manifold pressure at 1,300 RPM, speed dropped to 166 MPH at a fuel consumption of sixty-three gallons per hour.

Upon completion of training the volunteers departed Eglin Field, Florida on 23 March enroute to McClellan Field near Sacramento, California. This too was a training flight as Doolittle had given instructions to operate by the new long range cruise control procedure. A stop was made at Kelly Field, Texas and the aircraft continued on to McClellan on the 26th.

At McClellan Field all radio equipment was removed and any pitted propeller blades replaced. Machine gun stoppages had been a recurring problem which was solved by laborious honing of action surfaces. To Doolittle's irritation base mechanics made final carburetor adjustments in spite of the fine tuning done by Bendix technicians at Eglin Field. Fuel tanks were again checked for leakage.[6]

Admiral Halsey and Doolittle met on 30 March for initial briefing and on 1 April the sixteen B-25s and twenty-four trained crews departed McClellan for Alameda Naval Base near San Francisco. There fuel tanks were drained and the Mitchells hoisted aboard Hornet and lashed down.

On 2 April Captain Marc Mitscher's Hornet, accompanied by two cruisers, four destroyers and one oiler, steamed westward under the Golden Gate Bridge, destination unknown. Days later and north of Midway, the ships joined the other units of Vice Admiral Halsey's task force consisting of carrier Enterprise and two more cruisers, six destroyers and one oiler. Safely at sea Halsey announced to his anxious crews, "This task force is headed for Tokyo". All aircraft were then armed and bombs loaded.

The existence of the task force was unknown to the Japanese but their intelligence had intercepted some earlier communications and correctly deduced that some offensive operation was in the making.

The Japanese staff saw no cause for alarm. During the initial four months of the Pacific war their forces had ravaged the American fleet and continued to push Allied forces to near destruction on every front. Never would the Americans subject their precious carriers to the dangers in well protected home waters.

This view was not shared by Admiral Yamamoto, Commander in Chief of the Japanese Navy. As a naval attache in Washington D.C. he had come to know the Americans well and knew that these generally easy going people had become united in anger into a most formidable and determine foe. Equally disturbing to the Admiral was his knowledge of the untapped industrial might and the huge natural resources of the United States.

From available intelligence he concluded that a carrier based strike against Japan was possible between April 14th and 19th.[7] He immediately ordered defenses strengthened, moving additional fighter and anti-aircraft

One of the Tokyo B-25s under guard during the fuel tank modification program at Mid Continent Airlines, Minneapolis. (Mark Copeland)

Looking straight up through the open bomb bay doors shows the four 500 pound bombs under auxiliary fuel tank. (NAA)

units to strategic areas and posted a cordon of picket ships and patrol aircraft some 600 miles offshore. Yamamoto intended more than adequate defense. He intended to destroy any attacking American force. Heavy units of the fleet were strategically positioned. The Japanese trap was set.

But Japanese intelligence lacked one crucial bit of information. They logically assumed that carrier based single engine aircraft would make such an attack, then be recovered at sea by the waiting carriers, vulnerable within strike range of both sea and land based air power.

The possibility of early discovery by Japanese patrols could not be discounted. It was therefore decided that should this occur the B-25s would be launched and flown to Midway or Hawaii. If these island bases were out of range the airplanes would be pushed overboard making Hornet combat ready. Should discovery be made within reasonable striking range of Japan, all B-25s would be launched and the attack carried out as planned in spite of the additional distance to China.

On the morning of 18 April 1942 and approximately 623 miles from Honshu the latter possibility occurred when a Japanese picket boat was sighted by a scout plane from Enterprise and a second picket blundered into the approaching task force.

The near picket boat was destroyed but not before alerting Tokyo. The decision was made to launch all aircraft immediately, ten hours earlier and 220 miles farther from Japan than the maximum planned acceptable distance, creating a critical fuel situation. Hornet plowed into the stormy seas and at 8:20 AM Doolittle's B-25 was

the first to leave the pitching deck. All sixteen Mitchells launched successfully.

Flying low over the sea the raiders were on their own and took bearings on the target cities of Tokyo, Kobe and Nagoya with explicit orders to bomb military targets only. Hitting their targets at low level they inflicted all the damage that sixty-four 500 pound bombs and incendiaries could. Successfully hit were rail and dock yards, a fuel refinery, utility plants and vessels in port, but inevitably some landed in civilian areas. Despite the advance warning Japanese defenses were unprepared and the raiders met only sporadic, ineffective anti-aircraft fire.

Free of the Japanese defenses the Mitchells raced for the China coast, well aware that their arrival would be after nightfall on unlighted, unfamiliar terrain. Absolute radio silence being imperative, the Chinese could not be informed of their unexpected earlier arrival time. The increased flight distance did not deplete the fuel as seriously as expected due to a timely tail wind for eight hours. Although fuel became a critical problem, all aircraft reached China except for one that landed in Vladivostok.

Approaching the mainland of China through rain squalls and poor visibility and no available landing fields the crews were faced with the beggarman's choice of crash landing or bailing out. From both decisions a few deaths and serious injuries resulted.

Of the remaining fifteen aircraft eleven crews bailed out and two made crash landings. Three deaths occurred on landing and a few serious injuries. Sheltered and attended by courageous Chinese, the survivors were hunted ruthlessly by the occupying Japanese who exacted maximum penalties from the populace.

That the Tokyo raid of 18 April 1942 was a success or failure may well remain controversial. It inflicted no damage of serious or lasting effect; all B-25s were lost, seven men were injured and three killed, eight taken prisoner of which only four survived and one airplane landed in Russia where the crew was interned. Japanese vengeance was wrought in full measure. American captives were tortured and Chinese sympathizers were murdered by thousands.

Doolittle, awaiting departure from China, confessed to his men that he thought the mission a total failure and expected courts martial upon his return. The nation and his superiors emphatically disagreed, awarding their hero a double promotion from Lieutenant Colonel to Brigadier General and a grateful nation's highest award, the Congressional Medal of Honor, and prompt assignment to a new command of greater responsibility.

But was the mission a failure? Numerous positive results suggest otherwise. A highly secret and complex mission between the Army and Navy was accomplished without a hitch. The Navy suffered neither damage nor loss in performing their part. The American B-25 crews had done the impossible and shocked the Japanese into implementing significant changes in their conduct of the war and assigning more forces to home defense. It became clear to the Japanese that control of the Pacific was essential and could not be achieved without the neutralization of Midway and the Hawaiian Islands. Their subsequent unsuccessful attempt to take Midway turned into a debacle from which the Imperial Navy's carrier offensive capability never recovered.

American morale received a badly needed boost from the Tokyo Raiders, assuring the nation that it was not a question of winning the war but when.

The success of the mission resulted from many factors: thorough preparations and training and the anticipation of all known problems; dedication and courage of each individual concerned; airplanes and equipment that proved adequate for the job and air tight security. It must also be recognized that the Japanese were not prepared for an attack of this type and were caught by surprise despite Yamamoto's premonition and the picket's warning.

(See Appendix M for a complete listing of aircraft and crews of the Tokyo Raiders.)

Notes to Chapter 8
1. Craven, W.F. and Cate, J.L., **The Army Air Forces in World War II**, Chicago, IL The University of Chicago Press, 1953, Vol I, page 439-440
2. Glines, Col. C.V., **Popular Aviation**, March/April 1967, page 17
3. Craven & Cates Vol VI, page 336
4. Hq. AAF Division of Intelligence Services **The Tokyo Raid**, Informational Intelligence Summary (Special) No. 20, 18 Apr 1942
5. Wright Aeronautical Corp., Range Tests, R-2600-9/13 Engines, NAA B-25, Project F-240, Reports Nos. 74, 76, 77, 82, 10-26 Feb 1942
6. Letter, General James H. Doolittle to Norman Avery, 15 Apr 1974
7. Caidin, Martin, **Argosy Magazine**, Apr 1974, p. 43

Recovering from his injuries, Tokyo Raider Captain Ted Lawson (center) visited the North American plant in 1943. Shown here with field service technicians and Lt. Col. Stephen Barker, resident Air Corps officer at North American. (NAA)

For the 25th anniversary of the Tokyo raid B-25D-30/F-10, 43-3374, was converted by North American to replicate General Doolittle's 40-2344. The trimetrogon camera nose used on the F-10s was removed and replaced with a conventional "greenhouse". The only noticeable differences from the original are the Clayton exhaust stacks instead of the collector ring and long tail pipes. After completion by North American's Field Service Department the airplane was photographed with several of the raiders and NAA personnel. From l to r: John Casey, manager Field Service Dept., Ted Lawson, Duncan Harding, NAA Engineering Supervisor, Howard Sessler, Travis Hoover, unknown, John Hilger, Unknown, Griffith Williams. The airplane is now part of the collection on exhibit at the USAF Museum at Dayton, Ohio.(NAA)

PILOT'S OPINIONS REGARDING THE B-25

Ed Virgin
NAA Chief Test Pilot

North American hired me as a test pilot shortly after the first B-25 entered the flight test program and for four years after that it seemed like I had one of those great airplanes strapped to my backside most of the time. It had already been discovered that with constant dihedral wings the airplane lacked the stability for bomb runs as desired by the Army. After the outer wing panels were flattened out to zero degrees dihedral the B-25 became an absolutely superb flying machine with excellent stability. This was to be expected of an airplane tested and evaluated by both constructor and Army test pilots.

Its "settling" qualities were excellent. Control forces were well balanced and effective. I could set course, adjust power and trim and the airplane needed little or no attention even in reasonably rough air. It was as forgiving as any airplane I ever flew, a rugged, reliable old dreamboat and a pilot's airplane.

Lieutenant Ole Griffith
91st Photo Mapping Squadron

My transition to the B-25 was direct from the Beech AT-10 and the greater weight of the B-25 and the tricycle gear took a bit of getting used to. It was much higher than the AT-10 and when my instructor pilot opened the throttles those R-2600s really pushed me back against the seat.

I soon found it to be a beautifully flying airplane, very forgiving and free of objectionable characteristics. It worked well on a single engine and was a very stable platform for trimetrogon mapping. Landing and takeoff qualities were ideal for some of the smaller fields we operated from in South America.

Lieutenant William H. Cather
501st Bomb Squadron, 345th Bomb Group

(Lieutenant Cather flew B-25D, 41-30064, a "Townsville" strafer, on the famous unescorted raid by B-25 strafers against Rabaul on 18 October 1943)

After training in the Curtiss AT-9 the B-25 seemed like a monster. It was about 6 feet higher above ground level and the two 1,700 H.P. engines made quite a difference. I well remember being pushed back in the seat on my first takeoff but I soon got accustomed to it and found it an easy airplane to fly. The old C and D models we trained on at Columbia, South Carolina flew night and day and really piled up the hours. With new pilots and old airplanes we had some accidents but we all felt much safer than the B-26 trainees.

The 345th Group took sixty new airplanes across the Pacific to New Guinea; my squadron, the 501st had fifteen. Every airplane made it across safely and we experienced an extremely high rate of reliability in the twelve months I flew the B-25s in combat.

The B-25 was a very stable airplane. It was easy to fly close formation and easy to land and take off. I have seen them come back with parts shot away, tires shredded and an engine out. It got us home under some pretty rough circumstances.

After many of our medium bombers were converted to 8 gun nose strafers we found that the extra nose weight bothered us very little and we soon became accustomed to the flight characteristics.

My airplane survived a combat tour of over 140 missions between January 1943 and March 1944 when it was transferred to a service squadron as war weary.

PART V

9 Battle Line in the Pacific

Imposed on a map of the western Pacific Ocean a triangle with apices at the Fiji Islands, Jakarta in the Netherlands East Indies and the northern tip of Japan constitutes an expanse of some ten million square miles of sea, sky and islands. Beginning from the long southern side of the triangle early in 1942, Allied forces began their slow arduous and costly northward trek, constantly narrowing the area of operations to the final apex of Japan more than three and a half years later.

It all began against heavy odds. A great portion of the American Pacific Fleet and many aircraft were lost in the opening round in December 1941. Hawaii remained in danger and as the Philippines inevitably fell to the Japanese onslaught. Australia became the refuge of retreating Allied units and the base of operations in the Southwest Pacific.

Organizing to hopefully check the Japanese advances, American, British, Dutch and Australian forces formed ABDA, a temporary cooperative, until more efficient operations could be managed. Operating under a unified command, ABDA provided efficient management of supplies and equipment and the establishment of responsibilities. Logical divisions of effort resulted in American and Australian forces being assigned responsibility for the air defense of the Netherlands East Indies with the Dutch in support as they lacked a modern air force. The British were to hold the Burma-Malaya line from Singapore. [1]

In December a handful of B-17s arrived in Brisbane from the Philippines. Another dribble of fighter aircraft arrived by ship. They were few in number and to effectively protect the Dutch East Indies substantial reinforcements from the USA were urgently required. In January 1942 the Indies, Maylaya and Singapore fell, but the long supply line began to fill with the arrival in Australia of B-17s and LB-30s by air and more fighters by ship.

The transportation of men and equipment to Australia became a top priority as did the security of the newly developed South Pacific ferry route over which most would come. Following this route south from Hawaii to the Fiji Islands to Brisbane, the B-25 first went to war.

Jack Fox, one of North American's field service representatives, was assigned to escort the first four B-25s to the Netherlands East Indies Air Force at Brisbane. North American had equipped the airplanes with extra fuel tanks for the long, over water flights. Company pilots delivered the planes to the Air Corps at Long Beach where contract crews from Consolidated Aircraft Co. took over

for the ferry flight. Final preparations were made at San Diego and the airplanes were then flown to Hamilton Field near San Francisco for final processing. Departure was on 2 March.

Arriving in Brisbane, Fox was met by Captain Boot of the NEIAF who had anxiously awaited the first of his B-25s. As the first of the type in the area, the Mitchells attracted considerable attention and much to Fox's surprise, from some old friends of the 17 BG. As more B-25s arrived a training program for NEI pilots and mechanics was immediately implemented under Fox's direction.

The training program was soon interrupted by a surprise visit from Lieutenant Colonel J.H. Davies of the 3rd Attack Group who began negotiations with the Dutch for possession of ten of their new B-25s, including the release of Fox from his obligations to the Dutch. This was arranged to mutual satisfaction and Fox was soon in Charters Towers, the first and only NAA service representative in the area at the time. The sudden acquisition of Dutch airplanes by U.S. forces was conducted under somewhat mysterious circumstances and based on many technical questions regarding the B-25, Fox knew something important was planned. He was not informed and asked no questions.

Observing another B-25 landing at the base, Fox noted that the entire crew consisted of an American captain and a sergeant. As comparatively few pilots had been checked out the the B-25 by that time, and concerned about "his" airplane, Fox inquired of the Captain about his B-25 experience. Glaring at Fox he sternly replied, "Who needs checking out? Besides, the damn thing has a stick and a throttle, doesn't it?" This less than cordial meeting soon developed into a close and mutually respectful friendship with another recent arrival in Australia, Captain Paul "Pappy" Gunn. [2]

A retired Navy pilot instructor, Gunn had been pilot and operations manager for Philippine Air Lines until the Japanese attack on Manila. Appraised of Gunn's expertise and knowledge of the Philippines, General Brereton, Air Corps Commander in the area, commissioned him a captain in the Air Corps. Thoroughly familiar with the islands, his first assignment was participation in the evacuation of personnel and equipment to Darwin via Mindanao. Arriving in Brisbane, he was advised of the fall of Manila and that his family were prisoners of the Japanese. So began the colorful wartime career of this crusty character who spent the war years doing all he could to make life difficult for the enemy. [3]

The mysterious acquisition of the Dutch Mitchells by Colonel Davies was soon clarified. General MacArthur, direct from Corregidor, arrived in Brisbane to take command of Southwest Pacific forces. Soon thereafter he authorized a raid against the Japanese blockade hoping to permit badly needed supplies to reach his old friend, General Wainwright, and the beleaguered garrison on the Bataan Peninsula. With the fall of Bataan on 9 April this plan was canceled and replaced by a mission against Mindanao on the 12th.

Commanded by Brigadier General Ralph Royce, the strike force was comprised of three B-17s and the ten B-25s spirited away from the Dutch. The B-17s were led by Captain Frank Bostrom and the B-25s by Colonel Davies. It was a long and grueling mission on both men and equipment with unpredictable risks and results. Commencing in Brisbane the first leg of the mission was some 1,100 miles to Darwin and 1,500 miles from Darwin to Del Monte Field on Midanao. Strikes were made against Nichols Field, Davao and Cebu. Three Japanese aircraft were destroyed and two transports were believed sunk.

One B-17 was lost but all other aircraft returned safely to Darwin. Gunn and crew were the last to reach Darwin. Japanese fighters had strafed Del Monte when the Royce airplanes were out and holed Gunn's long range fuel tank hidden in the brush. Minimal, if adequate repairs were hastily made.[4]

For the effort expended little damage was inflicted and the little publicity received was completely overshadowed by the Doolittle raid on Tokyo on the 18th.

The following B-25s made up the medium bomber section of the Royce mission:

41-12441	Captain Lowery
41-12442	Lieutenant Heiss
41-12443	Lieutenant Smith
41-12455	Lieutenant Wilson
41-12466	Lieutenant Felthan
41-12472	Lieutenant Peterson
41-12480	Captain Strickland
41-12483	Colonel Davies
41-12485	Captain Gunn
41-12511	Lieutenant Maull

MacArthur was deeply concerned about the disappointing size of the forces in his new command and quickly became dissatisfied with early air operations. He lost little time reorganizing the air units as the Fifth Air Force. Major General George Kenney arrived in Australia in late July and assumed command of all Allied air forces on 4 August. An aggressive no nonsense heavy hitter, Kenney was the man MacArthur correctly believed could best organize an air force capable of a northward offensive all the way to Japan.

He chose Brigadier General Ennis Whitehead as Deputy Commander. The Fifth eventually expanded into the largest land based Allied air force operating in the Pacific.

This was followed by activation of the Thirteenth Air Force in New Caledonia on 13 January 1943. The

Colonel Davies and his crew of #483, lead Mitchell of the Royce Mission. Flak damage was taken on the right tail. L to R: Captain McAfee co-pilot, Corporal Neuman, Colonel Davies, Major Hubbard, Sergeant Young. (USAF via NAA)

Seventh Air Force, activated in Hawaii on 5 February 1942 worked its way across the Central Pacific to the final assault on Japan. The Northern Pacific was the territory of the Aleutian based Eleventh Air Force.[5]

The miscellaneous aircraft arriving in Australia following the fall of the Philippines and the NEI consisted of trainers, transports and obsolete bombers. The few modern fighters were in need of parts and maintenance. Slow though it was the westward flow of men and equipment arrived in sufficient numbers that Australian facilities were inadequate to accommodate the influx.

Maintenance was difficult as the slow supply of parts and service equipment became critical and problems persisted. Time consuming difficulties abounded. Transports and bombers arrived in Australia's temperate climate equipped with deicing and other winterizing equipment. By the end of September 107 B-25s had been laboriously de-winterized even after General Kenney's complaints failed to cause the necessary modification stateside.[6]

Combat units faced technical problems unforeseen when the aircraft were built. Inadequate armament was a common complaint from all theaters, particularly the Southwest Pacific. As a result many units added more guns to their airplanes to best meet individual area requirements, a practice fraught with hazards from weight and balance and structural considerations.

To perform the extensive maintenance, overhaul, repair and modifications required, major air depots were established late in 1942 at Brisbane, Charters Towers, Cairns, Townsville, and Port Moresby. The Townsville depot was constructed, equipped and staffed to a size and capability unequaled outside the United States.[7]

While the Japanese Navy was involved in the summer campaign in the Solomons, their army units attacked the Bismarck Islands and New Guinea, landing at Finschhafen, Salamaua, Milne Bay and Buna planning to take Port Moresby by May. Failure to win a decisive victory over the U.S. Navy in the Battle of the Coral Sea, and a stout Australian defense in the New Guinea highlands, forever denied them that prize. Australia, never quite out of danger, was thus given another, if temporary reprieve. New Guinea was essential to the northward Allied push and MacArthur was determined to hold the island at all cost. As a result, attacks on Japanese forces on the the Huon Peninsula and the Bismarcks dominated much of Allied air action late in 1942.

Complying with the established policy of the war in Europe being assigned first priority, Washington directed that offensive action in the Pacific be limited to the interdiction of communications and as much action against ground and sea forces as possible with the limited resources available.

Thus was the battle line established for the long northward drive to the heart of the Japanese Empire.

Notes to Chapter 9
1. Craven, W.F. and Cate, J.L., **The Army Air Forces in World War II**, Chicago, IL The University of Chicago Press, 1953, Vol I, pages 243, 367
2. Fox, Jack, **Personal Memoirs**, page 74
3. Kenney, General George C. **The Saga of Pappy Gunn,** New York, NY, Duell, Sloan and Pearce, 1959, pages 31-37
4. USAF, **The AAF in Australia to the Summer of 1942,** Historical Study 9, Albert F. Simpson Historical Research Center 1944, pages 62-64
5. Craven & Cate, Volume IV, page 98
6. Ibid., Volume IV, p. 154
7. Ibid., Volume IV, pages 103,104,199

This Australian field office was used by the North American company technical representatives. "South American Aviation" used the triangle from the official NAA logo with Pappy Gunn, President; Jack Fox, Operations Manager and Jack Evans, Interference Secretary. (NAA)

The legend and his handiwork, Major Paul "Pappy" Gunn in strafer #41-12437. The airplane is named in his behalf and marked with one of his common remarks. The fuselage blister guns are pitched slightly downward and the shape of the blast plate typifies most strafers. Field Service Rep, Jack Fox, stands alongside. (NAA)

10 Strafer-Bomber Development

Within weeks after the opening of hostilities at Pearl Harbor the desirability of minimum altitude attack on ships and troop concentrations was readily recognized and in January 1942 the subject was discussed between the Ordnance Department and the Director of Bombardment. A directive was subsequently issued for tests and development of low level bombing to be conducted at Eglin Field, Florida. The technique, yet to be proven, was generally referred to as skip bombing.[1]

No specific attack aircraft existed in the inventory and each theater commander was free to develop his own adaptation as he saw fit with the equipment available. In the Southwest Pacific in particular, range capability for attack aircraft was of great importance, other capabilities notwithstanding. General George Kenney, directing operations from Australia and New Guinea, first pressed A-20s and B-25s into service as low level attackers, a role quite different from that envisioned when the aircraft were designed. Both proved their good inherent qualities but lack of adequate armament became readily apparent.

Frontal attacks by Japanese fighters were all too successful and the .30 caliber nose gun in the early B-25s proved ineffective. Jack Fox developed a flexible mount for the .50 caliber gun to replace the .30 caliber. Tests proved successful and the mounts were made in considerable quantities and found extensive use on B-17s, B-25s and B-26s. [2]

Medium altitude bombing against Japanese shipping had achieved modest success at best. Torpedo attacks and dive bombing by A-24s had been done on a limited basis. Their limited range however, precluded operations from Port Moresby across the high Owen Stanley Mountains and the low speed required long range fighter protection.

It was General Kenney's opinion that development of skip bombing showed the greatest promise of improving hit ratios. There were serious misgivings. Skip bombing required low level approach against intense, accurate, defensive fire from heavily armed ships and crew morale was a serious consideration.

Early in October Kenney assigned Major William Benn of the 63rd Bomb Squadron to run skip bombing trials for evaluation. Tests with 100 pound bombs dropped from a B-17 determined the required speed, altitude and drop distance combinations. A five second delay fuse was found preferable but none being available, a modified eleven second Australian fuse was substituted. Benn's tests showed that a three bomb string gave a good probability of a hit. [3]

A-20 and B-25 crews began training in the technique and carried out limited skip bombing strikes coordinated with strafing Beaufighters and altitude bombing by B-17s. Results appeared encouraging but for effective skip bombing a crucial ingredient was lacking. Heavy forward firepower was needed to counter defensive fire from ships under attack [4]

In the fall of 1942 Captain Gunn and Lieutenant Tomkins, an engineering officer at Amberly Field, modified an A-20 to correct this deficiency. High speed, mast head level attack had no need for the services of a bombardier whose absence left the nose section free for armament. Tomkins installed a battery of four .50 caliber guns in the nose and attached a single gun in a blister pack on each side of the forward fuselage. Efforts were hampered by a shortage of basic materials such as structural steel shapes, plate, sheet metal and solenoids. To increase the limited range of the A-20, two 450 gallon fuel tanks were installed in the bomb bay, leaving space for a brace of parafrag bombs. [5]

An innovation generally credited to General Kenney, the parafrag was a standard twenty-three pound fragmentation bomb fitted with a proximity fuse and a parachute. Exploding a few feet above the ground, it proved extremely damaging to personnel and aircraft for a radius of 150 feet.[6]

At this point all problems were not solved to assure success of the strafer-skip bombing technique. Bomb fuses presented a problem demanding a quick solution. Deck level bombing brought the attacking aircraft in such close proximity to its target that without delayed action fuses, the airplane would probably be destroyed by its own bomb drops. In mid 1942 General Kenney initiated experiments to develop a five second delayed action fuse. Suitable production fuses did not become available for several months so Australian and standard M 106 fuses were modified.[7]

So equipped, the A-20 proved a highly effective attack airplane but was limited by a seriously reduced bomb load due to the added fuel tanks in the bomb bay. A program was begun to convert a number of A-20s to strafer bombers but the overall project was hampered to some extent by a limited supply of airplanes due to the priority of lend lease deliveries to Russia.

Pappy Gunn and Jack Fox had some serious conversations about modifying the B-25 to a similar configuration. In several respects the Mitchell was better suited and the projected rate of deliveries from the factory indicated an adequate supply. Although the B-25 was not as fast as the A-20 it had greater range without additional fuel tanks which permitted a normal bomb load. The larger nose section also provided adequate space for guns and ammunition containers.

Before modifying a B-25 as a prototype strafer it was necessary that General Kenney approve. After satisfying the General that the project was reasonably well thought out, Gunn and Fox received Kenney's enthusiastic blessing.[8]

Development of B-25C1/D1 strafer bombers to meet the needs of the moment proved the old adage that necessity is the mother of invention. The depot modified attackers marked the first major change in Mitchell configuration and directly influenced future factory design. The B-25 proved remarkably adaptable to numerous field and depot modifications and out in the Southwest Pacific became the object of more outright butchery, "cut to fit, bend to suit, weld to match and scrap if necessary," innovations than any other airplane."

In December, 1942 Jack Fox sent the following communication to the Field Service Department at North American explaining the changes necessary to modify the B-25 to a low level, skip bombing strafer.

A good example of Yankee ingenuity are the hand made gun mounts on MARGARET's fuselage. The blast protection plate differs considerably from the shape commonly used on subsequent airplanes. (NAA)

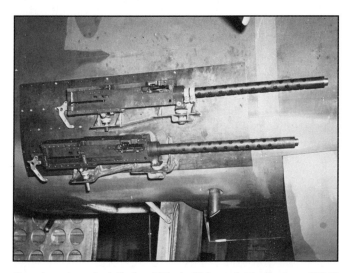

Guns have been installed and fitted with bore sight adjusters. (NAA)

To: NAA Field Service Department
Com. No. 1243
Subject:
B-25 Strafer Bomber, Required Modifications
The B-25 is considered well suited for the subject role as it has adequate range of action, sufficient airspeed and bomb capacity and will prove exceptionally effective if fitted with sufficient frontal fire power. The following points warrant close consideration and expeditious effort by all concerned as the trend out here is much in favor of the outlined changes.

a. The bombardier and his equipment must be removed to provide space for four .50 caliber guns and ammunition boxes for 500 rounds per gun. The flat bomb aiming panel will be removed and a Dzus attached panel will be installed around the protruding gun barrels. The top center plexiglass panel of the bombardier's compartment will be removed and a Dzus fastened cover substituted to permit loading the ammunition boxes. The bombardier's escape hatch will be bolted shut. It has been suggested that an installation also be made with four 20 mm cannon but it is improbable that space will be available for enough ammunition.

b. In addition to the above gun installation four more fixed .50 caliber guns will be installed externally on the center section - two on each side, the top gun staggered ahead of the lower gun. The ammunition boxes can be in the bomb bay.

c. The center of gravity problem worries me a bit but the people here are determined to make the installation. Even with blast tubes the blast might be troublesome to the pilots. Propeller clearance is small and there may be air flow interference. It may all turn out OK. I sure hope so. I grant you the benefit of the argument that these extra guns will add considerable weight but on the other hand this weight has advantages in the concentration of gun fire.

d. One B-25 is being fitted with A-20A fragmentation bomb racks (Douglas parts) three of which can be installed in tandem on the right side of the bomb bay leaving space on the left side for whatever is wanted at the time. The difficulty of the series installation is getting a properly controlled salvo position. Bomb controls must be revised for co-pilot operation.

e. The lower turret will probably be removed. This seems advisable as the airplanes will be used at very low altitude making lower turret use extremely difficult. Much weight will be saved.

I would like to bring up an interesting item here concerning a B-25C made into a transport and named "Not in Stock". Both turrets, armor plate, much radio equipment and certain other items not considered essential were removed. It is used to transport essential materials in combat zones. It

Nose gun installation was simplified by positioning all four through the bomb aiming panel making air sealing easier. (NAA)

performs very well indicating 240 MPH at 7,000 feet and twenty-seven inches of manifold pressure at 1,850 RPM. I must state that much of the credit for all of the above is due to the resourcefulness of Major P.I. Gunn.

Jack Fox

Gunn's personal disdain for engineers, slide rules and analysis was generally accepted among all concerned. In retrospect, however, regardless of the fine efforts and innovative capabilities of Gunn, Fox and others, the installation of the eight additional forward firing guns had to have been backed by a certain amount of competent design and stress analysis by the engineering personnel at Brisbane. Resistance to vibration and structural integrity under anticipated G loads was an obvious necessity. That considerable thought had been given to the B-25 strafer bomber concept for some months before the fact is evidenced by the station diagram gun installation sketch by the 81st Air Depot Group dated 1 June 1942. (See pg.106.)

Photographic evidence indicates that two nose guns were bolted to each side of a narrow, vertical structural beam attached to the nose section floor on the airplane center line. Ammunition cans were installed aft of the guns and ammunition was replenished through a quick detachable panel above. Special brackets were designed and made to secure the fuselage blister guns to reinforced primary structure.

Blast protection from the fuselage blister guns was achieved by blast tubes and large sheet metal plates on the fuselage covering the entire blast area. Felt pads

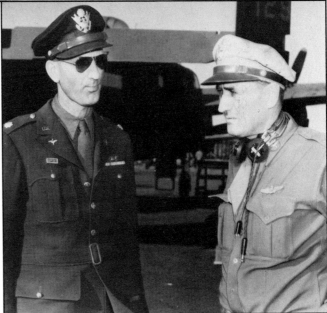

Lt. Col. R.L. Fry, Commanding Officer of the 81st Depot (left) and Major Gunn. (NAA)

were first used behind these plates but when wet and cold hardened so as to become ineffective. Rubber padding was found to function well and was used on all installations.

General Kenney expressed great interest in the strafer prototype which he referred to as his "commerce destroyers" and kept a regular watch on the progress.

The strafer prototype, appropriately named "Pappy's Folly", was put through initial flight and gun firing tests by Gunn, Fox and Sergeant Evans. The fuselage guns were found to be too far forward for acceptable

MORTIMER of 90th Bomb Sq. was a famous B-25. It was a veteran of the Royce mission, converted strafer and participant in the Bismarck Sea Battle. A good luck airplane, it flew over 445 combat hours without a crash landing or a crew injury. (NAA)

center of gravity of the airplane and were moved farther aft. Boresighting was done at nearby Amberly Field.

Satisfied that most of the bugs were worked out, Kenney sent Gunn and Fox and the new airplane up to seventeen mile strip near Port Moresby where Major Ed Larner and crews of the 90th Bomb Squadron, 3rd Bomb Group put it through extensive trials. Larner was sufficiently impressed that Kenney got the Eagle Farms people busy converting a number of identical examples. By the end of February twelve strafer bombers were completed and assigned to the 90th Squadron.

After receiving the strafers the 90th BS began extensive training exercises on a wrecked ship off Port Moresby. The developed technique was a target approach at an altitude from 1,000 to 1,500 feet until about three miles from the objective. Evasive action was then taken while reducing altitude to 500 feet at 1,500 yards range; then down on the deck for a high speed strafing-bombing run. Frequently attacking in pairs, one airplane strafed the target on a beam approach while the other attacked at mast head level.

Gunn, Fox and Sergeant Evans experimented with more gun installations on the strafers. A .30 caliber gun was installed in each landing light bay, an arrangement which functioned well on numerous missions. The innovation was short lived however, as when word of this reached the North American company orders went out to remove the guns for structural reasons. They next added a battery of .30 caliber guns in the bomb bay positioned to fire directly downward. Although functional and deadly on troops below, too much bomb bay space was used and the concept was abandoned.

In 1945 Lt. Col. and Mrs. Gunn toured NAA's Inglewood plant escorted by company president, 'Dutch' Kindelberger. Caught by a Japanese strafer, Gunn suffered severe burns on his arm and was sent to a California hospital for treatment. Mrs. Gunn and their four children miraculously survived the war in a Japanese prison in Manila. Gunn told Jack Fox in confidence that he had considered "appropriating" an airplane, flying to Manila, and with the help of the Philippine underground, attempting to free his family. That he had the courage is probable but the likelihood of success was extremely doubtful and either success or failure would have resulted in severe reprisals by the Japanese. He would also have been AWOL with an unauthorized airplane, probably a B-25 or A-20. Realizing that his desperate scheme bordered on madness, better judgement prevailed. (NAA)

Notes to Chapter 10

1. Craven, W.F. and Cate, J.L., **The Army Air Forces in World War II**, Chicago, IL The University of Chicago Press, 1953, Vol IV, page 107
2. Fox, Jack, **Personal Memoirs**, page 86
3. Hq. 5th Air Force **Report on Skip Bombing**, APP. 9, 14 Mar, 1943
4. Fox, Jack, **Personal Memoirs**, pages 117-120
5. USAF, **The AAF In Australia to the Summer of 1942**, Historical Study 9, Albert F. Simpson Historical Research Center, 1944, page 125
6. USAF, **The Fifth Air Force in the Huon Peninsula Campaign January - October 1943**, Historical Study 113, Albert F. Simpson Historical Research Center 1946, page 62
7. Craven & Cate, Volume IV, Page 107
8. Fox, Jack, **Personal Memoirs**, pages 116-117

11 Smoke on the Water

It was the Battle of the Bismarck Sea in March 1943 that primarily proved the effectiveness of the B-25C1/D1 strafer bombers. This action also constituted one of the most historic engagements of the Fifth Air Force and was instrumental in the campaign to drive the Japanese from New Guinea. The decisive outcome marked a major turning point for Allied forces in the Southwest Pacific.[1]

As continual Allied pressure throughout 1942 gradually weakened the Japanese hold on the Solomons, it was certain that they would increase their forces on New Guinea. By late December they had suspended reinforcement of the Buna detachment in favor of a build up at Lae by convoys from Rabaul. This effort met with some success although losses were sustained from Allied air attacks.

Throughout January 1943 photo reconnaissance showed a notable increase in activity and quantity of shipping at Lae, Alexishhafen, Gloucester and, particularly, Rabaul. Shipping and airfields in these areas were brought under continual strikes by long range bombers. Further intelligence disclosed that a sizable convoy would

depart Rabaul on 28 February and arrive at Lae on 3 March.

General Kenney meanwhile had hastened development of air bases at Port Moresby and Milne Bay and by January these facilities were capable of staging some heavy bombers. Most medium and light bombers were based at Port Moresby and had undergone considerable training for convoy interdiction. Kenney and his staff planned a well coordinated attack with a ready force of over 250 aircraft composed of fighters, attack Beauforts, heavy, medium and light bombers and the new B-25C1/D1 strafer bombers. Alternate plans were based on varying convoy routes and the ranges of various aircraft.

Stormy weather favored the convoy's departure and it was well underway when, in mid afternoon on 1 March, it was sighted by a B-24 from the 321st Bomb Squadron which reported fourteen ships with a fighter escort estimated at 100 aircraft from both Army and Navy units. Continued reconnaissance by B-17s of the 63rd

A B-25 strafer of the Bismarck Sea Battle undergoing field maintenance in New Guinea. (NASM No. 24076 AC)

Air Force B-25s attacking a Japanese transport in the Battle of the Bismarck Sea. Coordinated attacks by medium and heavy bombers and fighters with fighter cover devastated an entire convoy. (NAA)

and 65th Bomb Squadrons failed to locate the convoy due to deteriorating visibility.

Mid-morning on 2 March the convoy was located but could be reached by heavy bombers only. Eight 63rd Squadron B-17s attacked from medium altitude with 1,000 pound bombs. Five destroyers, one light cruiser and eight transports were reported. The B-17s made the final attack of the day as the convoy headed south from the Bismarck Sea through the Vitiaz Straights and into the Huon Gulf. By morning the convoy would be within range of Kenney's composite forces.

RAAF Beauforts opened the morning of 3 March with a torpedo attack but claimed no success. Heavily armed Beaufighters of No. 30 Squadron coordinated attacks with B-17s, B-25s and A-20s and their well timed tactics netted twelve enemy fighters.

If the day had not gone well for the Japanese, the combat introduction of Major Ed Larner's 90th Bomb Squadron B-25C1/D1 strafers made doubly sure. Selecting individual targets they barreled in for the kill at mast head height. During a twenty minute period their eight forward firing guns raked ship decks in a withering fire, making defense from the ships almost impossible. Their 500 pound bombs scored seventeen hits out of thirty-seven bombs dropped on eleven ships. The results of this brief encounter were five transports badly damaged. Concurrently A-20s of the 89th Squadron and six B-25 mediums of the 405th claimed eleven direct hits from low level with 500 pound bombs.

By mid afternoon more bombers roared off the airdromes near Port Moresby seeking the battered ships. The weather deteriorated over the Owen Stanleys and some aircraft failed to reach the target. However, coordinated assaults by B-25s, A-20s and B-17s took a further toll. Within minutes eight B-25C1 strafers of the 90th made four low level hits on each of two destroyers, sinking one and seriously damaging the other plus further damage to two cargo vessels. B-17s sunk another cargo

vessel with a direct hit and RAAF Bostons claimed a destroyer sunk.

Hazards form enemy fighters were compounded by dangers created by the attackers themselves. RAAF Bostons bombing from 1,000 feet were, at times, dangerously close to the mast head level B-25 strafers, while B-17s at medium altitude bombed through both, fortunately with no casualties.

Reconnaissance aircraft continued the search over a wide area to prevent damaged vessels from escaping during the night. Motor torpedo boats of the Seventh Fleet reached the scene of the wreckage on the night of 3 and 4 March, finishing off another cargo ship. The morning of the 4th B-17s and B-25s dispatched a damaged destroyer while Beaufighters, A-20s and B-25s searched and strafed survivors. For three days the fighters and B-25 strafers returned to the battle area with their merciless fire. Survivors, should they reach the safety of Lae, would become a further hazard for Allied ground forces. It was a bloody, unpleasant job that seemingly had to be done.

Modest losses to Kenney's aircraft were directly attributed to the excellent top cover provided by the P-38s and P-40s. Three P-38s and one B-17 were downed in the battle and a single B-25 crashed in a landing accident. Over 350 Japanese fighters were believed committed to protection of the convoy and approximately ninety were considered destroyed. It was finally determined that the original convoy consisted of eight destroyers and eight cargo and transport vessels and that all transports and four destroyers were sunk or beached. Surviving destroyers picked up survivors, transported them to Lae and returned to Rabaul.

As the smoke cleared from the Huon Gulf a number of significant facts became clear. Land based air power, well coordinated, proved highly effective against shipping. A number of factors contributed: coordinated attack by all types from several altitudes; effective top fighter cover; acquisition of good intelligence; thorough preparation and training and ingenious technical achievements. The heavy Japanese losses were of great strategic value to Allied operations and the battle stands as the greatest number of ships lost to air power in a single engagement, exceeded only by the American losses at Pearl Harbor.

Some forty sorties were flown against the ill fated convoy and of those approximately 76% were successful in reaching the objective. In all, 571 bombs totaling some 426,000 pounds were dropped. Post battle analysis credited the B-17s with a 9% hit ratio, the A-20s with 50%, medium altitude B-25s 14%, the RAAF Bostons above 1,000 feet with 10% and the B-25C1 strafer bombers with 43%.

The low level A-20s and the B-25C1/D1 strafer bombers proved conclusively that such craft, mounting heavy forward forepower, of adequate range and capable of carrying an effective bomb load were ideal air attack weapons. These depot modified strafers added a new dimension in attack aircraft, initiating a revised concept of operations and setting the design requirements for subsequent factory built B-25s.

Generals MacArthur and Kenney, upon receiving battle reports from the Bismarck Sea Battle and the results of the strafers, could not have been more pleased with the performance of both men and equipment. General Arnold immediately ordered Kenney to Washington and Wright Field for a briefing with the engineering staff regarding the strafers and future B-25 configurations. Kenney had previously forwarded copies of engineering drawings of the gun installations to Arnold who subsequently concluded that if mission requirements indicated a need for a considerable quantity of this type, work of such magnitude should be done stateside at the aircraft factories, leaving the theater depots free for the maintenance and repair. However, until the B-25G and H models became available the Service Command would continue modifying their airplanes.

Informed of Gunn's expertise and efforts in the strafer development, General Arnold ordered his transfer to the Engineering Division at Wright Field. Considering General Kenney's strenuous objections and desire to retain Gunn in his organization, a two week stay at Wright Field was agreed upon. Enroute back to Australia he spent several days at the North American plant with

Captain Chatt (above) of 90th BS piloting CHATTER BOX, scored two direct hits on a Japanese destroyer, stopping it dead in the water. Crew members Andrew Swain and Holbert Barnes (on ground, left to right). (NAA)

North American Aviation Field Service reps Jim Clemens, (left) and Larry York with MORTIMER, veteran of the Royce Mission and Battle of the Bismarck Sea. Piloted by Lt. Edward Solomon, MORTIMER hit a destroyer which was later scuttled. One of the first B-25s converted to a strafer, this 90th BS airplane had a charmed life. As of Sep 1943 it logged 715 total hours of which 445 were in actual combat. (NAA)

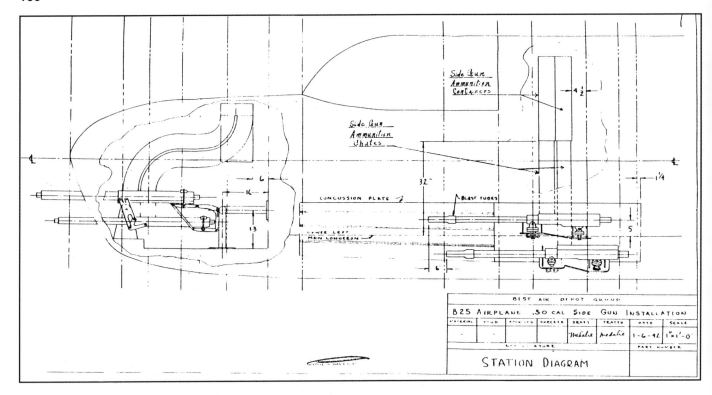

engineers and test pilots discussing changes to revise the B-25 into a completely factory built attack bomber.[2]

Before leaving for Washington Kenney ordered the strafer program into high gear. An unknown number were completed at Eagle Farms before the project was taken over by the 4th Air Depot Group at Townsville where a near production line was set up. By the end of April thirty strafers were completed and by late August five squadrons were so equipped.[3]

Notes to Chapter 11
1. **USAF The Fifth Air Force in the Huon Peninsula Campaign January - October 1943**, Historical Study 113, Albert F. Simpson Historical Research Center 1946. Pages 86 - 101
2. Kenney, General George C., **The Saga of Pappy Gunn**, New York, NY, Duell, Sloan and Pearce 1959, pages 60-65
3. Craven, W.F. and Cate, J.L., **The Army Air Forces in World War II**, Chicago, IL The University of Chicago Press, 1953, Vol IV, pages 135-149

Shortly after the Battle of the Bismarck Sea and before the B-25 strafer conversion project got underway at the 13th Air Depot Group in New Caledonia, the XIII Air Force had a number of their B-25C/D models converted by the V Air Force at Eagle Farms. With bomb aiming panel removed, the gun mount structure is visible. (NASM # 3A 4434)

12 More Strafers

When details of the victory at the Bismarck Sea got around, the merits of low level strafer-skip bombers were quickly recognized. General Kenney was a bit critical at first of other commanders for not implementing the concept as soon as he thought they should have. He readily acknowledged however, that the tactics required special airplanes flown by especially trained crews and that the bombs, technology and sighting were new. He was of the firm opinion that attack aviation would have a prominent place in much of the war ahead.

Major General Millard Harmon, Thirteenth Air Force Commander, lost no time establishing a strafer-bomber program. Seven months earlier the 75th and 390th Squadrons which became part of the 42nd Bomb Group, had undergone low level training. Colonel Harry Wilson, commanding the 42nd, continued this training at Fiji. To expedite getting some strafers in action Harmon asked Kenney to modify some 42nd Group B-25s until his depot at Tontouta could get organized to do the work. Kenney agreed to modify one airplane and supply blueprints but a number of Harmon's airplanes are known to have been altered by the Fifth Air Force in Australia.[1]

Not until early 1943 did the strafer modification get underway at the Thirteenth Air Depot Group. In January the 71st Service Squadron, 6th Service Group, arrived in Tontouta for B-24 maintenance and B-25 conversion. In February the Engineering Department of the Group initiated the long term, ambitious project to install eight .50 caliber guns in the B-25s. The same problems of supply were experienced as by the the Fifth Air Force at Eagle Farms and ingenuity and improvisation were the order of the day. To cope with a shortage of steel, truck beds were cut for raw stock. In addition to the installation of eight additional guns, in itself a substantial effort, a complete revision of bomb racks and controls was required.[2] Some of the work done was considerably beneath factory standards and in the opinion of one of the North American company representatives some of the initial work was "a bit savage".

Such were the means to get the strafer bombers into battle and by 10 July thirty-six B-25C1/D1 strafers had emerged from the Tontouta shops. During the summer months of 1943 the B-25 strafer program constituted one of the major tasks accomplished by the Service Command. By mid-summer the Fifth Air Force depot at Townsville had equipped the 3rd and 38th Bomb Groups with fifty-eight combat ready strafers and when the program was shut down in September no less than 175 B-25C1/D1 strafers had been completed.[3]

A nose gun installation designed by the 13th ADG mounted four .50 cal. guns on a base plate bolted to the floor of the nose section. The arrangement provided ample space for ammunition cans and feed belts. (Charles Porter)

An early 42 BG, XIII Air Force strafer from the Eagle Farms depot. (Charles Porter)

Operating with shortages of parts and raw materials the 13th ADG made gun mounts from whatever steel could be found. (Charles Porter)

Other innovations of the 13th ADG were twin .50 cal. guns in a tail turret (above) and a single gun at right and left waist stations (below). (Charles Porter)

The concept was however, picked up by other commands. The 341 Bomb Group in India and Burma made a considerable number of B-25 strafers with varying nose gun arrangements. They were used with success on railways, marshaling yards, highway transport and storage depots. The 41st Bomb Group, Seventh Air Force in the Central Pacific used strafers configured approximately the same as the famous models from Townsville. In April 1943 the 26th Air Depot Group in Egypt altered sixteen B-25s to a six nose gun configuration for an unspecified mission.[4] These few airplanes were later returned to the original medium bomber type, indicating that strafers received much less use there than in the Pacific.

By that time the cannon carrying B-25G was on the North American assembly line. The first of these was accepted in May to be followed by the more efficient B-25H. Not until the arrival in all theaters of the B-25J with factory eight gun nose was the effect of the famous "Townsville" strafers equaled.

The first B-25Gs allocated to the Southwest Pacific were assigned to the Fifth Air Force and began arriving in Brisbane in July 1943. General Kenney was less than enthusiastic about the G model and with some misgivings agreed to accept sixty-three with the understanding that they could be modified as he might see fit for operations in New Guinea. His doubts were justified as deficiencies were recognized and unforeseen problems arose.[5]

The airplanes were to have left the factory equipped with the 75 mm cannon, two .50 caliber nose guns, four guns in fuselage blister packs, two at waist stations and a single flexible tail gun. They arrived in Brisbane with two nose guns and the cannon, top and bottom turrets but without waist guns, blister packs or tail gun, all of which Kenney considered essential for low level attack.[6]

From mid-November through December the B-25G was given thorough trials by Major Gunn and crews of the 3rd and 38th Bomb Groups. As more B-25Gs arrived they were put directly into combat. The Cape Gloucester airdromes and nearby shipping were primary targets. More than 1,200 rounds of 75 mm shells were fired and hits were scored on a destroyer.[7]

Gunn was satisfied with the accuracy of the cannon but critical of the sighting and lack of an adequate number of forward firing .50 caliber guns. He strongly recommended adding two more nose guns and four more in fuselage blister packs believing that with these additions the B-25G would be an excellent attack aircraft.

Thus the Service Command undertook yet another extensive gun modification program extending from November 1943 through April 1944. Due to the weight of the factory installed armament and the addition of two more nose guns and ammunition, to maintain acceptable weight and balance the fuselage gun packs were positioned above the bomb bay doors. After several hundred test rounds were fired the muzzle blast rippled skins, loosened

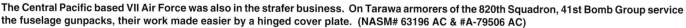

The Central Pacific based VII Air Force was also in the strafer business. On Tarawa armorers of the 820th Squadron, 41st Bomb Group service the fuselage gunpacks, their work made easier by a hinged cover plate. (NASM# 63196 AC & #A-79506 AC)

rivets, cracked leading edge skins and damaged adjacent fuselage structure.

By September effort was well underway at the Townsville depot to remedy these problems and make the B-25G suitable for the tasks ahead. Fuselage structure was reinforced and inspection panels added to the wing center section. Fuselage gun packs were fitted with ported blast tubes, gun charging cables routed to the cockpit and ammunition boxes installed in the bomb bay. The bomb bay doors were fitted with rubber backed blast protection plates. Nearly 100 new parts were required.[8]

Despite all the changes, the arrangement was not satisfactory in all respects. The fuselage gun packs were relocated forward to the same location as on the preceding B-25C1/D1 strafers, and balance was achieved by adding a twin .50 caliber tail turret. The ventral turret was

removed and conveniently deleted at the factory effective on the 200th airplane, 42-65001.

Although the 75 mm cannon was an effective attack weapon, repeated firing loosened nose skins adjacent to the blast, requiring continual repair. The cannon was subsequently removed from many G models and replaced by two .50 caliber guns in the crawl tunnel. When the B-25G gun modification program wound down at Townsville in April 1944, eighty-two airplanes had been modified at an average cost of 234 man hours per airplane. [9]

Unquestioned was the need for a continuing supply of B-25s in all theaters of operations. Early in September 1943, decisions were required for anticipated allocations for each type of new B-25 which would replace many of the C and D models then in use. Arrival in the Southwest Pacific of the heavily gunned and improved B-25H was

The potency of the 75 mm cannon notwithstanding, the first B-25Gs to arrive in the Southwest Pacific did not meet expectations and were generally considered inadequately armed. The cannon was removed from many SWP Gs and replaced with two .50 caliber guns in the crawl tunnel. Two more nose guns and fuselage blister gun packs were also added, a conversion common in the V and XIII Air Forces. (NASM # 71467AC)

A considerable number of B-25Gs were fitted with a dual .50 cal. tail turret installation, mostly by the 4th ADG at Townsville, Australia and the 13th ADG at Tontouta, New Caledonia. (NAA)

scheduled for September and the B-25J improved medium bomber was expected early in 1944.

The heavily armed Douglas A-26B was also expected early in 1944. General Kenney was indifferent to the A-26 preferring to finish the war with the B-25 which had proved highly successful. Neither was he particularly

Jack Fox at the North American Inglewood plant between assignments in the South Pacific is shown here on the flight ramp with a B-25G named in his honor. (NAA)

enthusiastic about the forthcoming B-25H, being more interested in the J Model with factory made eight gun strafer nose. He did, however, express his willingness to accept the B-25H as regular replacements with provisions that he could modify these too, should he find it advantageous to do so. Regarding allocations he preferred that 70% of his new B-25s be strafers and the remainder medium bombers.[10]

In the spring of 1944 the first allocations of B-25Js reached the Southwest Pacific. Early deliveries consisted mostly of the medium bomber configuration which were less suited to most missions than the attack variant. Many were retrofitted with the factory eight gun nose and by September most Js were being delivered so equipped. With the forward turret and four guns in blister packs, the airplane was the ultimate strafing weapon.

By early 1945 most B-25C and D models were among the oldest and weariest in combat inventory. Their workhorse assignments and constant modification and repair had taken a toll. The 405th Squadron the Fifth Air Force had received no new B-25s prior to September, 1944 after a period of thirteen months and one airplane had flown an impressive 160 missions.

Although deliveries of B-25Js continued in substantial numbers, by mid 1945 they were being augmented by initial allocations of the new Douglas A-26 Invader. Powered by the excellent Pratt & Whitney R-2800 engines, it was a fast and formidable aircraft, carrying a two ton bomb load at high speed with good range and armed with fourteen forward firing guns.

First tested by the 3rd Bomb Group, pilots reported that the broad nose and forward position of the engines reduced visibility for low level work as compared to the B-25. General Kenney stated that he preferred to finish the war with A-20s and B-25Js with the eight gun nose. By July however, A-26s were being allocated and Kenney was accepting limited numbers. By then the war was winding down, the jet age was dawning and the need for more strafers was nearly over.

Notes to Chapter 12
1. Craven, W.F. and Cate, J.L., **The Army Air Forces in World War II**, Chicago, IL The University of Chicago Press, 1953, Vol IV, page 226
2. USAF, **The Thirteenth Air Force, March - October 1943,** Historical Study 120, Albert F. Simpson Historical Research Center, 1946, pages 173, 174
3. Craven & Cate, Volume IV, page 199, 279
4. Carr, William C. Technical representative, North American Aviation Inc. to author, May 1987
5. Craven and Cate, Volume IV, page 170
6. USAF, **The Fifth Air Force in the Huon Peninsula Campaign January - October 1943,** Historical Study 113, Albaert F. Simpson Historical Research Center 1946, page 160
7. Craven and Cate, Volume IV, page 333
8. Historical Study 113, page 161
9. Craven and Cate, Volume IV, page 99
10. Historical Study 113, pages 145 and 146

13 North From Townsville

Those desperate early days of the Pacific war had proven again that necessity is the mother of invention. Starting with Pappy Gunn's Depot adaptations and ending with North American's factory variants in the States, the B-25's ability was enhanced to an awesome degree. Perhaps better than text, the photos on the following pages tell the story of these Pacific warbirds and warriors on the "march" north.

Amid puff balls of flak, a 71st BS strafer pulls up after bombing a freighter off Wewak, New Guinea in the summer of 1943. (NAA)

CORAL QUEEN, 42 BG, XIII AF out of New Caledonia. A B-25H/J flak plate was added above the blast plate. (John Hooser)

B-25C1 strafer of the 405 Bomb Sq, 38 BG "Green Dragons".(USAF)

Sep 1943 B-25D1 strafers of the 499 BS work over Japanese shipping at Victoria Bay, New Guinea. (NASM No. 80-13154, USAF 1640118)

The bastion of Rabaul on New Britain Island came under heavy attack by Army B-25s in Oct 1943. (USAF)

The "Crusader" logo of the 42 BG is well shown on the tail of this B-25J-10. (John Hooser)

Shown here, west of Cape Glocester, New Britain Island, Mitchells attack a corvette. (NASM No. 25989)

TORRID TESSIE was host to Joe E. Brown, left, when the comedian visited the 38 BG on a USO tour. (USAF)

On the 78th mission of RITA'S WAGON, 500th BS, the crew dropped the kitchen sink on Japanese forces in the Celebes. The B-25D1 #41-30055 was another famous Townsville strafer. (USAF)

B-25D1 strafer, 41-30278, HELLS FIRE, on a mission with other Mitchells of the 500 BS. This aircraft was shot down by fighters in the Celebes in Sep 1944 with loss of the crew. (NASM No. 116726AC)

B-25G, 42-64915, of the 820th BS, 41st BG, returned to base despite severe damage. Note field addition of waist and tail guns. (NAA)

Japanese ships under attack off New Hanover Island on 16 Feb 1944 by B-25s of the 345th BG. Two 500th BS aircraft can be seen in the distance near an exploding freighter while another straddles a corvette that stranded and was sunk. Note bomb in mid-air. (NASM No. 3A-33401)

PRIDE OF THE YAN-KEES, a VII AF 41st BG B-25G, is being serviced by armorers in the Gilbert Islands. Spent 75 mm cases make fine barrel covers for the .50 caliber guns. (NASM No. 27699AC)

PBJs of U.S. Marine Squadron VMB-423 over the Southwest Pacific. The near airplane is a PBJ-1J with factory 8 gun nose and wing tip radar. Farther back are PBJ-1Ds some equipped with APS-3 search gear. (Kenn Rust)

This tail stinger is believed to be a product of NAA's Mod Center at Fairfax Field, Kansas. It preceded and differs considerably from the tail gun on later B-25H and J models. Less space is availabe for the gunner than in the deeper aft fuselage of the later models. The airplane shown is a B-25G of the 48 BS, 41 BG, VII Air Force. (Charles Reese)

Lower position gun mount by the Hawaiian Air Depot to same design as the lower mount. Variations in detail have been noted and reported to have been incorporated on some PBJs. (Charles Reese)

14 **Bridge Busting**

In wresting Burma and its valuable resources and strategic transport arteries from the Japanese, continuous attacks were made in 1943 on the surface transport system. Although augmented by motor highways and extensive river traffic, a modern railroad was the primary means of moving troops, equipment and raw materials. To stem the flow of critical materials and military traffic, rail targets were of major importance. The rail lines generally followed the southward flowing rivers to the port city of Rangoon where both inbound supplies and outbound raw materials were transshipped.

In 1942 the Tenth Air Force was assigned the defense of Burma and India, responsibilities later redirected to defending Allied transport between India and China. Receiving new B-25C and D airplanes, the 11th, 22nd, 490th and 491st squadrons of the newly formed 341st Bomb Group began training in the fall. Early on the potential effectiveness of the Group was reduced by assignment of the 11th Squadron to Chennault's forces in China.

Among the responsibilities of the thinly spread Tenth Air Force was the destruction of the enemy land transport system in Burma. Rail yards and rolling stock came under attack by fighters, heavy bombers and the B-25s of the 341st. Due to the difficulties and time needed for repair, it was the bridges that were singled out for concentrated attack. The rail network in Burma utilized more than 100 bridges over 200 feet in span and many more of lesser size. They were difficult targets, often located in valleys or canyons, easy to defend with anti-aircraft guns, smoke or cross canyon cables. The spans were narrow, tough to hit and infinitely more difficult to destroy. Straight track was vulnerable and more easily attacked but surprisingly, bomb ricochets were frequent from the high speed, low level Mitchells. A number of schemes were tried to eliminate the problem. None were successful until the brain child of improvisation, a simple two foot long pointed spike threaded into a 100 pound bomb casing, was employed. The ricochet problem was thus simply solved and pilots of the 341st found that dropping "spike bombs" in pairs at two mile intervals created damage requiring the maximum time to repair.

Bridges were another matter. The ratio of hits from both heavy and medium bombers from varying altitudes was very low and this was compounded by the transfer of the 22nd and 491st Squadrons to China, joining the 11th, already there. Thus the number of missions was vastly reduced. The principal responsibility for bridge work was then left to the lone 490th Squadron.

The crew of B-25C, 41-13121, 22nd BS after completion of 100 missions. Many Mitchells of the 341 BG were fitted with additional .50 caliber nose guns for more effective results on CBI rail equipment. (William Bertholic)

The 341st BG made a formidable installation of six .50 caliber guns in this B-25C. The top two appear parallel to the line of flight and the others pitched slightly downward. The 341st used field modified strafers with great effect on supply areas and railway installations. Various combinations of from 3 to 8 guns bristled from their B-25s. (James A. Philpott)

Regardless of considerable effort and accompanying risks, the percentage of hits on bridges continued to be discouragingly low and the occasional destruction of a bridge was more frequently luck than not. By the end of 1943 Squadron morale hit a low ebb but the unit was determined to solve the problem. Trials were

Photographed near Mawlu, Burma, this B-25H of Col. Phil Cochrane's 1st Air Commando Group scatters incendiary bombs on an enemy target. (NASM #A3-7656)

made with variations in bomb fusing, release altitudes, speeds and approaches.

Skip bombing, as introduced by the Fifth Air Force, failed to work on bridges; bombs sometimes skipped underneath to explode on the far side, others skipped completely over or ricocheted off course. Bridges in wide valleys were open for dive bombing but no aircraft in Tenth Air Force inventory was suitable for the task, least of all, the B-25.

After almost a year of near futile effort to destroy a significant number of bridges, the winning combination

was discovered accidentally by Major Robert Erdin while leading a raid on the Mu River bridge. Attacking at low level he pulled up suddenly to avoid an oncoming tree while jettisoning the bombs, certain that it was another failed attack. Looking back, the crew discovered two spans toppled into the river. Subsequent analysis concluded that the shallow dive and bomb release at pull up caused the bombs to strike at the correct angle preventing ricochet and failure to explode on target.

SHERIDAN EXPRESS of the 491st BS in Burma, 1944. (Kenneth M. Sumney)

CALCUTTA COMMANDO of the 82nd Squadron, 12th Bomb Group, X Air Force. (John Stanaway)

No. 41-13122 of the 490th BS on another mission in the valley of the Irrawaddy River. (James A. Philpott)

Lieutenant Colonel Robert McCarten began an intensive training program to develop the technique. By combining glide and skip bombing the pilot could pick an aiming point with greater accuracy than in skip bombing

After 125 mission in CBI 41-13122 of the 341st BG, was retired from combat and returned to the U.S. for a publicity tour. On North American's Inglewood flight ramp the airplane was photographed with her trans-Pacific crew: (l to r) Major James A. Philpott, MSGT Donald Hyatt and Captain Dwight Potter. The scoreboard includes one locomotive, two Japanese fighters and five bridges. (NAA)

alone. At 1,200 feet altitude a half mile from the target a glide approach of approximately 30 ° was maintained at 260 to 280 MPH. Glide angle was reduced to 15° to 20° at 150 feet over the objective at bomb drop-pullout.

The new technique of "glip" bombing brought impressive results. Within a month the 490th took out eight bridges, receiving accolades from Major General Howard Davidson, commander of the Tenth Air Force. Congratulating McCarten he referred to the squadron as "bridge busters", a name which stuck with the Skull and Crossbones unit. They later labeled themselves the Burma Bridge Busters or the Dental Clinic, famous for their bridge work.

The three squadrons of the 341st in China with Fourteenth Air Force were, among other tasks, assigned the dangerous mission of destroying the steel and concrete bridges on the modern railway system in French Indo-China. From December 1944 to March 1945 the Mitchells of the 341st carried out a successful and aggressive program to deny the Japanese the use of as much of that efficient rail network as possible. Operating under conditions of intense anti-aircraft fire, rough terrain and frequent low visibility, the 341st destroyed twenty-one major spans and damaged an additional seventeen in twenty-three missions with an ordnance expenditure of 3.85 tons of bombs per bridge.

The cost of ordnance was low but the price in men and airplanes came high. In just the brief period from 27 February to 5 March 1945 the 341st Bomb Group lost four B-25s and sustained damage to an additional thirty-one. Twenty crew members were killed and twelve wounded.[1]

Notes to Chapter 14
1. GO 117, Hq, Fourteenth Air Force, 25 Aug 1945, per Unit Citation

JAUNTY JO, #43-36192, a B-25J of the 498th BS, 345th BG took fatal flak hits (above) over the Byoritsu refinery on Formosa. A gaping hole is visible through the co-pilot's side of the cockpit. The Air Apaches indian head insignia and yellow cowl ring are still visible at the moment of impact (below). Parafrag bombs are from the photographing B-25. (NASM #A58291AC)

15 Interdiction and Blockade of Japan

By late 1944 the gains made by joint operations of land, sea and air forces secured new bases nearer Japan from which Allied aviation operated with increasing effectiveness. The Japanese hold on the Central Pacific, East Indies, the Solomons and Bismarcks, China, Burma and the Philippines slipped and gave way as the Allied pincers closed. Vast areas were continually weakened, bypassed by the Allied advance, isolating enemy strongholds. From extensive bases on Saipan the B-29s began long range strikes on the industrial heart of Japan.

Heavily populated and possessing few natural resources, the island Empire was forced to rely on a continuing supply from her Asiatic conquests. With little protection from a weakened Navy, Japan was highly vulnerable to blockade. From Burma came oil, tungsten, cobalt and copper. From Manchuria came soy beans and the coal and iron for the furnaces of Japanese industry. More food and coal came from Korea. The China coast provided rail yards, land transport and the ports and harbor facilities for repair and fueling of convoys plying the sea lanes from Malaysia and the East Indies to Japan.

Formosa, the most developed of Japanese possessions, was a major source of copper, sugar, aluminum and alcohol and butanol production. Numerous air bases provided for the defense of China and adjacent shipping lanes and, late in the war, kamikaze operational bases. Formosa was, therefore, a priority target under continual attack. Due to its importance it was heavily defended and took a significant toll of American aircraft.

The blockade and interdiction of transport became a well established strategy to hasten the collapse of Japan and hopefully preclude the necessity for a costly invasion. By that time American submarines had sent a tremendous toll of Japanese shipping to the bottom and continued to be a major interdictive force until the end of the war, sinking 100,000 tons per month on a regular basis. By January 1945 the quantity of tonnage turned in favor of aviation which sank nearly double that amount. Carrier based aircraft continued wide ranging assaults as Iwo Jima and Okinawa were invaded. In March B-29s and B-24s began extensive aerial mining of principal Japanese ports and harbors.

As Japanese forces were pushed back ever closer to the home islands, their area of operations decreased accordingly, resulting in more concentrated and damaging attacks by American aircraft and submarines. The invasion of the Philippines provided new bases for attacks on supply lines between Japan and her southern garrisons. Reinforcement or supply of southern units became virtually

Mitchells of the 823rd BS, 38th BG, attacked a Japanese convoy attempting to reinforce their base at Ormoc, Leyte in November 1944. Protected by V Air Force P-38s and P-47s, the B-25s sunk 3 transports, 6 escort vessels, and damaged others. (USAF via NAA)

impossible as the lines of communication essential to survival came under continually increasing attack.

The B-25 in both strafer-bomber and medium bomber configurations was well suited for tactical missions against the numerous targets of the blockade. Land transport and coastal installations on the Chinese mainland were hard hit by Mitchells of the Fourteenth Air Force. Island based long range Mitchells of the Fifth, Seventh and Thirteenth Air Forces left a trail of destruction on the China Seas. Operating in some of the world's worst weather, Aleutian based B-25s and B-24s of the Eleventh Air Force and Navy Harpoons and Venturas harassed the Kuriles north of Japan. Due to threats of Russian aggression the Japanese kept a heavy troop concentration and badly needed air power in this northern chain.

After arrival at Oahu, Mitchells of the 41st BG were fitted with wing studs for mounting 5 inch HVAR rockets (below) and some of the B-25s were also equipped with factory 8 gun nose. The B-25J at right was photographed at Wheeler Field before departing for Okinawa in June, 1945. (Eldon Ray Ford)

In April 1945 off the coast of China, the freighter Luzon Maru falls victim to marauding B-25s of the 345th BG. A B-25J strafer pulls up after a stern attack on the already stricken vessel. (USAF)

On a July 1945 strike, B-25G No. 139 of 820 BS, 41st BG, took flak damage that cost the gunner a hand. (Harold P. Moody)

Waist gun installation modification is believed to have originated with the NAA Mod Center at Fairfax Field. This retrofit is on a 41 BG B-25G. (Fred Emmert)

Marine Sq VMB-612 underwent special training for deployment of the 11.75 inch Tiny Tim rockets. Shown on Okinawa on 2 Aug, a PBJ is being loaded with the big weapons. (National Archives)

A Tiny Tim rocket, less fins, on a modified MK 1 bomb trailer with jacks extended. All the PBJs shown are equipped with APS-3 radar search gear. (National Archives)

Those PBJs of the USMC VMB squadrons equipped with APS-3 search gear were characterized by ungainly nose radomes. This airplane of Lt. Col. Jack Cram's VMB-612 is readied for the first mission with Tiny Tim rockets. (National Archives)

Marine PBJs operated from the Philippines, Saipan, Iwo Jima and Okinawa. Many PBJs were equipped with five inch HVAR rockets and night search gear for long range missions against shipping trying to run the blockade. Strikes against Formosa, Hainan Island and the Asian coast were of long duration against heavily defended objectives which took a heavy toll of American airplanes. A lost engine near the target area almost certainly resulted in ditching.

In mid 1945 11.75 inch Tiny Tim rockets and related equipment were shipped to Marine Squadron VMB-612 on Iwo Jima. After a training period at Chimu Field, Okinawa in July, the Squadron was ready to carry the new weapon on continued night strikes against southern Japan.

During July VMB-612 made thirty attacks with conventional weapons against Japanese shipping and not until 11 August were the Tiny Tims used in the assault against Japanese supply lines. Between the atomic bombing of Nagasaki on 9 August and the Japanese agreement of surrender on the 14th, PBJs of VMB-612 flew two search and destroy missions against shipping in the Tsushima Straits. On 11 August two PBJs, each armed with eight five inch wing mounted HVAR rockets and two Tiny Tims, searched the straits between Korea, Kyushu and Honshu, one airplane covering the Southern tip of Korea. On the 13th, three identically armed PBJs returned to the straits. Twenty-three small craft were contacted, some visually, some by radar. The PBJs came under meager, inaccurate fire but sustained no damage.

Armed with 5 inch HVAR rockets, PBJs of VMB 612 prepare for attack on the Japanese industrial center of Kobe in June 1945. (National Archives)

Carrying glide torpedos, Js of the 47BS, 41st BG on 28 July, 1945 depart from Okinawa to Sasebo, Kyushu(left). 43-3905 is configured as a medium bomber and 43-3890 as a strafer. Another strafer #43-3980 is shown in flight (below). (NASM #3A4103 and E. Ford)

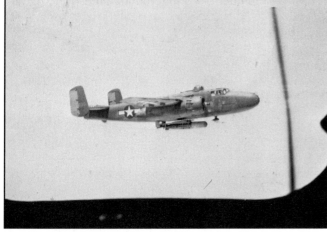

The small ships were considered unsuitable for attacks by the Tiny Tims which were never fired in anger.

On 12 August aircraft of 612 equipped with five inch HVAR rockets and APQ-5 bomb sights continued night searches from Chimu. Only small vessels were located and no attacks made, emphasizing the desperate state of Japanese shipping as the war drew to a close.

The night missions of VMB-612 were long, tiring strikes sometimes exceeding 1,500 miles round trip and were especially fatiguing due to night flying requirements. The squadron flew 630 missions, made 164 attacks, damaged 107 enemy ships of which eight were believed sunk. Total tonnage sunk or damaged was 195,180. The price was high, twelve airplanes, thirty-nine men killed or missing and three wounded.

From bases in China B-25s of the 341st Bomb Group struck land transport, railroad bridges and conducted extensive sea and river sweeps to stop the flow of essential materials to Japanese vessels in Asian harbors. Mitchells of the 341st also ranged the Formosa Straits, the East China coast and French Indo-China. The unit received its first B-25Hs in January 1944 and the 75 mm cannon was soon in use against river and coastal shipping. In April the J models began arriving, and fitted with the factory eight gun nose, mounted fourteen forward firing .50 caliber guns. The B-25J in the strafer configuration found greater favor than the cannon equipped Hs for attack against river and coastal shipping and proved devastating for strafing truck convoys, locomotives and airdromes.

So effective were the joint interdictive efforts of air and sea forces that by August 1945 little significant Japanese shipping remained afloat. Tactical units had begun preparation and training for pre-invasion assaults and the strategic B-29s continued methodical destruction of Japan. By then the nation was effectively defeated and only the final stage of invasion or surrender remained.

16 The 75 mm Cannon in Combat

The combat value and general effectiveness of the 75 mm cannon in the B-25 will probably remain controversial. Although thousands of cannon rounds were fired by B-25s in many theaters of operations, particularly the Southwest Pacific, the big gun was frequently removed and replaced by two .50 caliber machine guns.

Located in the bombardier's crawl tunnel with the breech extending back into the navigator's compartment, adequate if minimal space was provided for the gunner and the rack of twenty-one rounds of ammunition. Mechanical loading of the gun was considered in conceptual design of the installation but hand loading was selected as more efficient, took less space and weighed and cost less.

The best of gunners could usually fire a maximum of four rounds per target run. The cannon proved an effective weapon against barges, freighters and small craft and a single well placed hit could inflict considerable damage to a destroyer. The muzzle velocity of 1,930 feet per second resulted in a comparatively high trajectory which, combined with less than adequate sighting, failed to provide a suitable degree of accuracy. Accurate range determination was therefore critical, and aiming demanded a straight run on the target increasing vulnerability from enemy fire.

Arrival of the B-25H was anticipated with considerable enthusiasm by the 11th BS, Fourteenth Air Force for interdiction work in China. Twenty-four of this model were received by the 11th, the first taken on strength in mid January 1944, deliveries continuing until mid March 1945. When first employed on river sweeps

and similar missions, both success and disappointment were experienced. Targets specifically suited to cannon attack proved less numerous than first believed and many targets vulnerable to the big gun were equally so to a good brace of .50 caliber guns and/or deck level bombing. It was further found that the results achieved by strafer bombing on sea sweeps could not be equaled by cannon fire alone.

The cannons were bore sighted at 1,000 yards and were generally fired at altitudes from 1,000 feet beginning an attack to 500 feet at completion. Sighting was achieved with either the electric N-6A sight or the modified A-1 radar sight. With the N-6A fire was usually opened at 2,000 yards range with an average of three rounds fired by the time of closing to 1,000 yards. Using the radar sight reasonable accuracy was obtained by beginning fire at 5,000 yards range which permitted eight or ten rounds to be fired by the time of closing to 1,000 yards when cannon fire ceased and the .50 caliber guns became effective.

The number of 75 mm rounds fired using either sight depended on such variables as the condition of the gun, ability and experience of individual cannoneers, speed of the airplane and even shell cases. The cannon frequently shot out of alignment thereby requiring subsequent maintenance and bore sighting.

Sea sweep missions were generally conducted by flights of two airplanes. Although the B-25H provided design space for twenty-one rounds of 75 mm ammunition, storage for a far greater number could be made available based on mission requirements. Cannon accuracy proved lower than bomb attack results but the cannon had the

A new B-25G is given its required pre-delivery check flight by NAA production test pilots near Los Angeles in 1943. (NAA)

124

Sqd	1943 Dec	Jan	Feb	Mar	Apr	1944 May	Jun	Jul	Total
47th		299	37	71	422	20		329	1,178
48th		331	147	187	2	81	50	233	1,031
396th		85		45	34				164
820th	229	626	259	75	8	30		71	1,298
?						413			413
	229	1341	443	378	466	544	50	633	4,084

Number of 75 mm Rounds Fired by the 41st Bomb Group VII Air Force on Attacks in the Marshall and Caroline Islands

Unit	Date	Rounds Fired
345th BG	3 Dec 1943	96
38th BG	4 " "	96
"	6 " "	121
"	7 " "	224
"	9 " "	143
"	11 " "	111
"	14 " "	72
"	24 " "	227
"	25 " "	331
"	26 " "	224
"	30 " "	172
	Total	1,187

Number of 75mm Rounds Fired by the Fifth Air Force in the Bismarck Islands, December, 1943

Trajectory Grid

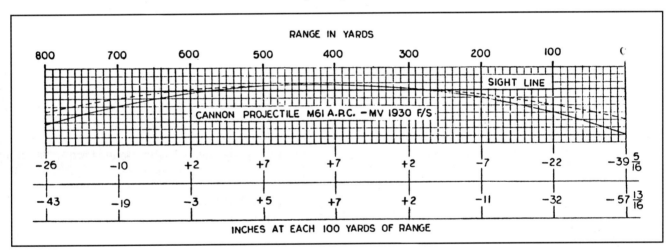

advantage of a far greater number of projectiles per sortie. Emphasis could therefore be placed on the cannon for lesser defended targets especially when coordinated with an air ground liaison team in the area "talking" the airplane in on target.

Precise accuracy of the cannon was difficult to assess on river missions as all direct hits were not always reported. An average of 50% was a conservative estimate.

Tactics for cannon attack were similar to those used by the Navy's torpedo planes where long, low level approaches without evasive action were the norm. This was a hazardous situation against heavily defended objectives and considering that the B-25H carried no co-pilot, freedom from enemy fighter attack was necessary so the pilot could give full attention to the airplane, sighting and firing.

In November the 11th Squadron received the new APG-13A radar range finding equipment for use with the 75 mm gun. This equipment identified a target and determined the precise range at all times during an attacking run. Operated by the navigator, the new units

began target tracking at 6,000 yards with accurate range determinations down to 1,000 yards providing the advantage of starting a run from far greater range. During the month the APG-13 was installed in B-25H airplanes 43-4584; 4971; 4924; 4989 and 4601.

Designed as an attack aircraft and therefore not fitted with a bombsight, the B-25H did not work out too well in bombing formations with the faster bomb sight equipped C,D and J medium bombers which served as lead aircraft. The heavier, slower Hs either used higher power or required that other aircraft reduce speed to maintain formation.

17 North African - Mediterranean Mitchells

Four primary responsibilities were assigned to Allied aviation in the Mediterranean theater of operations:
a. Destruction of enemy industry by heavy bombardment
b. Tactical support of ground forces
c. Protection of shipping, harbors, sea lanes and rear installations from enemy action.
d. Support of partisans.

Arrival of four B-25 medium bomber groups in the theater, beginning with the 12th Bomb Group "Earthquakers" in August 1942, occurred at a critical time. Rommel's Afrika Korps had blitzed their way to within seventy miles of Alexandria, then re-grouped at El Alamein for the final push through Cairo to the strategic prize of the Suez Canal.

To the four squadrons of the 12th fell a heavy burden of the early medium bomber operations against Rommel's superior forces. This situation improved for the Allies early in 1943 by the arrival of three additional B-25 units. The 310th and 321st Groups reached Africa in November and December respectively via the north Atlantic route. Both were assigned to the Twelfth Air Force. The 340th BG arrived at Cairo in March over the South Atlantic through Natal, Ascension Island and across Africa to Cairo to join the Ninth Air Force.

The B-25 medium bomber groups became part of the Mediterranean Allied Air Forces (MAAF), one of the most diverse international fighting teams of the war. Predominantly American and British Commonwealth, there were also units of Poles, Italians, Greeks, French and Yugoslavs.

The mediums helped blast the crack Afrika Korps and the war-weary Italians until the advance was checked and the enemy forces were driven from North Africa. Captured enemy airfields brought MAAF air units nearer their objective in Southern Europe.

Late in April 1943 the 341st Service Squadron, 26th Air Depot Group in Egypt modified sixteen B-25C-1, -5 and -10s into formidable strafers for the 487th Bomb Squadron, 340th Bomb Group.

A fourteen man crew working extended hours in an outdoor revetment completed the armament installations on two airplanes per day, the 16th and final being completed on 4 May. The single B-25C-1 required the addition of five guns and the B-25C-5 and -10 models with two nose guns installed at the factory, required four. A total of 1,500 rounds of ammunition was supplied. Guns were installed parallel to the line of flight instead of a slight downward pitch

characterizing the field modified strafers of the V, VII and X Air Forces and the factory eight gun nose. Following completion of the assigned missions all airplanes were returned to the original configuration.

The sixteen airplanes were: 41-13169; 42-32246; 42-32278; 42-32279; 42-32290; 42-32304; 42-53353; 42-53372; 42-53388; 42-53455; 42-53463; 42-53465; 42-53480; 42-53482; 42-53483; 42-53488.

It was in the Southwest Pacific early in 1942 where the B-25 was found lacking in defensive armament, a deficiency held responsible for the loss of a significant number of airplanes. The 321st BG entered combat with the advantage of having fifty-seven of their B-25Cs and Ds fitted with additional guns before departure for Africa.

The airplanes of the 321st, then stationed at DeRidder Army Air Base, Louisiana, were flown to the

Two 487th BS B-25s modified by the 26th Air Depot in Egypt. (Wm. C. Carr)

Over the Straits of Sicily 10 April 1943 the Luftwaffe suffers a bad moment and brave men died attempting to transport badly needed supplies to Rommel's Afrika Korps. A flight of Mitchells and P-38s took part in splashing 21 of the 35 Ju-52 transports. (USAF)

Warner Robins Air Logistics Center in Georgia where a busy month of round the clock efforts accomplished the required additions. The unpopular and cumbersome bottom turret was removed and the floor structured over. Large windows were cut in the aft fuselage to provide a single .50 caliber gun on each side at waist stations and a single gun was installed in the tail with a canopy similar to but unlike that used on the later B-25H and J models.

The value of the additional guns was readily appreciated after the unit was committed to battle. As a result a similar but more extensive project to continue this work on additional airplanes was set up at Sidi Ahmed Air Base at Bizerte, the program getting underway on 10 August 1943. In addition to the gun installations done at Warner Robins, the operation was more extensive and time consuming by the addition of armor protection under the pilot's seats, forward of the instrument panel, waist gun floor and the floor and sides of the tail gun position.

The forward area project at Sidi Ahmed was logistically no match for the well equipped and supplied facility at Warner Robins. Parts, materials, machine and hand tools were in short supply and service personnel scrounged salvage dumps, depots and air bases to locate required equipment and raw stock. Captured enemy materials were tested for suitability and put to use.

A Warner Robins airplane served as a prototype at Sidi Ahmed. No specifications or blueprints were available and to maintain the required uniformity and interchangeable parts, installation kits were fabricated and supplied with Depot blueprints, photos, parts lists, and instructions. Expediency dictated time limits for the aircraft removed from combat readiness. In the absence of skilled stress analysis, considerable judgment was required to determine the reinforcement around the large waist gun windows. The structural integrity was later proven when one of the modified airplanes with full bomb load was caught in the prop wash of the plane ahead. It was rolled with such force that all crew members suffered bruises and abrasions. The wing showed signs of local failure but the fuselage sustained no damage.

A near production line was set up with airplanes entering one side of the hangar and passing through stations where each operation took place. When complete the planes moved out the far side with armament added, cleaned, painted, inspected and ready for service.

During the first six weeks of the project about twenty-five Mitchells were completed and after the procedures were streamlined by experience, between 10 August and 31 December 183 B-25Cs and Ds of the 12th, 310th, 321st and 340th Bomb Groups were processed. When the Sidi Ahmed program wound down more than 300 B-25s of all four groups had been so modified under these difficult conditions, a credit to the personnel of the 1st Aircraft Assembly Squadron and the 18th, 41st and 319th Depot Repair Squadrons. Benefits from the added armament noticeably reduced loss rates and an increase in the number of enemy planes shot down, thirty-five during the first four months of operations.

Operating under the 57th Bomb Wing, the 310th, 321st and 340th Groups participated in every major campaign from Tunisia to the German surrender in Northern Italy.

In late May and early June 1943 the 57th wing made a major contribution to the reduction of the strategic islands of Pantelleria and Lampedusa. In the Straits of Sicily off the Tunisian coast, these heavily fortified islands blocked the northward Allied advance on the long road north to Europe. On these concentrated air attacks the B-25s dropped 1,140 tons of bombs, more than 18% of the total tonnage, a quantity exceeded only by the B-17s. Missions were extended to the Italian mainland, Corsica and Sardinia and a persistent interdictive effort was mounted against axis lines of communication. Arrival of the B-25G and the 75 mm cannon added to the effectiveness of the attacks.

Riding at anchor in the harbor at La Spezia, the Italian liner Taranto was useless to the Axis except as a threat to Allied operations. It was feared that the Germans would tow the ship to the channel where it would be sunk as a channel block, denying use of the port to the Allies after it was captured. To the 340th BG fell the task of thwarting such plans. Mounting an eighteen plane mission, six B-25s targeted the bow, six the mid section and six the stern. The attack was carried out with great precision and the ship sunk in twenty-five minutes. Mitchells of the 310th BG sunk an additional vessel in La Spezia to prevent it too from becoming a harbor block.

Late in October 1943 at the height of its many accomplishments in the African desert and the Mediterranean, the Ninth Air Force was effectively dismantled and reorganized in England as a tactical air force for the direct assault on Germany. Its many components were assigned elsewhere, the 12th going to the CBI and 340th transferred to join their companion 310th and 321st Groups in the rapidly expanding Twelfth Air Force.

By mid-January 1944 shiny, new, heavily armed B-25Js were coming on strength to replace the drab, desert pink and olive green, war weary B-25Cs and Ds. The new J models were factory equipped with more

POOPSIE, a veteran XII AF B-25C and crew with mascot. (USAF)

After 73 missions DESERT WARRIOR returns home to North American's flight ramp. Flown by a crew representing the four squadrons of the 12th BG "Earthquakers", the famous Mitchell began a stateside tour. The story of the airplane's combat travels is told by the colored map on the tan fuselage. (NAA)

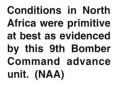
Conditions in North Africa were primitive at best as evidenced by this 9th Bomber Command advance unit. (NAA)

SAN ANTONIO ROSE of the 340th Bomb Group. (John Sutay via Jeff Ethell)

SWEET LORRAINE (left above), LEROY'S JOY (upper right) and TEXAS GAL (above) all of the 81st BS, 12th BG. (USAF via Kenn Rust)

PLUTO, B-25C 41-13167 flew with the 83rd BS, 12th BG and wore a coating of desert "pink". (USAF via NAA)

SHADRACH, 10th BG, reached North Africa by way of England in Aug 1942. Piloted by Capt. Clyde Grow (left) and kept airworthy by crew chief T/Sgt. Frank Gularte (right), she flew 72 missions and accumulated over 500 hours in the air. Hard hit by fighters and AA fire on the 64th mission the B-25 suffered damage to one engine, both wings and with both tires shot out, was forced to crash land at Palermo. After extensive repairs it was back in business. (NAA)

In all probability the greatest non-combat loss of aircraft was 88 B-25s of the 340th BG from the eruption of Mt. Vesuvius on 22 Mar 44. When eruptions began a week earlier the aircraft were considered safe and removal to other fields would have resulted in severe logistical problems and effect on missions. When conditions deteriorated the airplanes were caught in the fallout at Pompeii Airdrome and were virtually destroyed, only salvageable for parts. (NAA)

armament, defensive and offensive, than earlier counterparts.

It was the battle of the Brenner Pass in November, 1944 that marked one of the greatest undertakings of the medium bombers. The vital railway link through the Italian Alps between Germany and Italy was defended proportionally to its importance to the critical Axis supply line. Electrified and highly efficient, the railway was vulnerable because of its many bridges and tunnels. These became primary objectives of both heavy and medium bombardment but of greater possible importance were continuing raids to wipe out the many transformers. These were destroyed in such numbers that the use of electric locomotives was abandoned in favor of less efficient steam power, cutting the tonnage hauled by half. When the Brenner was finally closed, German forces could no longer carry on in Italy.

In the latter part of 1941 American lend lease aircraft to Britain began to reach Africa by ship and after assembly on the Gold Coast, they were ferried across Africa to Khartoum. This was a long and dangerous operation at best over a primitive route established in the 1930s.

To assist the British in the maintenance and operation of these airplanes, the Air Corps sent a few officers and enlisted men as technical observers and advisors in March 1942. This also provided a golden opportunity for these people to observe the desert air war and report to Washington on battle field conditions, the latest combat requirements, logistics, successes and failures and recommended changes. As more airplanes reached Africa from the U.S. the manufacturers began sending their own representatives to the area to further augment this effort. The aircraft companies established sizable departments where their service personnel were trained and dispatched as needed.

The efforts of these skilled engineers and

Probably from the 12 BG this B-25 made it home after being struck by anti aircraft fire. The fate of the bombardier is unknown. (NASM #61630AC)

Ground crewmen speculate on the damage inflicted by an 88 mm anti-aircraft round on Lt. Col. Malcolm Baily's PATCHES. The 12 BG B-25 flew in this condition for more than two hours after being hit over Yugoslavia. (NASM #3A-22795)

Supporting General Mark Clark's Fifth Army B-25Js of the 340 BG wing over the Tyrrhenian Sea to attack German forces in Northern Italy on 3 Jan 45. (NASM #3A26344)

technicians cannot be overemphasized in the successes and operational efficiency of their respective products. Known as field service men in those days, the reps lived the same primitive existence as their military counterparts, wore the same issue clothing, ate the same GI food, bathed in unheated water and sloshed in the same mud. As civilians they frequently flew combat missions at considerable risk in case of capture, worked with mechanics and air crews, helped develop new ideas, listened to gripes and forwarded suggested improvements to the home office that better product might result.

A few of the many North American people involved in this critical work throughout the world were Bud Snyder, Jack Fox, Paul Brewer, Jack Watson, Bill Carr and Ralph Oakley.

With a British unit in North Africa, Bill Carr contributed to the development of spike bombs based on the 250 pound British teardrop general purpose bomb. A two foot long rod was pointed at one end and the other threaded into the bomb nose. Exploding at ground level it proved devastating to aircraft and personnel.

Wing bomb racks were slow to achieve popularity. Mechanics found them bothersome to keep clean and adjusted and many pilots were convinced that loaded racks caused a significant reduction in air speed. Some units flatly refused to use them. This was readily apparent in the 12 BG where Carr found a pile of discarded racks exposed to the weather and drifting sand, expensive and usable parts rapidly becoming unusable. After cleaning and adjustment and with liberal instructions for the mechanics, Carr persuaded a few pilots to use them. Bulletins were posted on the squadron board identifying the pilots and respective airplanes with the weight of wing stores, power settings, takeoff, climb and cruise performance. It was soon recognized that the external bomb loads caused less drag than originally believed. More airplanes were fitted and carried greater bomb loads per mission with proportionally increased damage to the enemy.

Jack Watson and an ingenious 310 Bomb Group armament officer increased the B-25's maximum load of 500 pound bombs to eight and rigged the bomb bay for an alternate of four 1,000 pound bombs, a load equal to that carried by a B-17. The "Reps" also served.

B-25Js of the 445th BS, 321st BG, parafrag a target in the assault on German supply lines at Brenner Pass. (NAA)

18 Transports and Trainers

Resplendent in shiny aluminum finish, the first B-25 personnel transport on the company flight ramp. It was much lighter and cleaner than combat examples and moved out at a very respectable speed. (NAA)

Between November 1942 and February 1950 North American modified five B-25s to personnel transports, company designations RB-25(1) through RB-25(5). The RB, according to one of the engineers on the project, signified "rebuilt". In 1949 a sixth airplane was far more extensively revised as a prototype transport and pilot trainer for the Air Force. Immediately after the outbreak of World War II the urgency of military air transport resulted in the appropriation of over half of the nation's commercial airline fleet. Civilian travel became inconvenient at best, passenger priorities were established and travel by air or rail was crowded and frequently delayed.

As the new North American plants came on line at Dallas and Kansas City it became an immediate necessity for company personnel to make frequent trips to these and many other locations nationwide. Inefficient travel could not be tolerated.

In November 1942 after 278 hours of flight test time, the first B-25, 40-2165 was transferred from test status to the experimental department for modification as a company transport. Number 1 was built with incomplete and temporary tooling and many parts were not interchangeable with production examples. It was an orphan airplane and the Army, satisfied that value had been received, released it to North American.[1]

Following removal of all military equipment, passenger accommodations were installed. Five seats were located in the aft fuselage and for business while flying, a desk and intercom system. Two more seats were installed ahead of the bomb bay directly behind the flight deck. The bomb bay was converted for baggage and a bunk was installed on the crawlway above.

Only the absence of armament and the windows in the aft fuselage suggested that it was not a combat machine as the Air Corps insignia and tail numbers remained. Notable changes from production models were primarily the nose and windows. The aft side windows on both sides of the cockpit and the top window escape panel above were skinned over to provide protection from the sun. This feature would also be true for future similar conversions. Four windows were installed on each side of the aft fuselage, one on the right being an escape hatch. The greenhouse nose was fully skinned to a solid configuration which housed the radio and navigation equipment. Removal of the tail turret provided space for an installation of emergency flares. Deicer boots, which did not appear on B-25s until the C model, were also installed.

Completed and parked on the flight ramp near North American's engineering building, the new transport attracted considerable attention by employees and was soon tagged with the unofficial title, "Whiskey Express". Company pilot Ed Stewart was usually at the controls and made countless flights to many parts of the country with Mr. Kindelberger and other personnel.

On January 8 1945, Stewart, co-pilot Theron Morgan and crew chief Jack Maholm were on a routine check flight after an engine change. As a check, one engine was feathered but failed to unfeather. Descending through considerable overcast on final approach, Stewart maintained an intentional above normal approach speed as standard single engine procedure. The landing gear failed to lock in the down position and the hydraulic system failed to build adequate locking pressure before too much runway had been used. The airplane could not accelerate to climb-out speed under these conditions and a crash landing was made in the open fields near the present location of the Los Angeles International Airport tower. No fire occurred and no injuries resulted. No. 1, however, had made its final flight, damaged beyond repair [2]

All good things must come to an end. After four and a half years of testing and corporate service the first B-25 personnel conversion was lost due to a small, improperly manufactured part. Fortunately none of the crew was injured. (NAA)

Subsequent inspection of the hydraulic system revealed that a small, inexpensive fitting had been made with an erroneously oversize orifice which had prevented adequate hydraulic pressure buildup.

On a business trip to North American in 1943, General Arnold expressed considerable interest in the company's converted B-25 transport. He subsequently arranged for B-25, 40-2168, to be diverted to North American for identical modification for his personal airplane. All work was accomplished by the Field Service Department under a master change record with government funds.

North American modified the airplane exactly as done on the company transport, 40-2165. Few drawings and sketches were made, most work being done by verbal direction with approval of structures engineering and procedural inspections.

All was complete in June and between 19 June and July the airplane was flown for over four hours by NAA test pilot, Bob Chilton and company flight test personnel. On 10 July Major Harris of the Army completed the final flight check of four more hours preparatory to delivery.[3]

The extent of General Arnold's use of the airplane is unknown. Colonel Claire Peterson was the general's regular pilot for 2168 and his services continued for Arnold's second airplane, a B-25J.[4]

In July 1945 after some 300 hours of flight time, 2168 was turned over to the War Assets Commission for final disposition. Fortunately it escaped the scrap yard and was sold on the civilian market. With an executive interior it attracted considerable interest as a potential business aircraft.

Sold in 1947 to a Chattanooga business man, it remained in that ownership until November 1948 when purchased by Bankers Life and Casualty Company of Chicago. Mr. MacArthur of Bankers Life frequently flew the airplane to Los Angeles on business and had arranged for landing and tie down with the Hughes Aircraft Company at Culver City. It was a simple matter of time before Mr. Hughes discovered the slicked up Mitchell on his flight ramp and soon decided he couldn't get along without it. Mr. MacArthur reportedly rejected several offers from Hughes but subsequently finding a check for a most unusual amount in his mail, sold 2168 to the tycoon in June 1951.

The airplane remained in the Hughes stable with little use until it was sold in 1962. From that time until the present the airplane has passed through a number of ownerships and remains in airworthy condition.

Late in February 1944, B-25J, 43-4030, was flown from North American's Kansas City plant to the Inglewood division for conversion as a transport for General Dwight Eisenhower. Part time engineers for stress, structures, fuel, electrical, heat and vent and two shifts of mechanics, all under the direction of the Field Service Department, completed the work under a government funded sales order and master change record.[5]

It was directed that the airplane be completed as soon as possible causing considerable speculation at North American regarding the date of the anxiously awaited D-Day in Europe.

Considering the importance of the recipient and the transatlantic delivery flight, more extensive revisions

General Arnold's transport, 40-2168, on North American's flight ramp soon after conversion by the Field Service Department. (NAA)

General Eisenhower's customized B-25J-1, 43-4030, on the weight and balance scales at North American's Inglewood plant in May 1944. The revised tail cone housed a jettisonable life raft. Upon completion the airplane was flown directly to England for the General's use. (NAA)

were made than on the previous two transports. North American management directed that a more detailed engineering record be kept rather than rough sketches and hand waving.

The Field service hangar was temporarily equipped with limited engineering accommodations where changes could be adequately recorded and new drawings made as required.

The airplane was stripped of all camouflage paint, armament and other military hardware and equipment not needed for a personnel carrier. Waist gun windows were structured over as were the aft pilot windows and the escape window panel above.

For the General's comfort, a bunk was installed on the crawlway over the bomb bay and a narrow passage on the left side of the bunk provided passage between fore

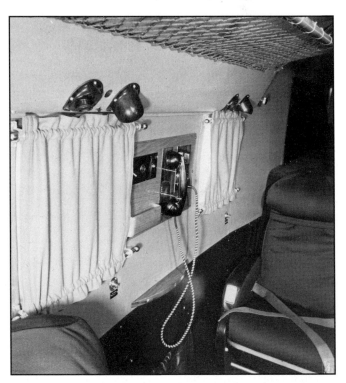

Interior appointments of 43-4030 were considerably improved over the less extensively modified B-25s for North American and General Arnold. Soon after hostilities ceased the airplane was sold through government surplus sales. (NAA)

134

and aft fuselage compartments. The top of the bomb bay was lowered considerably requiring additional structure for the wing center section carry through. The remaining bomb bay space was fitted with a bullet proof fuel tank. Immediately aft of the bomb bay two side by side seats were installed and behind these, a fold down table extended the full width of the airplane. Two additional tandem seats were positioned aft of the table.

A walnut cabinet, superbly crafted by one of the mock up wood workers, provided space for coffee, other beverages, dry ice and easy to carry snacks. Walnut scraps remaining from the cabinet work were soon gathered by members of the company rifle and pistol club for custom pistol grips.

For easy access to the aft cabin area the aft hatch was revised and enlarged and fitted with a collapsible sliding stair. In the aft most section was a small toilet compartment complete with medicine chest, folding wash basin and overboard drain. A telephone and mesh luggage rack completed the interior furnishings.

The interior walls were insulated and paneled like a commercial airliner. Lower side walls were upholstered in blue fabric and upper walls were tan. Blue carpet was installed throughout. The seats, also done in blue fabric, were purchased from the Douglas Company.

Removal of the tail gun provided space for a life raft which could be jettisoned. It was installed with few drawings and minimal instructions by a very competent mechanic.

The flight deck remained essentially unchanged from other B-25J models except for the addition of two comfortable seats aft of the flight deck and ahead of the bomb bay. These accommodated the radio operator and an additional passenger. [6]

While work on the airplane continued at a brisk pace to meet the "as soon as possible" completion date, word was received from the Army that the airplane was to be complete, flight checked and ready for delivery on 1 June. This left no doubt that the invasion date was imminent. All was done however, in good time as the North American pilot staff made the first check flight on 12 May.

After arrival of the airplane in England little information filtered back down to North American. Press dispatches reported that 4030 reached its destination two days after leaving Inglewood and shortly thereafter that the General had flown over the front in a fast, well appointed twin engine craft. Eisenhower apparently used the airplane on but few occasions and is well known to have subsequently flown over the combat zone in a specially modified two seat P-51 which provided increased safety with higher speed.

RB-25 (3) survived the war and was returned to the United States. In 1947 as a CB-25J, it was busied in cargo service out of Bolling Field near Washington, D.C. The following year it was designated VB-25J with the 1100th Special Air Mission Group flying VIPs within the United States. In early 1953 it operated with the 1254th Air Transport Group at Washington National Airport and in August, 1958, was assigned to the 1001st Air Base Wing at Andrews AFB.

Four months later, in December, 4030 basked in the Arizona sun at the scrap and storage facility at Davis-Monthan AFB and was struck from Air Force inventory in February 1959.

Fortunately, the saga of 4030 did not end with the scrapper's tools of destruction. It was marketed through government surplus sales and subsequently passed through a number of private owners, none probably aware of the airplane's history. [7]

In 1981 after thirty-seven flyable years 4030 was purchased by the Air Force for the museum at Ellsworth Air Force Base near Rapid City, South Dakota. Coming full circle back to the original owner, the airplane had been restored and is now on display as created for the supreme commander. [8]

In 1944 General Arnold relinquished 40-2168 in favor of a newly revised B-25J, 44-28945, duplicating exactly the airplane customized for General Eisenhower. The work was done by the Field Service Department. Inasmuch as the drawings and sketches from Eisenhower's airplane were retained and an experienced staff of engineers and mechanics were available, the modifications were a routine assignment.

A series of antennas were located under the forward fuselage and a direction finder positioned on top of the nose. The deicer system was retained and the "S"

General Arnold's second B-25 transport, 44-28945, ready for the General's acceptance on the North American flight ramp. The 'S' type exhaust stacks were replaced by full collector rings from B-25C inventory. (NAA)

North American president "Dutch" Kindelberger with General Arnold as he takes delivery of his second B-25. (NAA)

type Clayton exhaust stacks were replaced by less noisy full collector rings as used on the B-25C.

Between 24 November and 11 December the airplane was flight checked by test pilot Ed Virgin for a total time of three hours and twenty minutes.

General Arnold used the B-25J until January 1946 when it was released back to general service, redesignated VB-25J for personnel transportation. It remained in transport service until struck from Air Force inventory and released to surplus sales in 1953.

In 1963 and 1964 the airplane was owned by the Edwards Oil Company of San Angelo, Texas; from 1965 to 1968 by the Bendix Company and from 1969 to 1972 by the Double A Leasing Corp. of Miami, Florida. It was carried on the civil register as N3184G.

Under Bendix ownership the airplane was flown to the Horton and Horton Company at Meacham Field near Fort Worth, Texas where an air stair system was installed in the aft fuselage.

No record of the airplane appears in the civil register since 1972. It was reported sold to a former major of the Cuban air force who sold it soon after. The ultimate fate of 44-28945 is unknown but probably went derelict and was junked.

The crash of the first B-25, 40-2165, left North American without a company transport and in January 1945 conversion was begun on B-25J, 44-30047. Interior arrangements and appointments were essentially the same as the airplanes for Generals Arnold and Eisenhower

but the airplane incorporated a number of system and other technical advancements. A standard eight gun nose shell was used and the large door on each side provided easy access to heater and radio equipment within. The direction finder was mounted on the underside.

The airplane was completed late in 1945 and first flown on 18 October by Ed Stewart and George Krebs. Joe Barton made most of the test flights but other company pilots including Ed Virgin, Bob Chilton and George Welch were also involved. Late in December a test program was begun leading toward commercial certification by the C.A.A. During intermittent testing the airplane served as a company transport accumulating a total of thirty-two flight hours through 27 February 1946.[9]

The C.A.A. program was directed toward the civil community where a market existed for professionally modified medium bombers economically obtained from government surplus sales. Hundreds of low time aircraft and engines had become available immediately after the war. Such work could have kept many NAA employees busy following the massive post war contract cancellations. It is doubtful however, that North American's overhead could have met the competition from smaller fabricators.

On 27 February 1946 pilot Joe Barton, test engineer Cowles and CAA inspector McCutcheon were on a routine certification flight off the California coast near Malibu. A radio message was received from Barton reporting a fire. A Malibu resident reported seeing an off-shore flash which was assumed to be the exploding airplane. Little debris was recovered.

The loss of the airplane and certification program was insignificant to the loss of the personnel. Barton was one of North American's most competent and highly

In the late 40s and early 50s, 43-4030 was designated VB-25J and used by the A F as staff transport. Shown here with command plate at San Francisco in Oct 1947, it is now in the museum at Ellsworth AFB, Rapid City, S D (Wm. T. Larkins)

In post war service 44-28945 was re-designated VB-25N to serve as a staff transport based at Bolling Field. Upper 'S' stacks have been replaced with a semi collector ring. Shown at San Francisco in Nov 1952. (Wm. T. Larkin)

B-25J-25, 44-30047 was the fifth B-25 converted by North American to transport configuaration. It was developed for the purposes of company transport and prototype of a prospective commercial series of post war business craft. After 36 hours of flight time the airplane crashed in the ocean due to a fire during CAA qualification tests. (NAA)

A standard 8 gun nose shell was used on 44-30047 and was ideally suited for heater and radio gear, the large doors providing excellent accessibility for maintenance. The nose port is for heater ram air intake and is shown during blower tests. (NAA)

respected test pilots whose prominence was well earned through a great portion of B-25 testing and high speed dive tests of P-51s. [10]

Stripped of combat equipment B-25s were used in considerable numbers as advanced pilot trainers during the immediate post war period. More than 1,000 near new B-25Js and new engines remained in the USAF inventory. Further interest was expressed by the USAF in additional and more extensively modified B-25s for personnel transports, pilot and radar bomb and fire control trainers. Trainers had been a major part of North American's production since Dundalk, Maryland days in the 1930s and although the company was busy with F-86, T-28, AT-6G and B-45 airplanes, management desired to continue the trainer business.[11]

Early in 1949 North American submitted a proposal describing a pilot trainer, a radar directed bombing and fire control trainer and a ten place personnel transport. Cost per airplane was estimated at less than $100,000 as compared to $500,000 for the navigation trainer version of the Convair 240 airliner.

A wide selection of engines was quoted; the Wright R-2600-13 and R-1820 and the Pratt & Whitney R-2000, R-2800-CA-3, R-2800-CA-5, R-2180 and the R-1830. The proposal specified a wider and longer nose

section which provided space for a total of six seats forward of the bomb bay. Four additional seats, two side by side and two in tandem, were placed in the aft fuselage. [12]

Provision was made in the radar bomb and fire control trainer for two pilots, one instructor and four students. All student stations were equipped for radar bombing. Wing racks carried eight 100 pound bombs and bomb bay racks held nine 100 pound cluster bombs.

The navigation trainer utilized the same seating arrangement as the radar bomber. The student stations were equipped for four types of navigation, celestial, Loran, radar and dead reckoning. Additional equipment was installed at the instructor's station. The pilot trainer seated a pilot, co-pilot, instructor and student.

In mid 1949 North American purchased B-25J, 44-30975, Buaer 35848 from government surplus sales. The airplane was taken to the Experimental Department for modification as the prototype trainer/personnel transport under a sales order and master change record. This sixth and final B-25 conversion was by far the most extensively modified transport by North American. Nothing was spared to make this airplane a highly refined demonstrator, the plush interior and other refinements far exceeding military requirements. It seems incongruous however, that all documentation was titled EXECUTIVE TRANSPORT, indicating the probability that North American intended to use it as a company personnel transport and a prototype commercial conversion as well.

The nose section forward of the propeller was completely redesigned and bore no resemblance to preceding examples. It was extended forty inches farther forward than on standard Mitchells and widened to a comfortable seventy inches, fairing back to the original contour at the propeller line. This prompted the unofficial designation as the "Bulbous Nosed B-25". Moving the pilot's seats forward provided adequate space for four more seats ahead of the bomb bay. The floor of the forward section was raised to the level of the flight deck continuing aft to the bomb bay.

As described in the proposal the aft fuselage had four more seats, two side by side and two in tandem. A chemical toilet, electrical and radio gear and a 100,000 BTU Janitrol cabin heater were installed back of the aft bulkhead. A long tail cone fairing housed oxygen bottles and mounted the intake scoop for cabin heater ram air.

On the civil register as N5126N, 44-30975 Navy #35848, the prototype trainer/transport has the longer, wider nose section and additional window. De-icer boots were removed and the "S" type exhaust stacks of the top cylinders were replaced by a semi collector ring. (NAA)

The expanded forward section of N5126N featured a Convair 240 windshield and instrument panel and comfortable seating for six forward of the bomb bay. (NAA)

The large radome nose section of the prototype provided easy access to equipment. Transition of the fuselage contours is clearly shown. (NAA)

The bomb bay carry-through structure was considerably modified. A bunk with storage space underneath occupied the right side above the bay and a narrow passageway on the left connected the fore and aft cabin areas. The lower part of the bomb bay was converted to a baggage compartment which was raised and lowered by a modified electric bomb hoist.

Noise level in the cabin was reduced to approximately 120 decibels, reportedly below that of the commercial DC-3. The fuselage was soundproofed by a micaceous coating on the skin, fiberglass insulation and a layer of balsa wood in the floor.

Wright R-2600-13 engines equipped with Holley carburetors powered the demonstrator. Clayton "S" type exhaust stacks were retained for the lower cylinders and a semi-collector ring was fitted for the upper cylinders. Hydraulic fluid was controlled by the propeller feathering

Aft cabin interior of N5126N (NAA)

switch and auto shut off for fuel and oil was provided at the firewall.

On 15 February 1950 the completed transport was first flown by Ed Virgin, North American's chief test pilot, and Miles Towner, a former Marine Corps pilot of the Field Service Department. Some concern existed regarding stability with the extended nose but normal flight characteristics remained. Removal of guns, armor, turrets and other aerodynamic improvements resulted in a notable increase in performance over standard Mitchells. At 28,000 feet the airplane had a top speed of 300 MPH compared to 272 MPH for the combat ready B-25J, further indicating that the expanded nose section had no detrimental effect.

On 1 March a seven man team headed by pilot Miles Towner and co-pilot Jack Steppe of Customer Relations, structural and instrumentation engineers, a C.A.A. inspector and crew chief began a demonstration tour of a number of Air Force bases. The first stops were at Hamilton and Mather Fields in northern California. After a brief return to Inglewood the sales team departed for the east coast on 5 March via Albuquerque and St. Louis, arriving at Wright Field on 14 March. USAF and Navy personnel received the sales pitch and some flight time at Washington National Airport, Bolling and Langley Fields.

The return to California from Wright Field was via Little Rock, Arkansas and El Paso, Texas. On 25 March a short distance east of Phoenix, Arizona a storm front of extreme turbulence was encountered. The crew of an eastbound airplane reported the worst of their experience. The B-25 transport failed to make it through, crashing near the town of Chandler. Wreckage was widely scattered

and investigation attributed the cause of the crash to structural failure in severe storm conditions.

The loss of seven prominent employees was a severe blow to the company and took much of the steam out of the project, but Lee Atwood, North American vice president, expressed to company supervision his confidence in the probability of a sizable contract for the B-25 trainers.[13] Had the project gone forward it is doubtful that it would have continued. In June communist forces crossed the 38th parallel into South Korea and overnight North American's assembly lines looked like World War II all over again. With the demand for all the F-86 Sabre Jets that could be rolled out the back door, there would have been no place for reworked B-25s in the company's priorities.

North American's considerable effort notwithstanding, the B-25 pilot trainer contract went to Hayes Aircraft Co. of Birmingham, Alabama and the B-25 bomb and fire control trainer contract was awarded to Hughes Aircraft Co. of Culver City, California.

Following the end of World War II a considerable number of B-25s were used by the USAF as trainers, utility airplanes and staff transports. Sixty were converted to trainers and designated AT-24. Sub designators A, B, C and D were meant to represent production variants D, G, C, and J. In 1947 all such aircraft were redesignated TB-25D, G, C and J respectively.

Under the contract with the Hayes Aircraft Company of Birmingham, Alabama seventy-nine B-25J airplanes were modified for specialized, advanced pilot training, designated TB-25L. Deliveries began in April

TB-25N was retrofitted with semi collector rings and Bendix carburetors. It carries the logo of the Air Research Defense Command and the Cambridge Research Center. (San Diego Aerospace Museum)

TB-25J carries a ventral radome, date unknown, but the author recalls making the initial developmental drawings of the radome at Inglewood in 1950. The part would have been fabricated at NAA plant in Downey. (USAF)

B-25J at Patterson Field, OH in Jan 1946 was an early post war conversion to a CB-25J utility transport and was later processed through Hayes Aircraft as a TB-25N. The purpose of the odd chin radome is unknown. (Wm. T. Larkins)

Los Angeles smog provides a perfect background for this TB-25M. (Hughes Aircraft Co.)

Six B-25Js were modified as USAF personnel carriers: 43-4030; 44-28945 (above); 44-30319; 44-30971; 44-30976 and 45-8891. Number 44-30971 was further modified with Bendix carburetors and semi collector rings for the top cylinders. The VB-25s were assigned to the 1100th Special Air Missions Group at Bolling Field near Washington, D.C. and were later taken over by the 1254th Air Transport Group. They were marked with Bolling Field insignia and numbers 50 through 55. All were processed through the Hayes Aircraft Co., Birmingham, Alabama. 44-30976 (below) ended its days in Paraguay and was scrapped in 1987. (Howard Naslund)

1952 and continued through December. These airplanes differ from standard B-25Js based on the following changes:

a. Removal of armament and armor protection.

b. Modernized instrument panel with revised lighting.

c. Revised oxygen system.

d. Revised and improved radio and interphone system.

e. Improved fire detection and extinguishing system.

f. Pilot's three piece windshield replaced with one piece safety glass and equipped with windshield wiper and anti-icing system.

g. Additional soundproofing and interior trim and upholstery.

h. Enlargement of front entrance hatch and addition of escape hatches.

i. Exhaust semi-collector ring replaced "S" stacks on top seven cylinders of each engine. (Some airplanes only)

j. Two passenger seats added just forward of the bomb bay.

k. Five passenger seats added in the aft fuselage.

l. The flight deck floor revised to continue aft to the bomb bay.

m. Mechanical up latch emergency release for main landing gear.

From November 1953 through December 1954 the Hayes Company modified an additional 380 B-25Js, designated TB-25N, to the same configuration as the preceding TB-25Ls. These variants were similar to North American's highly modified prototype trainer but without the longer, widened nose and many deluxe refinements.

The modification of B-25Js for the installation of the E-1 fire control system came about late in 1950 when the USAF decided to use some of the many Mitchells then in service as trainers for fire control radar operators. The initial contract was awarded to the Hughes Tool Company of Culver City, California for twelve airplanes, designated TB-25K. Follow on contracts increased the total to 117.

All armor and armament was removed. A nose radome of special design was fitted for part of the radar equipment. Instrumentation was housed in the modified bomb bay and an astrodome was installed at the navigator's compartment. Monitoring equipment for one instructor and the students were installed in the aft fuselage.

Artist's cutaway illustration shows the interior arrangement of the trainer/transport prototype. (NAA)

As the TB-25K contracts neared completion, Hughes was contracted for the modification of an additional thirty-five B-25Js designated TB-25M. These variants, modified from TB-25L airplanes, were essentially the same as the K models except for the installation of the more advanced E-5 fire control system equipment. Deliveries began in December 1952.

From 1952 through 1954 a total of 979 B-25Js were processed through IRAN (Inspection, Repair As Needed) at the Hayes Aircraft Company at Birmingham. These airplanes were also equipped, seemingly at random, with some or most of the following items: auto pilot, bomb bay fuel tanks - fixed or droppable, AN/ARN-14 radio gear, dual UHF-VHF and demand oxygen systems. Sixty airplanes were fitted with the solid eight gun nose shell.

All were initially powered with Wright R-2900-29 engines and Holley carburetors although many were later fitted with Bendix Stromberg carburetors and the engines redesignated -35.

Another group was modified as transports and designated VB-25.

Hayes records show that the 979 airplanes were processed to the following designations and quantities:

B-25J	3
JB-25J	6
JTB-25J	5
TB-25J	98
VB-25J	6
TB-25K	90
TB-25L	79
TB-25M	35
TB-25N	627
VB-25N	27
JTB-25N	3

Notes to Chapter 18
1. Letter, J.L. Atwood to Norman Avery, 3 May 1982
2. Letter, Edgar Stewart to Norman Avery, Jun 1972
3. North American Aviation, Inc. Flight Data Record Card No. 40-2168
4. Letter, C.A. Peterson to Norman Avery 20 May 1976
5. Letter, Don H. Kennedy to Norman Avery, 16 Sep, 1982
6. North American Aviation, Inc., Report No. 8183, **Conversion of B-25 to Transport,** 30 May 1944
7. Correspondence, Planes of Fame and Norman Avery, 1977
8. Thomas, John W. Aerospace Historian
9. North American Aviation, Inc. Flight Data Record Card No. 44-30047
10. North American Aviation, Inc. **Skywriter** 8 Mar 1946.
11. North American Aviation, Inc. Internal Memorandum, J.L. Atwood to Supervision, "The Training Airplane Program", 14 Apr 1950
12. McSurely, Alexander, **Aviation Week** 27 Mar 1950 page 15
13. North American Aviation, Inc. Internal Memorandum, J.L. Atwood to Supervision, "The Training Airplane Program"

19 Mitchells in the Air National Guard

Based on the concept of the citizen soldier, the National Guard and Air National Guard constitute organized, trained and equipped units ready for mobilization in times of emergency. Until shortly after World War II National Guard aviation was generally comprised of reconnaissance and observation units and equipment. Significant changes occurred soon after the war when, in 1947, the U.S. Air Force was accorded status as a separately constituted service, equal in status to the Army and Navy, a goal long sought since the days of General Billy Mitchell. Concurrently, National Guard aviation was redesignated the Air National Guard.

Mandated as a military force, each ANG unit serves under the administration of its state government for intra state purposes of assisting in the preservation of public order, safety and rescue. While reporting to the state governor as commander in chief during peace time, if mobilized and called to active federal duty for a national emergency, the ANG then comes under federal control with other armed forces under the President of the United States as Commander in Chief.

By regular training with modern equipment the ANG maintains a continuing standard of proficiency ready for an immediate call to service.

Soon after World War II many first rate combat aircraft were assigned to the ANG. A great number of B-25Js were retained in the post war inventory and hundreds were modified as pilot trainers, radar control trainers and transports. A limited quantity of TB-25Ks, modified for training fire control operators, were assigned to certain fighter interceptor squadrons in support of F-89 and F-94 fighters for rocket attack. A few TB-25Ns served with ANG squadrons as weather reconnaissance and personnel transports. Common to ANG B-25s were the inflatable deicing boots on wing and tail and most, but not all, were retrofitted with Bendix carburetors and the accompanying high intake scoops. For unknown reasons the nacelles and occasionally the cowlings, were painted black.

TB-25K

AN ALBUM OF AIR GUARD MITCHELLS

TB-25K

TB-25K

TB-25N

TB-25K

TB-25K

TB-25K

TB-25K

TB-25K

All photos courtesy of Dave Menard or Doug Olson

143

B-25s of the AIR NATIONAL GUARD

Serial No.	Type	State	Unit	Base
44-28790	TB-25N	New York	102 RDCFT	Suffolk Cty Apt, Long Island
29125	TB-25J	California	146 WRS	Van Nuys MAP, Van Nuys
29199	TB-25N	California	112 RDCFT	Van Nuys MAP, Van Nuys
29250	TB-25K	Idaho	190 FIS	Gowen ANGB, Boise
29257	TB25-N	California	195 FIS	Van Nuys MAP, Van Nuys
29395	TB-25K	Minnesota	179 FIS	Duluth ANGB, Duluth
29444	TB-25N	Missouri	110 FIS	Robertson ANGB, St. Louis
29728	TB-25K	Maine	132 FIS	Bangor IAP, Bangor
29834	TB-25K	Vermont	134 FIS	Burlington IAP, Burlington
29860	TB-25K	New York	137 FIS	Westchester County Apt, White Plains
29915	TB-25K	Massachussetts	131 FIS	Barnes MAP, Westfield
30125	TB-25N	California	115 FIS	Van Nuys MAP, Van Nuys
30126	TB-25K	Michigan	107 FIS	Selfridge ANGB, Mt. Clemens
		Massachussetts	131 FIS	Barnes MAP, Westfield
		Maine	132 FIS	Bangor IAP, Bangor
30133	TB-25K	Indiana	109 FIS	Hulman Field, Terra Haute
30150	TB-25K	North Dakota	178 FIS	Hector Field, Fargo
		Washington	116 FIS	Spokane IAP, Spokane
30156	TB-25K	New York	138 FIS	Hancock Field, Syracuse
		Montana	186 FIS	Great Falls IAP, Great Falls
30207	TB-25K	New York	136 FIS	Niagara Falls MAP, Niagara Falls
30378	TB-25M	South Dakota	175 FIS	Joe Foss Field, Sioux Falls
30444	TB-25M	Wisconsin	176 FIS	Truax Field, Madison
30480	TB-25K	Oregon	123 FIS	Portland IAP, Portland
		South Dakota	175 FIS	Joe Foss Field, Sioux Falls
30488	TB-25K	New York	102 FIS	Suffolk Cty Apt, Long Island
		South Dakota	175 FIS	Joe Foss Field, Sioux Falls
30489	TB-25K	North Dakota	178 FIS	Hector Field, Fargo
30584	TB-25K	New York	136 FIS	Niagara Falls MAP, Niagara Falls
		Michigan	171 FIS	Selfridge ANGB, Mt. Clemens
30622	TB-25K	Wisconsin	176 FIS	Truax Field, Madison
		Minnesota	179 FIS	Duluth ANGB, Duluth
30643	TB-25K	Massachussetts	131 FIS	Barnes MAP, Westfield
30724	TB-25K	New York	138 FIS	Hancock Field, Syracuse
30734	TB-25N	New York	102 RDCFT	Suffolk Cty Apt, Long Island
		Texas	111 FIS	Ellington AFB, Houston
		California	115 FIS	Van Nuys MAP, Van Nuys
30852	TB-25K	Massachussetts	101 FIS	Otis ANGB, Fallmouth
		Wisconsin	176 FIS	Truax Field, Madison
30858	TB-25K	New Hampshire	133 FIS	Pease AFB, Portsmouth
30870	TB-25N	Missouri	110 FIS	Robertson ANGB, St. Louis
30979	TB-25J	New York	102 RDCFT	Suffolk Cty Apt, Long Island
		New York	137 FIS	Westchester County Apt, White Plains
		California	195 FIS	Van Nuys MAP, Van Nuys
31508	TB-25K	New York	137 FIS	Westchester County Apt, White Plains
86746	TB-25K	Indiana	109 FIS	Hulman Field, Terra Haute
86814	TB-25K	Massachussetts	101 FIS	Otis ANGB, Fallmouth
86815	TB-25K	Michigan	172 FIS	West Kellogg Apt, Battle Creek
		New Hampshire	133 FIS	Pease AFB, Portsmouth

Key

ANGB	Air National Guard Base	MAP	Municipal Airport
Cty Apt	County Airport	RDCFT	Radar Calibration Flight Test
FIS	Fighter Interceptor Squadron	TFS	Tactical Fighter Squadron
IAP	International Airport	WRS	Weather Recon Squadron

144

This classic transport, B-25H-10, 43-4899 (N37L), is similar to NAA conversions as to pilot's side window and distinctive nose contour. The "S" type exhaust stacks were replaced by two semi collector rings. Unusual for civilian B-25s are the tip tanks and unique tail cone. Number 4899 is one of a surprising number of surviving Mitchells and may be seen on display at the Kalamazoo Aviation Museum, MI. (L.S. Smalley via Wm. T. Larkins)

At San Francisco in 1948, this beautiful B-25J, 45-8829, NL66548, was owned by the National Motor Bearing Co. (Wm. T. Larkins)

B-25H 43-4336 was transformed into a superbly customized B-25 transport for Wheeler and Ryan, an oil and gas exploration firm, shown here at Fort Worth, TX. (Robert T. O'Dell)

20 Post War Civilian B-25s

Shortly after the end of World War II a great number of military aircraft were made available to the public through the Surplus Property Division of the Reconstruction Finance Corporation. Buyers were obligated to sign an understanding that all airplanes sold by that organization were on an "as is" basis and were not considered eligible for certification by the CAA. In January 1946 new B-25s, almost entirely J models, were listed at $8,250, terms strictly cash at the listed site of the sale. New and nearly new engines were abundant and available on similarly modest terms.

The popular Mitchells were soon flown nation wide in an ever increasing number of uses. The factory converted transports served as examples for conversions to personnel carriers. Some were used as charter craft,

many were used by the film industry and a considerable number found employment by the U.S. Forest Service as fire fighting aerial tankers. By 1970 few "civilianized" bombers remained in those services having been superseded by smaller multi engine aircraft designed specifically for passenger use.

The post war trend in establishing aeronautical museums was almost too late as the numbers of World War II airplanes began to rapidly diminish. This trend did, however, create additional interest in the old warbirds and many B-25s, among other types, were acquired by the military for air shows and museum exhibits. Less functional examples became gate guards at military bases, others were easily obtained for public parks and junkers were eagerly acquired for parts.

B-25H, 43-4643, civil registry N1203 was owned by Tallmantz Aviation, Orange County Airport, CA. It was widely used for film work including the spectacular Cinerama. The rounded wing tip was replaced with a square tip a la NA-98X. Holley carburetors were replaced by Bendix and collector rings replaced the S stacks. (NAA)

Notable as one of the photo planes from the film "Battle of Britain", B-25J-30, 44-31508, ex TB-25N was photographed at Caldwell, NJ in August 1969. N6578D has been restored to airworthy condition and is based at Ocala, FL. (Robert T. O'Dell)

B-25J, 44-31104, N39E, was used as a flying test laboratory by General Electric. Shown at Teterborough, NJ in Nov 1958 it has been reported vandalized and derelict and probably now non-existent. (Robert T. O'Dell)

General Arnold's second personal transport, 44-28945 an ex VB-25J, was owned by the Edwards Oil Company as N3184G. Fitted with a revised aft hatch and collapsible air stair, Bendix carburetors and semi collector rings at Fort Worth. (Merle Olmstead)

Former B-25J, 45-8882, served in the early 1950s as the company airplane of Albert Trostel & Sons of Milwaukee. It is fitted with the 8 gun nose shell, tail fairing and dual semi-collector rings and was one of 72 incomplete but flyable B-25Js at war's end. The civil registry number was later changed to N-32T. Shown at San Francisco in Dec 1952. (Wm. T. Larkins)

B-25J-30, 44-30996, ex TB-25N was typical of many converted Mitchells. De-icers were removed from the wings although retained on the tail surfaces. Bendix carburetors replaced original Holleys and the top exhaust stacks were replaced by semi-collector rings. (AAHS)

B-25J, 45-8835, was one of the last 72 uncompleted Mitchells. This is one of the less common examples retro-fitted with two semi-collector rings on each engine. Shown at the Bendix Lab at Teterborough, NJ in Feb 1959. (Robert T. O'Dell via Paul Stevens)

Former B-25J-25, 44-30690, was photographed at Long Beach, CA in 1962. Modidfied by Hughes as a TB-25K radar trainer it still carries the radome common to such aircraft. (A.R. Krieger)

VB-25J, 44-28945, was purchased by Bendix for use as a test bed for new developmental equipment by Bendix Radio Division at Towson, MD. It is shown here with a TB-25K nose radome and classy paint job. The airplane, the facility and the air field are all gone now. (Bendix)

Modified as a fire fighting aerial tanker, former B-25J, 44-30734 was photographed near Phoenix, AZ. This airplane is another survivor and has been restored to airworthy condition by BOM Corporation, Wichita Falls, TX. (Harry Gann via Wm. T. Larkins)

148

B-25D of the RAF over Kansas shows the tail, waist and fuselage blister gun packs common to many modified 41st BG Mitchells for use in the Central Pacific. The waist and tail guns are also common to those airplanes modified for the B-25 units in North Africa and this example is probably destined for an RAF unit in that theater. (NAA)

This B-25J shows the Russian color scheme and insignia characterizing Russian Mitchells during the latter part of the war. (NAA)

PART VII

21   B-25s in Other Air Forces

The extensive use of the B-25 by Netherlands units, both in the Southwest Pacific and over Europe has already been defined in Part IV, Chapter 7. While the Dutch had a unique relationship with North American Aviation, they were but one of a legion of nineteen nations employing the B-25 under Lend Lease or various Inter-American programs.

No less than eleven South American countries had the Mitchell in their inventory, some still flying in the mid-1960s.

The Soviet Union acquired some 870 and Nationalist China received over 100, some of the latter falling into the hands of the People's Republic of China in 1946.

Three British Commonwealth nations, Great Britain, Canada and Australia, operated Mitchells as did two "national" squadrons serving within the RAF, Poland and France.

Such details as are available regarding these B-25 aircraft of foreign air forces are displayed in Appendix N.

The facing page and those following provide a picture profile of Mitchells in foreign colors.

Over Brisbane, July 1945 Flight Lieutenant Egan of the Royal Australian Air Force checks out A47-44, B-25J-25, 44-30896 from Amberly Field. (RAAF)

RCAF Mitchells B-25D-20, 41-30760, (left) and B-25D-30, 43-3303, (right) were photographed at Saskatoon, Saskatchewan, Canada in October 1958. Both show common post war exhaust system where the top S stacks were replaced by a semi-collector rings. (R. T. O'Dell)

MK II Mitchell of 98 Squadron, RAF, bombing objectives in Northern France. (NAA)

B-25D-10 of 342 Squadron (Lorraine, Free French). (E.C.P. Armees)

B-25J-30, 44-31387, top turret removed. Republic of China. (Robert T. O'Dell)

RAAF 2 Squadron at Hughes Strip, Northern Territory, Australia. KO-G in right foreground is fitted with fuselage blister gun packs as used on the V Air Force Townsville strafers. (RAAF)

Uruguayan B-25J FAU 150, 44-30269 was photographed in 1962 at Montevideo. At least three other Mitchells are hidden from view beyond No. 150. (Neky Mendiburu via Dan Hagedorn)

Venezuelan CB-25J at Opa Locka, Florida. (Dr. Gary Kuhn via Dan Hagedorn)

Propeller blades bent after a crash, Brazilian B-25J No 5135 appears to be headed for the salvage wreckers. The airplane is probably 44-30783. (Andras Keleman via Dan Hagedorn)

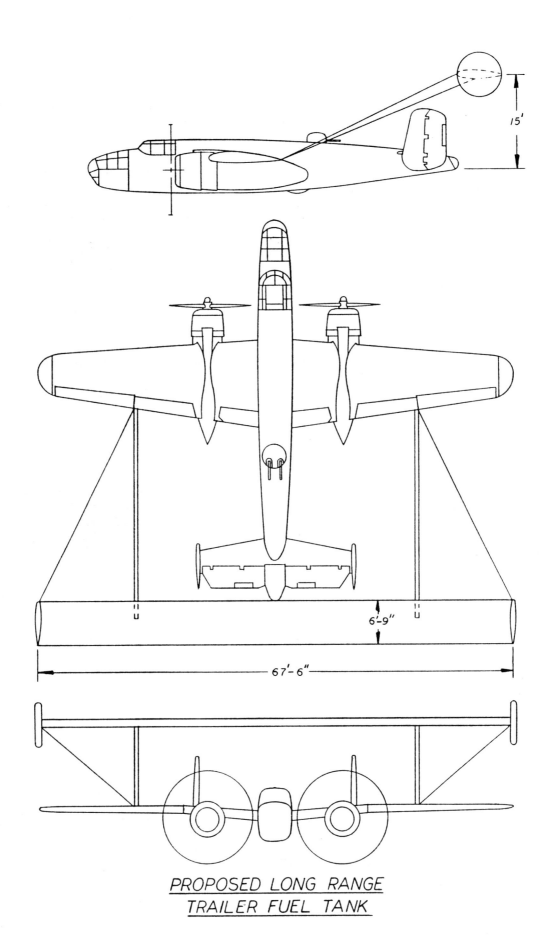

15'

6'-9"

67'-6"

PROPOSED LONG RANGE
TRAILER FUEL TANK

22 Mitchell Miscellany

In order to implement a directive to indoctrinate new flight training personnel in the "Concept of a Fighting Air Force", a demonstration team of B-25Js was organized in September, 1952 within the 3500th Pilot Training Wing at Reese AFB, Texas. The four plane unit was led by Captain Wallace McDannel, project officer and originator of the idea.

Within three days after arrival at the unit, new students were assembled on the flight line to witness precision maneuvers by the TB-25Js. The basic purpose of these demonstrations was to encourage further authorization of similar units at all Air Force Primary Schools to further motivation and competence.

Safety was paramount. All local traffic was cleared and the formation notified by the tower of any unusual circumstances or transient traffic hazardous to the demonstration. Each maneuver demonstrated the precision performance and capabilities of the TB-25 all of which had been accomplished in combat areas by less experienced pilots without undue hazard and within the performance limits of the aircraft.

Programmed maneuvers were:

a. Take-off and assembly. Elements of two takeoff simultaneously and join up within thirty seconds after the lead airplane is airborne.

b. A high speed pass at 1,000 feet in wing tip formation followed by a break-away and join-up in the opposite direction above 1,000 feet.

c. Trail formation pass at normal trail interval. The formation makes a high speed run over the runway at 50 feet, followed by a normal join-up at 1,000 feet.

d. Circuit of building area. Two 360° turns in box formation performed at 1,000 feet. Track over ground outside building area, utilizing 45° to 50° angle of bank.

e. Tactical landing from echelon utilizing 360° degree overhead approach.

Because of experience gained in the early months of the war, the necessity for very long range ferry flights appeared probable. Early in 1942 a number of schemes were investigated for increasing to 6,000 miles the range of B-17E, B-24D, B-25B and B-26C aircraft.

The choice of tank-wing trailers was made after consideration of the following other devices which were rejected because of excessive overloading of wings and landing gears.

1. Additional tanks in wings and fuselage.
2. Streamlined tanks on or under the fuselage.
3. Streamlined tanks mounted under the wings.
4. Biplane wing shaped tanks mounted on the fuselage.

Calculations were made for each aircraft to determine loading and dimensional requirements to provide the specified range with military load, cruising speed and takeoff distance to clear a fifty foot high obstacle.

Fortunately the progress of Allied forces negated the necessity of ever testing such a concept but it is presented to show its unique design fostered out of the desperation of 1942. (See drawing on Page 152)

AIR CRAFT	GROSS WT. W/TRAILER LBS.	TAKEOFF SPEED	GROUND RUN	TOTAL DIST. TO CLEAR 50' OBSTACLE
B-17E	75,900	120	3,750	4,700
B-24D	74,500	120	3,670	7,300
B-26C	54,100	150	5,380	6,900
B-25B	47,000	135	4,440	5,700

The USAF B-25 Demonstration Team at Reese AFB, Texas preparatory to one of their outstanding performances. (Wallace McDannel)

154

Developed for blind bombing of land targets from high altitude and as a navigational aid, the AN/APQ 7 high resolution "Eagle" radar was developed by the Radiation Laboratory of MIT and Bell Telephone. Production manufacturing was by Western Electric. The 18 foot span airfoil shaped unit was made of plywood and the entire system weighed 775 pounds. Too late for the war in Europe, it proved highly efficient by B-29s of the 315th Bomb Wing against Japan. B-25J, 44-30646, was one of the APQ 7 test aircraft. (NAA)

The droppable fuel tank, developed for use on fighters was tested on this B-25J at North American's Inglewood plant. (NAA)

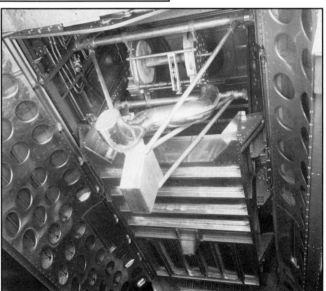

B-25 tasks included lowly duty as tow target tugs. The windless mechanism was installed in the bomb bay and a duct provided cooling air to the spool. (NAA)

B-25D equipped with BTO (Bombing Through Overcast) radar gear. (NAA)

Bendix B-25H, #43-4106, N5548N, equipped for testing the nose gear for the McDonnell F-101 Voodoo. (Bendix)

In 1951 B-25H, 43-4106, was acquired by the Bendix Aviation Corp and registered as N5548N. Terms of the purchase restricted the use of the airplane to Bendix only and for the exclusive purpose of testing and experimental work. On 17 August 1951 the company requested and received the NX designation for use in taxi tests of new brake linings, anti-skid devices, sink rate sensors, autopilot and automatic approach systems for the Air Force and Navy. The NX status was extended on 19 August 1952 so that further tests could be run for development of a steerable nose wheel and cross wind landing system.

In November 1955 No. 4106 was fitted with a full operational McDonnell F-101 Voodoo nose gear for high speed taxi and brake tests. A separate hydraulic system, wheel well and doors were required and the standard nose gear was in normal retracted position secured against actuation.

In 1960 the airplane was modified as a flying test bed for ESAR Airborne Pattern Mapping Equipment. Designated AN/FPS-46, the ESAR was an electronically steerable array radar of long range and high resolution used in space technology and communications. It was further used in developmental flight testing of the Wide Band Phased Array steerable beam radar.

The Doppler Radar System, later referred to as the Bendix Airborne Doppler Navigation System, was also tested on N5548N. This equipment provided a comparison of values of precisely measured distances against Doppler computed readout distances and was later used on transoceanic commercial aircraft.

Bendix sold the airplane in 1967.

A sink rate sensing gear was mounted under the fuselage between the main gears. Photographed at Towson, MD in 1955. (Bendix)

A second type of sink rate sensor was attached to the main gear. The bulk of the unit prevented gear retraction. (Bendix)

For crosswind landings Bendix developed a special piston type landing gear capable of limited left-right rotation. This picture clearly shows the rotated relationship of the wheel direction to the axis of the nacelle. A similar system was later used on the C-5 military transport. (Bendix)

Attempting to minimize shock strut stroke and nacelle space taken by the retracted landing gear, Bendix tested a unique eccentrically mounted main gear wheel. Much of the landing shock was absorbed by hydraulic shock mechanisms within the wheel and bearings were distributed at the periphery. The B-25 nacelle was not large enough to accommodate this unit with a pneumatic tire so the solid tire was used. (Bendix)

An all Black organization, the 477th Bomb Group was constituted on 13 May 1943 as a medium bombardment unit and assigned to the Third Air Force. Initial training was on B-26 aircraft. After a brief time the outfit was redesignated as the 477th Composite Group with one fighter and four bomber squadrons and assigned to the First Air Force. Training commenced on B-25s and P-47s and was still underway when the war ended. The 477th was inactivated in 1947.

Pilots of the USAAF 477th Composite Group, with one of their B-25Js. (NASM #90-3833)

23 Dimensional Data

Dimensional data was derived from the following drawings and documents:

NAA Report NA-5707   Design Description of Prototype
B-25H Mortimer II

NAA Report NA-5925   Aerodynamic Dimensional Data
for the B-25H Airplane
17 January 1944

USAAF AN 01-60GE-2   Erection and Maintenance
Instructions B-25J-5, -10, -15,
-20-NC; Mitchell III and PBJ-1J
Page 416

NAA Drawings:
62-00001   3 View and General Arrangement B-25
62A-00001 3 View and General Arrangement B-25A
62-00005   Fuselage Ordinates B-25
62-02114   Nacelle Ordinates B-25
      (B-25 through B-25J)
62-32003   Cowling Installation B-25
      (B-25 through B-25J)
82-42006   Exhaust Collector B-25C/D
82-00001   3 View and General Arrangement B-25C/D
98-00001   3 View and General Arrangement B-25H
98-61901   Installation - 8 Fixed .50 Caliber Nose Guns
Note: Fuselage contours between stations 70 and 304
are the same for all B-25s

HEIGHT

B-25	16' 4"
B-25 A, B, C, D	15' 9"
B-25H & J	16' 4.2"

LENGTH OVERALL

B-25, B-25A	54' 1'
B-25B, C, D	53' 0"
B-25G	50' 10"
B-25H	51'3.75"
B-25J	53' 5.75"

LANDING GEAR

Landing Gear Track	19' 4"
Main Gear Tire	47" Diameter
Nose Gear Tire	30"Diameter

TRAVEL, CONTROL SURFACES

	B-25, B-25A	B-25C, D, G	B-25H, J
Flaps	- 60°	-45°	-45°
Ailerons	+30° - 15°	+28° - 14°	+28° - 14°
Aileron Tabs	+13° - 13°	+13° - 13°	+13° - 13°
Elevators	+30° - 20°	+28° - 18°	+25° - 10°
Elevator Tabs	+12° - 12°	+4° - 20°	+4° - 20°
Rudder	+30° - 30°	+30° - 30°	+20° - 20°
Rudder tabs	+12° - 12°	+12° - 12°	+12° - 12°

Basic Data

WING

Span	67' 6.7"	Aileron area (total)	32.13 sq. ft.
Chord (at center of airplane)	154.6"	Flap area (total)	75.80 sq.ft.
Airfoil (at center of airplane)	NACA 23017	Dihedral, center of airplane	
Incidence (at center of airplane)	3° 0' 30"	to wing station 157	4° 38' 23"
Incidence at Wing Station 157.00	1° 57' 30"	Dihedral, outer wing panels	0° 21' 39" (negative)
Airfoil at Tip (Wing Station 380.38)	NACA 4409-R	Mean aerodynamic chord	116.16"
Incidence at tip (Wing Station 380.38)	0° 30' 0"	Leading edge of MAC* from leading	
Area, including ailerons	609.73 sq. ft.	edge of wing at center of airplane	12.68"

EMPENNAGE

Span between centers of rudders	22' 2"	Area, vertical stabilizers	47.80 sq. ft.
Area, horizontal stabilizer	81.8 sq. ft.	Area, rudders, including tabs	
Area, elevators, including tabs	50.6 sq ft.	and 9.6 sq. ft. of balance	43.20 sq. ft.
and 5.05 sq. ft. of balance		Area, rudder trim tabs	3.18 sq. ft.
Area, elevator trim tabs	3.12 sq. ft.		

* **Mean Aerodynamic Chord**

158

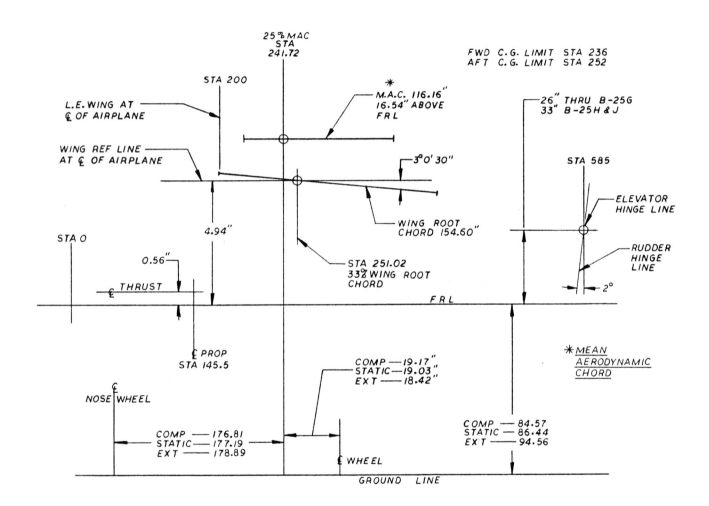

DIMENTIONAL DIAGRAM

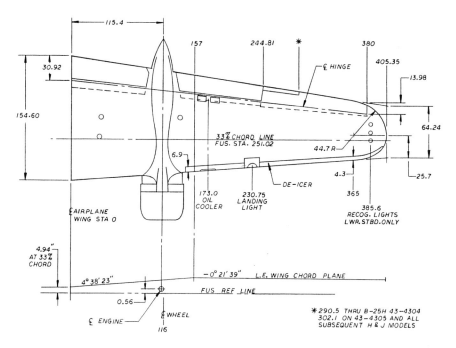

WING GEOMETRY

% OF CHORD	WING STA #0			WING STA #157			WING STA #380.37		
	DIST FROM L.E.	ORDINATES UPPER	LOWER	DIST FROM L.E.	ORDINATES UPPER	LOWER	DIST FROM L.E.	ORDINATES UPPER	LOWER
0	0	3.87		0	2.45		0	1.33	
1.25	1.93	8.01	0.16	1.49	5.37	0.30	0.84	2.36	0.22
2.50	3.86	9.80	1.54	2.99	6.67	1.21	1.68	2.82	0.32
5.00	7.73	12.14	3.32	5.99	8.37	2.37	3.36	3.48	0.89
7.50	11.59	13.68	4.62	8.98	9.53	3.18	5.03	3.98	1.13
10	15.46	14.74	5.70	11.94	10.36	3.83	6.71	4.39	1.19
15	23.19	15.95	7.49	17.96	11.38	4.88	10.07	5.04	1.15
20	30.92	16.34	8.87	23.95	11.83	5.64	13.42	5.50	1.06
25	38.65	16.28	9.88	29.93	11.93	6.20	16.78	5.80	0.95
30	46.38	15.88	10.57	35.92	11.77	6.56	20.14	5.96	0.82
40	61.84	14.33	11.25	47.90	10.84	6.89	26.85	5.90	0.68
50	77.30	12.09	11.27	59.87	9.28	6.91	33.57	5.35	0.70
60	92.76	9.33	10.81	71.84	7.24	6.72	40.28	4.35	0.89
70	108.22	6.17	9.99	83.82	4.87	6.33	47.00	3.16	1.13
80	123.68	2.73	8.86	95.79	2.30	5.74	53.71	1.89	1.30
90	139.14	-1.02	7.45	107.76	-0.40	4.86	60.42	0.68	1.15
95	146.87	-3.07	6.62	113.75	-1.82	4.29	63.78	0.17	0.91
100	154.60		5.46	119.74		3.43	67.14		0.44
L.E. RADIUS	4.92			3.20			0.75		

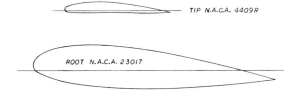

TIP N.A.C.A. 4409R

ROOT N.A.C.A. 23017

ORDINATES
WING AIRFOIL

STA	ABOVE WL 0				BELOW WL 0			
	AT ℄	BL 10	BL 20	BL 25	AT ℄	BL 10	BL 20	BL 25
4.0	11.58	5.81			6.54	0.21		
11.5	18.46	16.88			16.86	15.32		
19.0	22.13	20.78			24.94	22.96		
28.0	25.42	24.05	16.03		27.87	26.88	16.91	
40.0	28.93	27.49	20.71		29.79	29.13	23.26	
70.0	34.52	33.18	27.54	19.34	33.00	32.42	28.17	15.63
82.5	35.86	34.65	29.48	22.22	33.90	33.31	29.34	19.08
151.0	51.00	50.47	47.08		36.42	35.89	32.43	25.26
181.0	51.00	50.47	47.08					
199.0	51.00	50.47	47.08	40.27				
208.0	51.00	50.47	47.08	40.27	37.00	36.46	33.10	26.34
304.0	50.06	49.52	46.17	39.43	37.00	36.46	33.10	26.34
354.0	47.48	47.24	46.30	35.35	35.20	34.65	31.03	22.77
403.0	44.76	44.18	39.80	24.45	31.20	30.59	26.22	10.95
490.5	38.41	37.70	28.42		20.71	20.00	10.72	
576.5	34.72				7.72	6.04		
593.5	40.00	30.33			4.94	2.76		
610.0	36.28	28.73 / 1.03			2.11			
628.0	31.35 / 0.70	23.70 / 3.00						

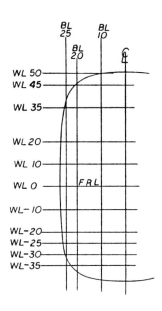

FUSELAGE
ORDINATES

HEIGHTS

STA	WL -35	WL -30	WL -25	WL -20	WL -10	WL 0	WL +10	WL +20	WL +35	WL +45	WL +50	MAX H B
4.0						10.04	7.48					10.28
11.5					14.58	16.95	16.36					17.10
19.0				14.0	18.79	20.08	19.75	11.98				20.18
28.0			14.52	18.80	21.34	22.00	21.86	17.01				22.10
40.0			18.68	21.52	23.35	23.83	23.83	20.51				23.91
70.0		17.62	22.31	24.15	25.62	26.04	26.08	24.77				26.09
82.5		19.20	23.12	24.80	26.15	26.56	26.62	25.73	8.57			26.63
151.0	14.50	22.46	25.10	26.39	27.56	27.94	28.00	27.77	26.13	22.16	12.78	28.00
181.0				26.65	27.78	28.18	28.22	28.00	26.44	22.30	12.78	28.22
199.0					27.85	28.22	28.25	28.04	26.50	22.30	12.78	28.26
208.0	16.35	23.07	25.48	26.72	27.86	28.25	28.26	28.06	26.53	22.30	12.78	28.26
304.0	16.35	23.07	25.48	26.72	27.86	28.25	28.11	27.93	26.33	21.40	3.50	28.15
354.0	6.57	21.13	24.24	25.68	26.90	27.29	27.31	27.04	25.10	17.84		27.33
403.0		12.99	21.02	23.38	25.09	25.58	25.61	25.33	22.89			26.63
490.0				9.98	20.18	21.34	21.51	21.21	16.26			21.51
576.5						14.96	16.27	16.29				16.29
593.5							15.03	14.50				15.07
610.0							13.69	13.36	4.45			13.78
628.0							12.86	11.38				12.42

FUSELAGE ORDINATES
HALF BREADTHS

Former B-25D/F-10, 43-3374 restored by NAA for 25th anniversary of Doolittle's Tokyo Raiders. Now at the USAF Museum at Dayton, OH. (NAA)

Beautifully restored, former TB-25J-30 was fitted with a TB-25K nose. (Robert Davisson)

Russian B-25, 43-1162

162

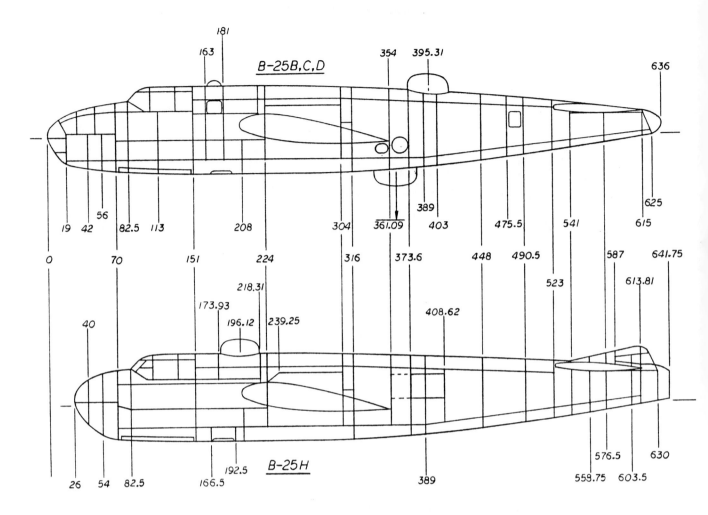

STATIONS DIAGRAM

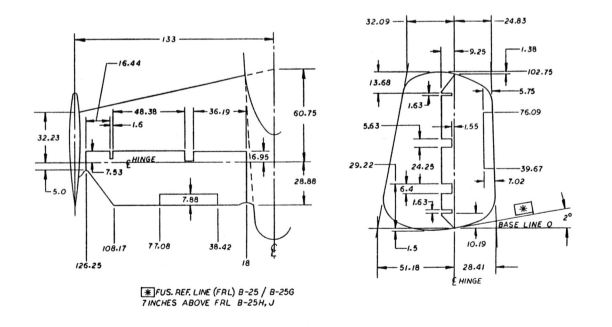

⊛ FUS. REF. LINE (FRL) B-25 / B-25G
7 INCHES ABOVE FRL B-25H, J

EMPENNAGE DETAILS

ARMAMENT DETAILS

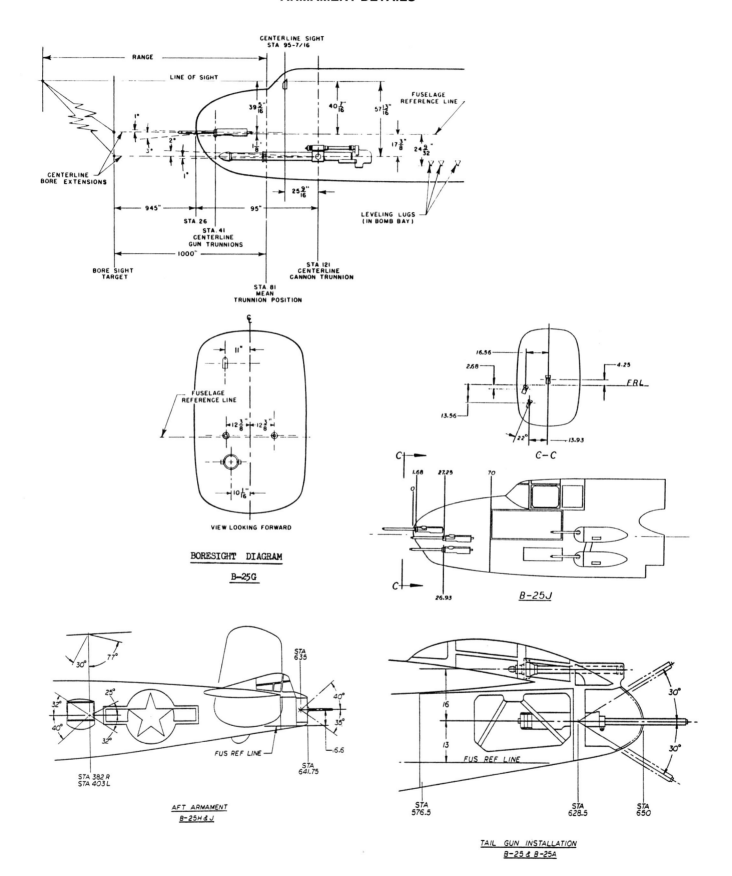

164

Fourth B-25 built, 40-2168, was factory modified for General Arnold's personal transport. (NAA)

B-25H on a test hop over the California desert. (NAA via Charles Smith)

B-25G, # 35099

B-25 No. 1, 40-2065 shown at Muroc Dry Lake, now Edwards AFB. Test pilot Vance Breese, in tie, facing the camera. (NAA)

Restored by the USMC Museum at Quantico, Virginia, B-25J-30, 44-86727, shown in 1975 at a fly-in at George AFB, CA. (Jack Urbanski)

Venezuelan B-25J believed to be taken at Fort Worth, TX. (Kenneth Wilson)

Purchased from the Catch 22 inventory, B-25J, 44-30801, is shown at Van Nuys, CA after restoration by Challenge Publications. (Norm Avery)

YELLOW ROSE, B-25J-5, 43-27868, as restored by the San Antonio wing of the Confederate AF. (CAF)

Ted Melsheimer's "Tootsie", 44-30606, a B-25J-25 in April 1992. (Charles Smith)

166

		B-25 MODEL
A	30.81	H J
B	29.50	H J
C	12.38	G
D	13.50	G H
E	2.62	H
F	3.50	H
G	1.12	G H
H	11.00	G H J
I	40.43	G H J
J	10.06	G H
K	17.38	G H
L	3.25	H J
M	18.37	H J
N	5.88	
O	11.75	
P	3.25	
Q	13.75	
R	5.25	
S	22.25	

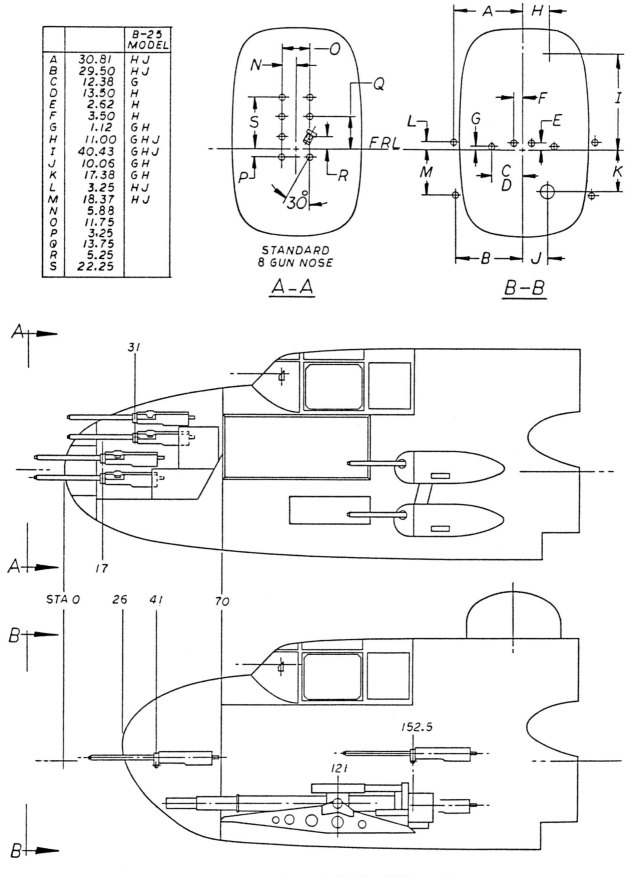

STANDARD
8 GUN NOSE

A-A

B-B

ARMAMENT DETAILS

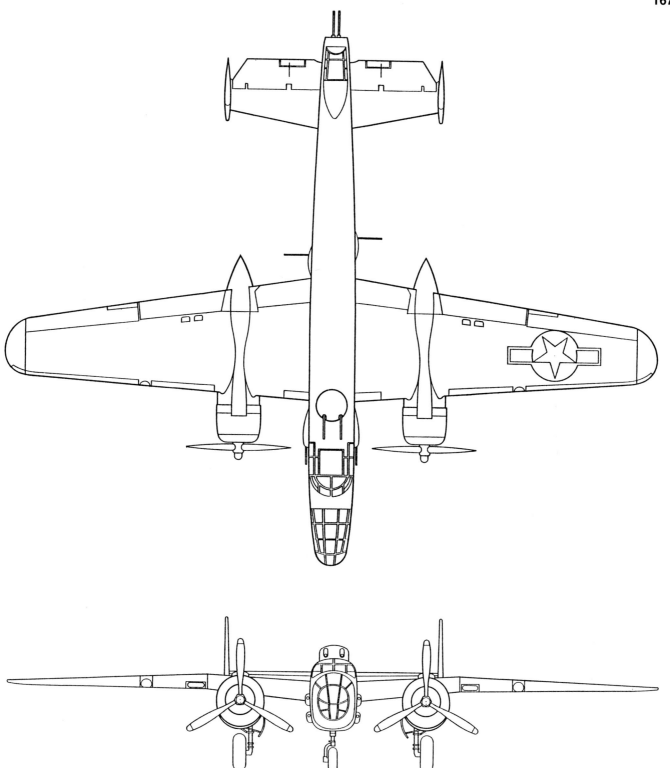

168

Engine installations on B-25, A and B models (above) were characterized by long exhaust pipes which were shortened on the first B-25C (below). Unfortunately, these pipes at night left a bright blue trail visible from such a distance as to delight the heart of any night fighter pilot. The Bendix carburetors on these early Mitchells were fitted with two different shapes of intake scoops. (NAA)

24 **Power Plant**

A product of the Wright Aeronautical Company, R-2600 engines powered all of nearly 10,000 B-25s. Headquartered at Paterson, New Jersey, WAC operated plants at Wood-Ridge, New Jersey and Lockland, Ohio and was further assisted during the war effort by the Dodge and Studebaker companies, licensees from the automotive industry. Between July 1940 and August 1945 WAC and the automotive partners produced 218,632 aircraft engines of which 47,420 were R-2600 types.[1]

A proven engine when selected for the B-25, it presented minimal risk of the engines then available or being developed. The early "A" series were built around a three piece aluminum alloy crankcase which was discontinued in favor of steel forgings which were used throughout the remainder of production.

BASIC ENGINE DATA

TYPE	TAKEOFF HP / RPM	RATED HP / RPM	LBS WEIGHT	QUANTITY	PRODUCTION DATES
R-2600-9	1700 / 2600	1500 / 2400	1987	522	4/41 - 12/41
R-2600-13	1700 / 2600	1500 / 2400	2000	13,494	4/41 - 1/44
R-2600-29	1700 / 2800	1500 / 2400	2000	18,784	6/43 - 7/45
R-2600-20	1900 / 2800	1600 / 2400	2045	14,620	2/43 - 10/45

-9, -13 and -29 engines to Wright AC Specification GR2600B655
and -20 engines to Wright AC Specification 776C-14BB-1
-9 engines equipped with Bendix Stromberg PD-13E-2 carburetors
-13, -20 and -29 engines equipped with Holley 1685HA carburetors
Post war some engines were equipped with Bendix Stromberg PR48A4
carburetors and designated as -35

Type	Radial, Static, Staggered, Twin Row, Air Cooled
Number of Cylinders	14
Bore	6.125 inches
Stroke	6.312 inches
Piston Displacement	2603 cubic inches
Compression Ratio	6.90:1
Impeller Low Gear Ratio	7.06:1
Impeller High Gear Ratio	l0.06:1
Propeller Reduction Gear Ratio	16:9
Propeller Shaft Spline Size	AN50
Overall Engine Length	76.85 inches

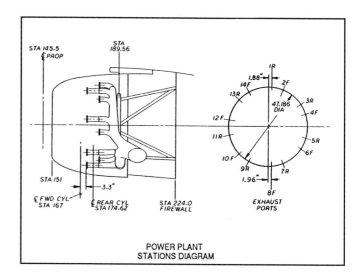

POWER PLANT
STATIONS DIAGRAM

170

This large cumbersome design from Britain was excessively heavy, high in drag and resulted in only moderate flame quenching. (NAA)

This design by the Solar Aircraft Co. also proved to be heavy, high in drag and was only partially successful. Nacelle reinforcement was necessary. It did, however, have the lowest back pressure of all the devices tested. (NAA)

NAA's fish tail design resulted in the best flame quenching of the types tested, but was heavy, high in drag and made the accessory section relatively inaccessible. Back pressure was high but within acceptable limits. (NAA)

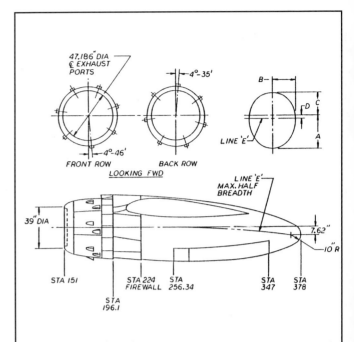

Wright Field produced this fish tail design. Night test flights showed an insignificant reduction in flame visibility. (NAA)

An improved NAA collector design. (NAA)

B-25, B-25A and B-25B models were fitted on the production line with Bendix carburetors but Holley carburetors were installed effective on the first B-25C. Although the Bendix was favored for easier maintenance it required more effective anti-icing provisions than the Holley.

There were several reasons for these changes which were considerably more involved than might be supposed. The S type exhaust stacks which attached individually to each cylinder, provided good flame dampening and low weight but occasionally broke loose from the top cylinder. The semi collector ring was therefore safer and provided better carburetor heat.

The revision to the exhaust system also necessitated removal of the S stack fairings on the cowling and the installation of patches over the resulting holes. Cowl flaps adjacent to the collector ring port were cut and reinforced. Redesigned baffles were fitted and the heat rise system was extensively modified.

Quenching of the exhaust flame was attempted with several variations. The cleanest design was the North American finger type of collector which ported the exhaust through groups of small rectangular outlets from under the trailing edge of the cowl flaps. Flame dampening was good resulting in visibility under certain conditions no farther than 300 feet. Weight was higher than desired and cracking became a frequent problem. This type was produced in considerable numbers and was fitted to several hundred C and D model airplanes, most of which were later retrofitted with the earlier collector rings or the Clayton S stacks.

This most acceptable result of the extensive flame quenching program was the individual Clayton S stack attached to each cylinder. This type became effective on the production line with the first B-25C-15, 42-32383, and all subsequent B-25s except for those airplanes fitted with the finger type collectgor. Made of porcelain enameled SAE 1020 steel, they provided a weight reduction of 53 lbs. per engine compared to the full collector rings. Cutouts and fairings were required for the cowl panels where the stacks protruded, giving an otherwise clean cowl design a rather cluttered appearance. The resulting speed loss of 9 MPH was considered an acceptable trade off. At rated power the exhaust was a dull, blue flame visible to a maximum of 150 feet. At maximum cruise, auto rich, the flame was a brighter blue and visible to 300 feet. At maximumpower, auto lean, a bright yellow exhaust was visible to a maximum of 600 feet. Field maintenance was improved with the S stacks although prolonged service resulted in some cracking problems and occasional separation of stacks on the top most cylinders with the accompanying hazards. The increase in noise as compared to collector rings ported on the outboard side of the nacelles was a general crew complaint.

The Bendix carburetor required a new intake scoop of higher and narrower shape than used on the Holley and this increase in height required revision to the

The Clayton S stack proved to be the ultimate refinement. (NAA)

For general cold weather use in Alaska and the ferry route to Russia, North American produced a winterization kit for a reduction in cooling air. Installation was quite easy. (NAA)

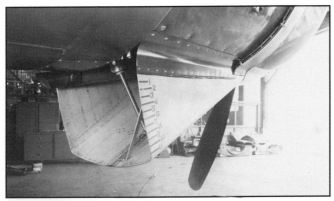

Attempting to provide increased ground cooling with another flame suppressing exhaust collector, NAA briefly experimented with a large adjustable air scoop. Little or no cooling improvement was achieved and considered a monstrosity, it was quickly forgotten. (NAA)

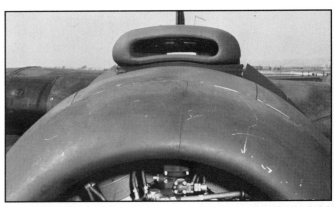

This odd carburetor intake scoop was tested on a B-25C with NAA designed finger type exhaust collector. The scoop is believed to have been fabaricated for tests with the Bendix PR48A4 carburetor. (NAA)

Four blade propellers were tested on this B-25 but the results are unknown and the type was never used on production airplanes. The type of carburetor scoop indicates that this airplane, B-25C, 42-32383, was equipped with Bendix Stromberg carburetors. (NAA)

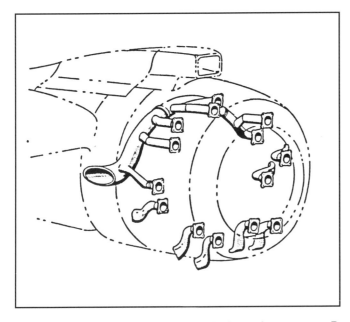

Ryan's two conversion kits were extensively used on post war B-25Js as shown on the accompanying illustration. One kit provided the necessary parts and equipment for replacement of the Holley carburetor with the Bendix Stromberg PR48S4 carburetor with a higher, narrower intake scoop. The other kit provided for the removal of the top seven S type exhaust stacks and replacement by a semi collector ring.

engine hoisting sling. Changes were also necessary to the hydraulic and fuel lines at the fire wall, carburetor quadrants, propeller controls, left nacelle heater fuel lines, pilot's auxiliary control quadrant, related electrical systems and the relocation of the oil separator and deicer system forward of the firewall.

These modification were accomplished utilizing kits fabricated by the Ryan Aeronautical Company of San Diego, California.

Notes to Chapter 24

1. Craven, W.F. and Cate, J.L., **The Army Air Forces in World War II**, Chicago, IL, The University of Chicago Press, 1953, Vol VI, pages 309,315,356

First affixed to the nation's military aircraft in 1921, the national aircraft insignia was changed four times, the final version from early 1947, continuing in use today. First flown in 1940 in military markings, B-25s continued in active service until 1958 and during that period successive models were marked with each type of insignia.

The original Type 1 comprised a white, five point star within a circular blue field equal in diameter to that of the star. A red disk equal to .31 of the star diameter was centered in the star. This insignia of forty-five inches diameter was initially applied to the B-25 fuselage and one of fifty inches diameter marked the top and under surfaces of both wings. Until December 1941 the letters US were painted under the right wing and ARMY under the left wing. Painted black, the letters were twenty-four inches high and eighteen inches wide.

Rudder stripes were standard concurrently with the Type 1 cockade. On the leading edge of the rudder a vertical blue stripe was painted equal in width to one third of the rudder width. The aft two thirds of the rudder was equally divided into seven red and six white alternating horizontal stripes spaced about the aft edge of the blue stripe. Rudder stripes were discontinued in August 1940 on B-25s leaving North American Aviation.

In February 1941 a Technical Order required removal of the cockade from the right upper wing surface and the left underwing surface and in December 1941 the large underwing letters US ARMY were discontinued.

Unchanged for twenty years, the Type 1 insignia was revised in August 1942 by the deletion of the red disk within the star. The result is illustrated as Type 2.

As World War II progressed the necessity for instant recognition of friend or foe became increasingly vital. Insignia of other air forces, Allied and enemy alike, were also of a circular field and split second recognition was frequently difficult and the range of positive identification remained relatively close.

A two inch wide yellow circle was subsequently added as a surround to the blue field. It was some improvement and was used mostly in the North African and Middle Eastern theaters of operations. Some B-25s showed a much wider yellow surround, probably the result of available paint brushes. Shown as Type 2A, its period of use was quite brief.

Progressive testing of various cockade designs indicated that the addition of rectangular white bars to each side of the circular blue field provided the best and quickest resolution. The length of the white bar was made equal to one half of the star diameter and equal in width to one fourth of the star diameter, extending outward on each side, the top edges continuous with the top edge of the horizontal star points. A red border, one sixteenth of the star diameter was added as a complete surround. This design is shown as Type 3. Aerial observations showed a marked improvement in rapid discernibility.

Although the Type 3 design was readily distinguished from German and Japanese insignia at a far greater distance than the Type 2A, it was found that at more distant ranges the red border tended to fade from view. Thus in September 1943 it was directed that the red surround be replaced by extending the blue field to replace the red and the result is shown as Type 4.

In the case of Navy or Marine aircraft painted black or midnight blue, the insignia was limited to the star and adjacent white bars. Navy gray was an authorized substitute for white on upper wing insignia.

The final insignia change became effective in early 1947 with the addition of horizontal red bars equal in width to one twelfth the star diameter, located horizontally across the centers of the white rectangular bars of the Type 4 insignia.

The prototype B-25, 40-2165, remained at North American as a test aircraft and retained the natural aluminum finish, Type 1 insignia and rudder stripes on the initial pear shaped tails only. Beginning with 40-2166 aircraft were painted olive drab at the factory and the yellow tail numbers were added by the using squadrons. At some undisclosed point the undersides of the fuselage and nacelles were painted neutral gray. This factory color scheme continued into production of early B-25H and J models but later examples of both types left the factory in natural aluminum finish to be painted in the field as circumstances warranted. Black tail numbers were standard on such aircraft.

Preparatory to the Allied invasion of Europe distinctive markings were applied to those American and British aircraft participating in the assault to assure ready identification by ground and naval forces and other aircraft. On April 18, 1944, Supreme Headquarters, Allied Expeditionary Force, issued an operational memorandum prescribing special assault markings which soon became known as invasion stripes.(See final markings panel.) The instructions set forth in this directive were to become effective on the day of invasion and to continue in use as long thereafter as considered advisable. The standard American and British national insignias remained unaffected by the addition of the invasion stripes.

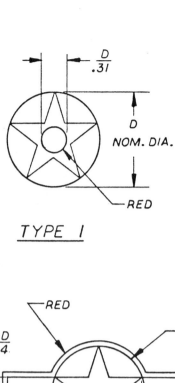

TYPE 1

BLUE FIELD
WHITE STAR
ALL INSIGNIA

TYPE 2

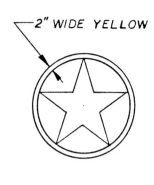

2" WIDE YELLOW

TYPE 2A

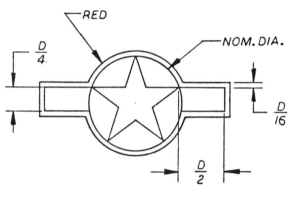

TYPE 3

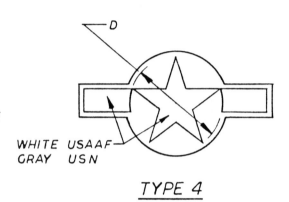

WHITE USAAF
GRAY USN

TYPE 4

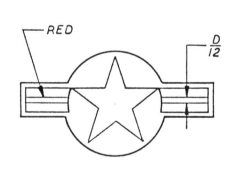

PRESENT

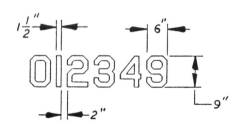

TAIL NUMBER
DETAILS

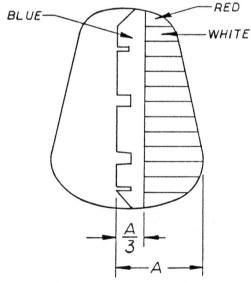

13 EQUALLY SPACED
ALTERNATE RED AND
WHITE STRIPES ON
PEAR SHAPED TAIL OF
PROTOTYPE ONLY

INSIGNIA
USA

175

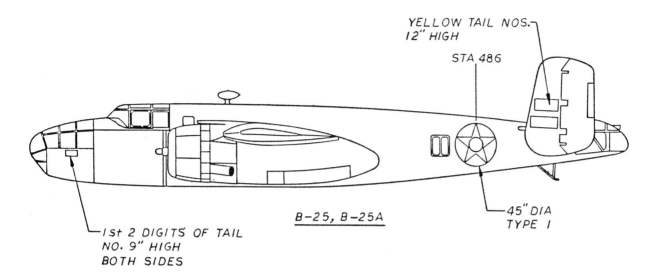

YELLOW TAIL NOS.
12" HIGH

STA 486

45" DIA
TYPE 1

B-25, B-25A

1st 2 DIGITS OF TAIL
NO. 9" HIGH
BOTH SIDES

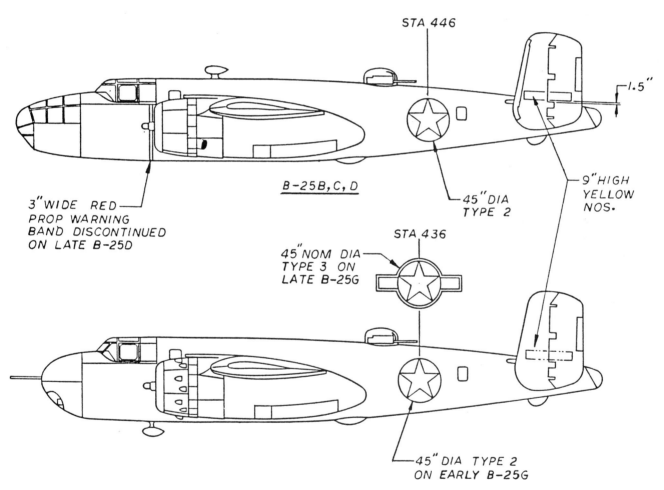

STA 446

1.5"

B-25B,C,D

45" DIA
TYPE 2

9" HIGH
YELLOW
NOS.

3" WIDE RED
PROP WARNING
BAND DISCONTINUED
ON LATE B-25D

STA 436

45" NOM DIA
TYPE 3 ON
LATE B-25G

45" DIA TYPE 2
ON EARLY B-25G

MARKINGS — USA

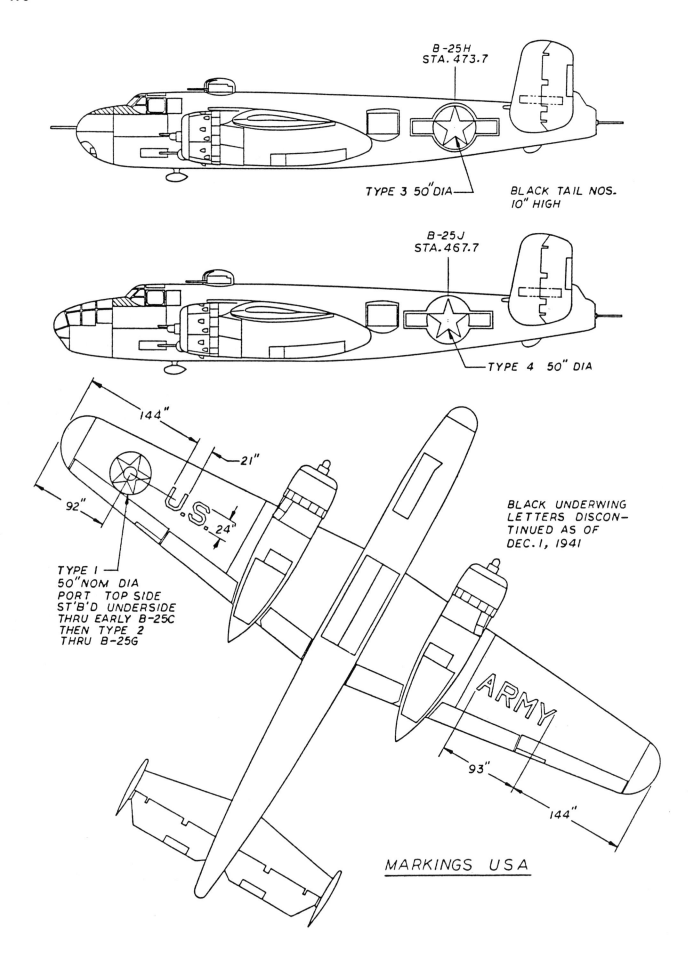

B-25H
STA.473.7

TYPE 3 50"DIA

BLACK TAIL NOS.
10" HIGH

B-25J
STA.467.7

TYPE 4 50" DIA

144"

21"

92"

U.S.

24"

TYPE 1
50"NOM DIA
PORT TOP SIDE
ST'B'D UNDERSIDE
THRU EARLY B-25C
THEN TYPE 2
THRU B-25G

BLACK UNDERWING
LETTERS DISCON-
TINUED AS OF
DEC.1, 1941

ARMY

93"

144"

MARKINGS USA

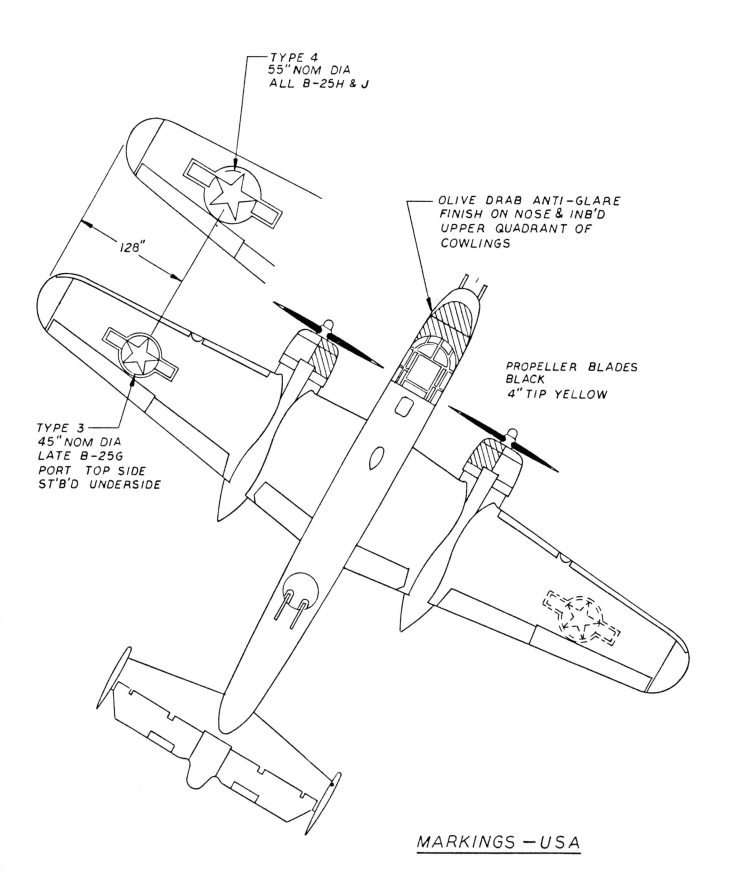

TYPE 4
55" NOM DIA
ALL B-25H & J

128"

OLIVE DRAB ANTI-GLARE
FINISH ON NOSE & INB'D
UPPER QUADRANT OF
COWLINGS

PROPELLER BLADES
BLACK
4" TIP YELLOW

TYPE 3
45" NOM DIA
LATE B-25G
PORT TOP SIDE
ST'B'D UNDERSIDE

MARKINGS—USA

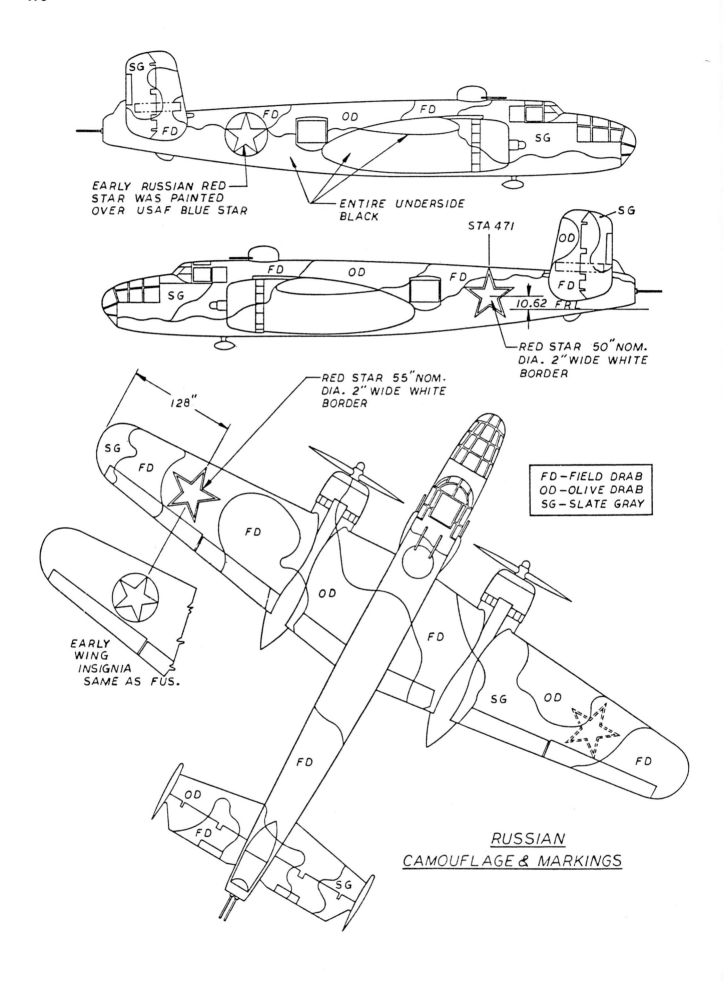

EARLY RUSSIAN RED STAR WAS PAINTED OVER USAF BLUE STAR

ENTIRE UNDERSIDE BLACK

STA 471

10.62 FRL

SG

RED STAR 50" NOM. DIA. 2" WIDE WHITE BORDER

RED STAR 55" NOM. DIA. 2" WIDE WHITE BORDER

128"

EARLY WING INSIGNIA SAME AS FUS.

FD — FIELD DRAB
OD — OLIVE DRAB
SG — SLATE GRAY

RUSSIAN
CAMOUFLAGE & MARKINGS

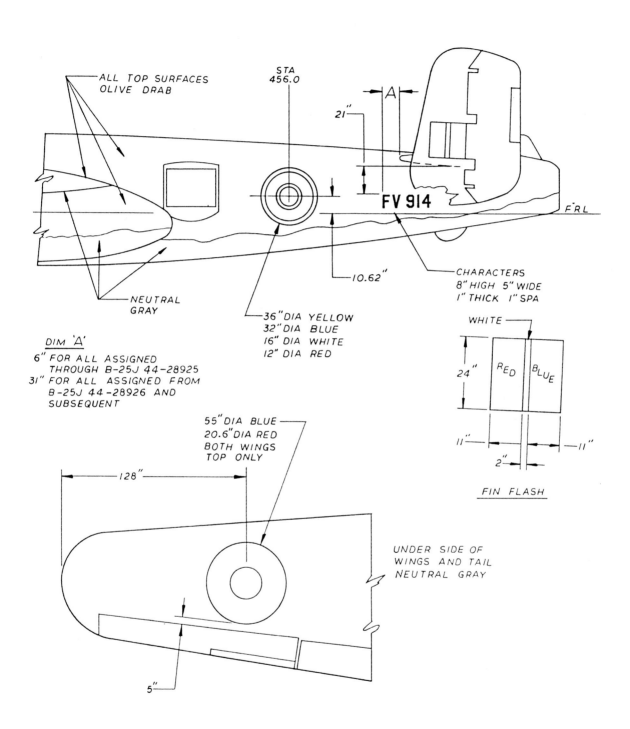

ALL TOP SURFACES OLIVE DRAB

STA 456.0

21"

A

FV 914

F·RL

NEUTRAL GRAY

10.62"

CHARACTERS 8" HIGH 5" WIDE 1" THICK 1" SPA

DIM 'A'

6" FOR ALL ASSIGNED THROUGH B-25J 44-28925
31" FOR ALL ASSIGNED FROM B-25J 44-28926 AND SUBSEQUENT

36" DIA YELLOW
32" DIA BLUE
16" DIA WHITE
12" DIA RED

WHITE

24"

RED BLUE

11"   11"

2"

FIN FLASH

55" DIA BLUE
20.6" DIA RED
BOTH WINGS
TOP ONLY

128"

UNDER SIDE OF WINGS AND TAIL NEUTRAL GRAY

5"

MARKINGS R.A.F

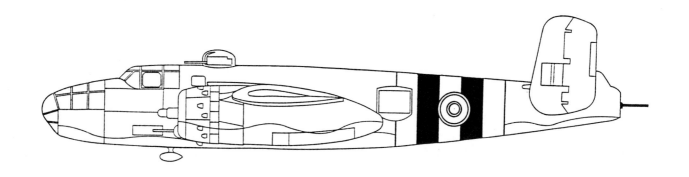

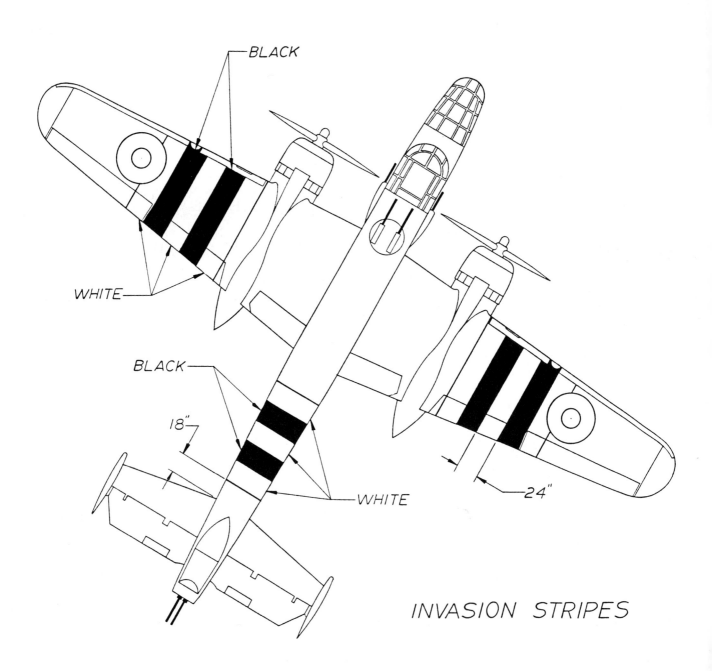

BLACK

WHITE

BLACK

18"

WHITE

24"

INVASION STRIPES

26 Existing Mitchells

Fairfax Field at Kansas City ceased to be an airport years ago and the B-25 plant and modification center turned to other uses. Mines Field, near Inglewood, California was about a mile square during WWII and has since been swallowed by the huge Los Angeles International Airport complex. Only one of the original Spanish style flight line buildings remain, preserved for posterity. The North American factory at the south east corner of the field was razed in 1979 and replaced by an air cargo loading facility.

The B-25s have long outlived the company and the plants that produced them. It is remarkable that fifty-two years after the first flight of the B-25 126 examples remain in existence world wide. Of these thirty-eight (twenty-eight in the U.S.) are airworthy and some fourteen others are being restored to airworthy condition. The list of survivors found in Appendix Z represents the efforts of several people and is believed to be the most accurate compilation to date. Because of continual changes of ownership some of the information will be obsolete at the time of printing but every effort has been made to give the reader current information.

The photographs below show a few existing B-25s as they appeared years ago.

TB-25N-25, 44-30606, N201L as it looked in November, 1958 at Oxnard, California. (Paul Stevens)

B-25J-30, 44-30988, as it looked at Reading, PA in June 1960 before acquisition by the Confederate Air Force. (Roger Besecker)

Texas Instrument used B-25J-35, 45-8811, as a company transport, retrofitted with Bendix carburetors and top semi exhaust collectors. (Merle Olmsted)

Operated as a borate bomber by Avery Aviation of Greybull, WY in 1966, B-25J-25, 44-30077, is restored to original airworthy configuration. (A.R. Krieger)

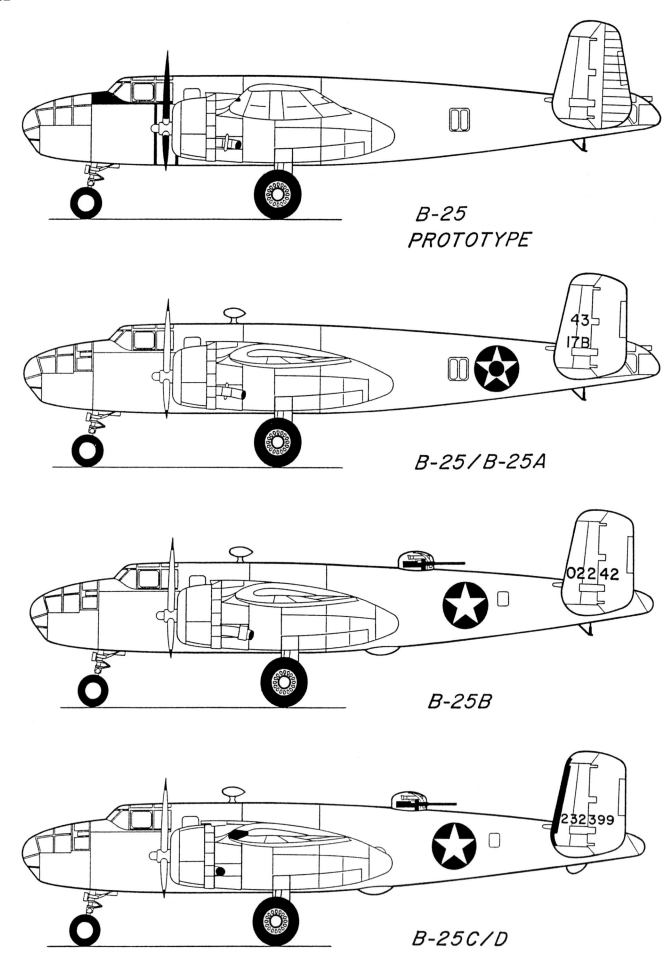

B-25
PROTOTYPE

B-25/B-25A

B-25B

B-25C/D

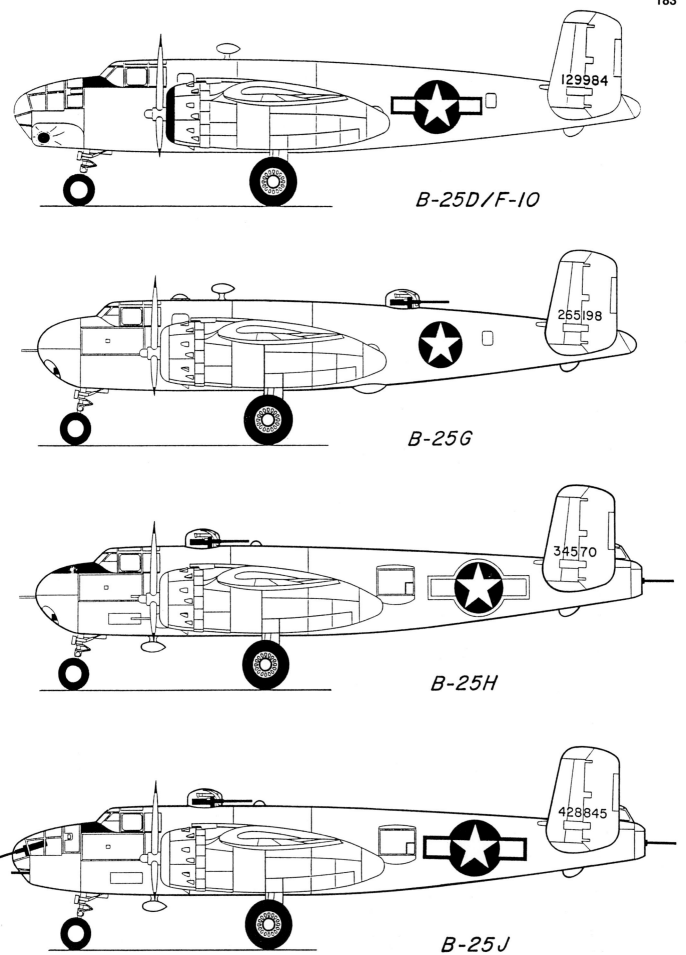

B-25D/F-10

B-25G

B-25H

B-25J

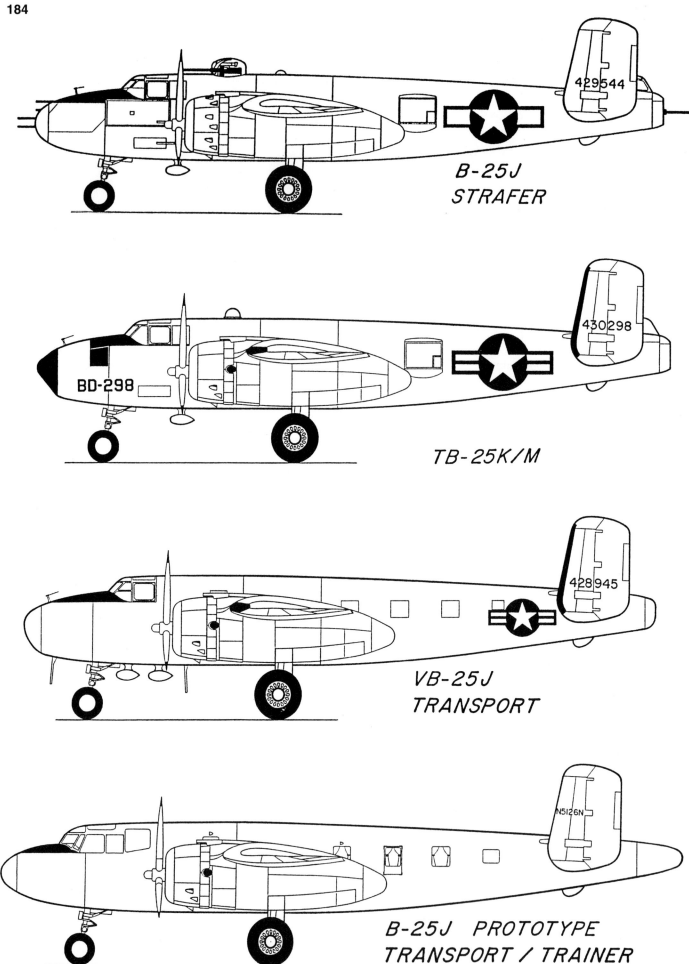

B-25J
STRAFER

429544

430298
BD-298

TB-25K/M

428945

VB-25J
TRANSPORT

N5126N

B-25J   PROTOTYPE
TRANSPORT / TRAINER

APPENDIX A
INITIAL DELIVERIES

B-25   Total 24   1 (40-2165) retained by North American
  2 Wright Field
  19 McChord Field
  2 (40-2177 & 40-2178) Chanute & Lowry Fields

B-25A   Total 40   16 17th BG McChord Field, Washington
  6 30th BG New Orleans, Louisiana
  6 43rd BG Bangor, Maine
  6 39th BG Spokane, Washington
  6 44th BG MacDill Field, Florida
  (1) to Wright Field until B-25B available

B-25B   Total 120   3 40-2229/2231 to Patterson for service tests
  3 40-2232/2234 to Wright Field
  2 40-2236/2237 Lend Lease to Russia

APPENDIX B
B-25s MODIFIED AS F-10s

41-29875	41-29927	41-30427
41-29876	41-29929	41-30554
41-29877 RCAF 894	41-29930	41-30580*
41-29878	41-29932	43-3371
41-29879	41-29970	43-3372
41-29880	41-29984	43-3416
41-29881	41-29987	43-3419
41-29883	41-29988	43-3433
41-29884	41-29989	43-3434
41-29885	41-29990	43-3437
41-29886 RCAF 891	41-29991	43-3438
41-29887	41-30132	43-3439
41-29888	41-30181	43-3440
41-29924 RCAF 892	41-30195 RCAF 893	43-3444
41-29926	41-30426	43-3446

*Probably F-10 stationed Talara, Peru

APPENDIX C
USN/USAAF PBJ SERIAL NUMBERS

Type	USN	USAAF
PBJ-1C	34998/35002	42-64502/42-64506
	35003/35022	42-64602/42-64621
	35023/35047	42-64708/42-64732
PBJ-1D	35048/35072	41-30730/41-30754
	35073/35096	42-87157/42-87180
PBJ-1G	35097	42-65031
PBJ-1D	35098/35122	42-87181/42-87205
	35123/35147	43-3320/43-3344
	35148/35183	43-3570/43-3605
	35184	43-3651
	35185	43-3655
	35186/35193	43-3771/43-3778
PBJ-1J	35194/35195	43-3985/43-3986
PBJ-1D	35196/35202	43-3837/43-3843
PBJ-1J	35203/35207	43-27511/43-27515
	35208/35214	43-27681/43-27687
	35215/35221	43-27904/43-27910
	35222/35228	43-28174/43-28180
	35229/35238	44-28792/44-28801
	35239/35248	44-29064/44-29073
	35249	44-29276
PBJ-1H	35250/35251	43-4659/43-4660
	35252	43-4667
	35253	43-4669
	35254/35256	43-4671/43-4673
	35257	43-4676
	35258	43-4710
	35259	43-4656
	35260	43-4670
	35261	43-4675
	35262/35279	43-4685/43-4702
	35280	43-4471

APPENDIX C (cont.)
USN/USAAF PBJ SERIAL NUMBERS

Type	USN	USAAF
PBJ-1H	35281	43-4482
	35282	43-4492
	35283/35285	43-4542/43-4544
	35286/35288	43-4591/43-4593
	35289/35291	43-4682/43-4684
	35292	43-4655
	35293	43-4658
	35294/35296	43-4664/43-4666
	35297	43-4709
PBJ-1J	35798/35820	44-30509/44-30531
	35821/35824	44-30353/44-30356
	35825/35829	44-30693/44-30697
	35830/35837	44-30703/44-30710
	35838/35840	44-30716/44-30718
	35841/35844	44-30961/44-30964
	35845/35848	44-30972/44-30975
	35849/35860	44-30980/44-30991
	35861/35876	44-31089/44-31104
	35877/35879	44-30849/44-30851
	35880	44-30856
	35881/35900	44-31277/44-31296
	35901/35920	44-31444/44-31463
	38980/38988	44-29277/44-29285
	38989/38998	44-29290/44-29299
	38999/39012	44-29604/44-29617
	64943/64948	44-29618/44-29623
	64949/64955	44-29788/44-29794
	64956/64962	44-29801/44-29807
	64963/64968	44-29814/44-29819
	64969/64972	44-29510/44-29513
	64973/64987	44-29870/44-29884
	64988/64992	44-29897/44-29901
PBJ-1H	88872	43-4530
	88873	43-4638
	88874	43-4654
	88875	43-4661
	88876	43-4703
	88877	43-4704
	88878/89050	43-4711/43-4883
	89051	43-4705
	89052/89071	43-5028/43-5047

APPENDIX D
PBJ's IN CONTINENTAL USA
(As of 31 December 1944)

Cherry Point, NC

HQ. MAG-62	1	PBJ-1C
	1	PBJ-1D
SS-62	1	PBJ-1C
	1	PBJ-1D
	151	PBJ-1H
	57	PBJ-1J
VMB-453	6	PBJ-1D
	3	PBJ-1H
	5	PBJ-1J
VMB-463	6	PBJ-1H
	2	PBJ-1J
VMB-473	1	PBJ-1C
	1	PBJ-1D
	2	PBJ-1H
VMB-621	1	PBJ-1D
	6	PBJ-1H
	1	PBJ-1J
VMB-623	2	PBJ-1D
	12	PBJ-1H
VMB-624	2	PBJ-1D

Cherry Point, NC (cont.)

VMB-624	10	PBJ-1H
	1	PBJ-1J
Edenton, NC		
MTS-812	17	PBJ-1C
	1	PBJ-1D
MTS-813	7	PBJ-1C
	5	PBJ-1D
	3	PBJ-1H
Kingston, NC		
VMB-483	2	PBJ-1D
	1	PBJ-1G
	1	PBJ-1H
	2	PBJ-1J
Newport, AR		
SS-1P	14	PBJ-1H
VMB-614	1	PBJ-1J
VMB-622	8	PBJ-1H
	1	PBJ-1J
San Diego, CA		
HQ.Mar F Air West	1	PBJ-1H

Pool: Undergoing Reconditioning 9 PBJ-1C
       Minimal Repairs 2 PBJ-1H

Total 348

APPENDIX E
PBJs ON STRENGTH
30 June 1944

VMB-423	10	PBJ-1D	Mag 14	Pacific
VMB-433	15	PBJ-1D	Mag 61	Pacific
VMB-443	15	PBJ-1D	Mag 61	Pacific
HQ SQ 62	17	PBJ-1C	Mag 62	Cherry Point, NC
	158	PBJ-1H	Mag 62	Cherry Point, NC
	12	PBJ-1J	Mag 62	Cherry Point, NC
VMB-611	15	PBJ-1D		Pacific
VMB-612	4	PBJ-1C		
	16	PBJ-1D		
VMB-613	20	PBJ-1H		Pacific
	4	PBJ-1J		
VMB-614	20	PBJ-1H		
	4	PBJ-1J		
VMB-621	15	PBJ-1H		
	2	PBJ-1J		
VMB-622	6	PBJ-1H		
	2	PBJ-1J		
VMB-623	5	PBJ-1H		
	2	PBJ-1J		
MCAS	34	PBJ		
Edenton,NC		Total 376		

PBJ Acceptances by Year

1943	188
1944	395
1945	123

APPENDIX F
PBJ ASSIGNMENTS

VMB-412 43-64964
VMB-413 43-64950, 64954, 64958, 64960, 64963, 64967
VMB-423 43-64946, 64947, 64959
VMB-433 43-64949, 64961, 64966
VMB-443 43-64943, 64944, 64945, 64946, 64947, 64949, 64962
VMB-453 43-88906, 88907, 89018
VMB-463 43-88883, 88904, 88980, 88988, 88999
VMB-473 43-88908,88911
VMB-483 43-88911
VMB-611 43-64951, 64957, 64965, 64971, 64974,64975, 64980
VMB-612 43-64952, 64956,64970, 64973, 64979, 64981, 64983, 64988
VMB-614 43-88874, 89019
VMB-621 43-88879, 88881, 88884, 88888, 88889, 88895, 88913, 89024, 89030
VMB-622 43-88996, 88997, 89019, 89021, 89031, 89032, 89033, 89034, 89035, 89036
VMB-623 43-88889, 88890, 88891, 88902, 88905, 89000, 89015, 89016, 89026, 89030
VMB-624 43-88894, 88896, 88898, 88899, 88901, 89001,89024

APPENDIX G
DUTCH LEND LEASE FOR 60 AIRCRAFT

U.S. NO.	ACCPTD N.E.I. HAMILTON FLD	ASSIGNMENT ALL DATES 1942 UNLESS NOTED
41-12457	6 Feb	Not ferried out, to Russia 31 May
41-12440	13 Feb	Not ferried out*
41-12445	2 Mar	To India, RAF 12 April*
41-12468	2 Mar	To India, Crashed Accra, Africa on delivery
41-12508	2 Mar	To India, RAF 12 April, later to 7 BG
41-12439	3 Mar	To Australia, 18 Sq NEI, 12 Apr*
41-12444	3 Mar	To Australia,direct to 3 BG
41-12464	3 Mar	To Australia*
41-12466	3 Mar	To Australia to NEI; to 3 BG 6 April
41-12502	7 Mar	To Australia to 2BG 23 April
41-12437	11 Mar	To Australia to 18 Sq NEI, 12 April*
41-12515	11 Mar	To Australia 3BG 18 April
41-12441	13 Mar	To Australia, 3 BG 6 April
41-12511	13 Mar	To Australia, 3 BG 6 April. Write off in USA, 26 Nov
41-12462	14 Mar	To Australia to NEI, Damaged, to 3BG in Aug.
41-12489	15 Mar	To Australia, direct to 3BG 18 April

APPENDIX G (cont.)
DUTCH LEND LEASE FOR 60 AIRCRAFT

U.S. NO.	ACCPTED N.E.I. HAMILTON FLD	ASSIGNMENT ALL DATES 1942 UNLESS NOTED
41-12500	15 Mar	Not ferried out
41-12487	16 Mar	To Australia, arrival 29 April
41-12442	17 Mar	To Australia to NEI; to 3 BG 6 April
41-12455	17 Mar	To Australia to NEI; to 3BG 6 April
41-12494	17 Mar	To Australia to NEI; Cannibalized; to USAAF 12 July
41-12495	17 Mar	To India 10th AF 9 June; remained with RAF 681 Sq
41-12496	17 Mar	To Australia to NEI; to 3BG 6 April
41-12507	17 Mar	To India to 10th AF 9 June. Remained with RAF 681 Sq
41-12509	17 Mar	To India to 10th AF 9 June. Remained with RAF 681 Sq
41-12443	18 Mar	To Australia to NEI; to 3 BG 6 Aprll
41-12498	18 Mar	To Australia to NEI; to 3 BG 6 April
41-12472	19 Mar	To Australia to NEI; to 3 BG 6 April
41-12480	19 Mar	To Australia to NEI; to 3 BG 6 April
41-12481	19 Mar	To Australia to NEI; Written off April
41-12483	19 Mar	To Australia to NEI; 3 BG 6 April
41-12485	19 Mar	To Australia to NEI; to 3 BG 9 April
41-12499	19 Mar	To Australia to 3 BG 6 April
41-12482	20 Mar	To Australia to NEI; 18 Sq 12 Apr; to USAAF 3 Sep
41-12514	20 Mar	To Australia to NEI; to 3 BG 6 Apr
41-12476	21 Mar	To Australia to NEI; to 3 BG 6 April
41-12478	21 Mar	To Australia to 3 BG 18 Apr
41-12484	21 Mar	To Australia to 3 BG 18 Apr
41-12501	21 Mar	To Australia to NEI 18 Sq 1 Apr, to USA 3 Sep
41-12438	26 Mar	To Australia to 3 BG 26 Apr
41-12470	26 Mar	To Aust. to AAF 16 Apr, to NEI 27 Jul
41-12497	26 Mar	To Australia to 3 BG 26 Apr
41-12447	1 Apr	To Australia to 3 BG 28 Apr
41-12448	1 Apr	To Australia to 3 BG 28 Apr
41-12449	1 Apr	To Australia to 3 BG 30 Apr
41-12450	1 Apr	To Australia to 3 BG 23 Apr
41-12451	1 Apr	To Australia to 3 BG 23 Apr
41-12452	1 Apr	Not ferried out; to USA
41-12486	1 Apr	To Australia to 3 BG 22 Apr
41-12488	1 Apr	To Australia to AAF 30 Apr; to NEI 1 Jun 1943
41-12490	1 Apr	To Australia to 3 BG 22 Apr
41-12491	1 Apr	To Australia to 3 BG 28 Apr
41-12503	1 Apr	Not ferried out. To USA crashed 11 July
41-12506	1 Apr	Delayed on ferry. To China 20 Jul 1943
41-12512	1 Apr	To 10th AF, USA, 21 May
41-12513	1 Apr	To AAF, wrecked in Liberia 4 Oct
41-12454	22 Apr	Not ferried out
41-12460	22 Apr	Not ferried out
41-12493	Unkn	To India, damaged in ferry. Returned to USAAF
41-12510	Unkn	To India, damaged in ferry. Returned to USAAF

*Eventually to USAAF

APPENDIX H

NETHERLANDS PURCHASING COMMISSION
10 Rockefeller Plaza, New York, New York

In Reply Refer to : Luchtvaart Dept.   No. 4558L/NA
September 8, 1942

Lt. Col. C.H. Dyson
Materiel Command, A.A.F,
Room 4337 Munitiions Building
Washington, D.C.

Subject: Delivery of Airplanes to the Netherlands Indies Government

Dear Col. Dyson:

I wish to summarize the status of the subject matter. It is my understanding that you will try to make the following disposition of our aircraft:

The six(6) planes which left West Palm Beach will be considered as Lend-Lease deliveries to the Royal Air Force

The two (2) planes which were damaged at West Palm Beach will be returned to the U.S Army Air Forces.

You will assume that the twenty-four (24) planes which left from Hamilton Field were delivered to us, and that General MacArthur has only loaned us eighteen (18) aircraft which will be replaced by eighteen (18) planes to be delivered to him on Project MX.

The eighteen (18) planes which, after arriving in Australia, should be transferred to the Netherlands Indies Squadron are:

41-12885	41-12912	41-12914
41-12916	41-12919	41-12933
41-12934	41-12935	41-12936
41-12716	41-29722	41-29717
41-29715	41-29723	41-29725
41-29719	41-29705	41-29798

It is, therefore, our understanding that the Netherlands Purchasing Commission will pay for the twenty four (24) planes which left from Hamilton Field.

Very truly yours,
NETHERLANDS PURCHASING COMMISSION
Army Aviation Department
(s) Major E.J.G. teRoller

APPENDIX I
ROYAL NETHERLANDS FLYING SCHOOL B-25s *

B-25 Model	US No.	Contract	Cost to Dutch	Date del to Dutch	Date Ret to USAAF
C-5	42-53394	NPC 7131	$165,759	19 Nov 42	24 Feb 44
C-5	42-53395	"	"	16 Jan 43	7 Mar 44
C-5	42-53396	"	"	19 Nov 42	6 Mar 44
C-5	42-53397	"	"	19 Nov 42	7 Mar 44
C-5	42-53391	"	"	22 Dec 42	21 Feb 44
C-5	42-53407	"	"	26 Nov 42	21 Feb 44
C-5	42-53490	"	"	15 Dec 42	24 Feb 44
C-5	42-53491	"	"	15 Dec 42	9 Mar 44
C-5	42-53492	"	"	16 Jan 43	8 Mar 44
C-5	42-53493	"	"	16 Jan 43	8 Mar 44
C-25	42-64781	AC 27390	$151,216	22 May 43	10 Mar 44
C-25	42-64782	"	"	22 May 43	5 Mar 44
C-25	42-64783	"	"	22 May 43	21 Feb 44
C-25	42-64784	"	"	22 May 43	21 Feb 44
C-25	42-64785	"	"	22 May 43	2 Mar 44
D-15	41-30472	AC 19341	$195,538	24 Apr 43	21 Feb 44
D-15	41-30491	"	"	24 Apr 43	21 Feb 44
D-15	41-30499	"	"	24 Apr 43	21 Feb 44
D-15	41-30500	"	"		Crashed
D-15	41-30501	"	"	24 Apr 43	2 Mar 44

* At Jackson, Mississippi

APPENDIX J
B-25s of 320 SQ (RAF) ROYAL NETHERLANDS NAVAL AIR SERVICE

MLD No **	Code Letter	US No	Taken on Charge	Struck Off Charge	Disposition
FR 141	B	42-32272	3 Aug 43	20 Mar 44	Lost in Action
FR 142	F	73	19 Apr 43	26 Apr 44	Lost in Action
FR 143	A,S	74	17 Mar 43	9 Aug 44	Lost in Action
FR 144	B	75	20 Mar 43	30 Jul 43	Ditched
FR 145*^	P	76	15 Jan 45	15 Aug 45	to RAF
			6 Mar 47	30 Sep 49	Scrapped
FR 146	O	77	6 Jul 43	26 Nov 43	Lost in Action
FR 147	C	80	19 Mar 43	20 Aug 43	Ditched
FR 148		82		29 May 43	Crashed in ferry
FR 149	D,N	83	17 Mar 43	12 Jun 44	Lost in Action
FR 150	W	84	1 Jun 44	8 Jun 44	Crashed. Mid Air
FR 151	C	85	6 Sep 43	20 Jun 44	Lost in Action
FR 152	W	86	5 Jan 43	28 Apr 43	Accident
FR 153			Nt issued		Lost in transit
FR 154			"		"
FR 155			"		"
FR 156*^	V,Y	42-32342	18 Jul 43	15 Aug 45	To RAF
			6 Mar 47	30 Sep 49	Scrapped
FR 157*^	X,D	43	23 Jul 43	15 Aug 45	To RAF
			6 Mar 47	30 Sep 49	Scrapped
FR 158	W	44	21 Jun 44	29 Jul 44	Lost in Action
FR 159*^	N.J.B	45	6 Jul 43	15 Aug 45	To RAF
			6 Mar 47	30 Sep 49	Scrapped
FR 160*#	J	42-32346	23 Apr 44	15 Aug 45	To RAF
			6 Mar 47	30 Sep 49	Scrapped
FR 161*^	O	47	22 Jun 44	15 Aug 45	To RAF
			6 Mar 47	30 Sep 49	Scrapped
FR 162	P	48	14 Jul 43	25 Oct 43	Write off
FR 163*#	R	49	Jan 45	15 Aug 45	To RAF
			6 Mar 47	30 Sep 49	Bttle Dmge,Scrp
FR 164	D	50	26 May 44	25 Dec 44	Write off
FR 165	S,K	51	26 Jul 43	9 Feb 45	Crshed, Mid air
FR 166	R	52	17 Jul 43	25 Oct 43	Lost in Action
FR 167*	V	53	29 May 44	19 Nov 44	Landing Damage
			6 Mar 47	26 Mar 54	Write off
FR 168*	E	42-32513	14 Apr 43	7 Nov 43	Lndg dmg, reprd
			6 Mar 47	6 Feb 54	To school
FR 169*	L	14	27 Jun 43	25 Oct 43	Lding dmg,reprd
			6 Mar 47	15 Aug 51	Write off
FR 170*#	G	15	16 May 43	15 Aug 45	ToRAF
			6 Mar 47	30 Sep 49	Scrapped
FR 171*		16	6 Mar 47	11 Feb 48	Scrapped
FR 172		42-64688	19 Jul 43	14 Aug 44	Write off
FR 173*	J	89	15 Jun 43	22 Mar 44	Dmgd, reprd
			6 Mar 47	24 Jul 53	To museum
FR 174	K	90	23 Jun 43	28 Oct 43	Lost in action
FR 175*#	W	91	12 Nov 43	4 Apr 44	Dmgd, repaired
			6 Mar 47	30 Sep 49	Scrapped
FR 176	P	42-64786	9 Nov 43	24 Oct 44	Crashed
FR 177	M	87	22 Nov 43	18 Mar 44	Emrgncy Lnding
FR 178	W	88	21 Jul 43	25 Oct 43	Lost in Action
FR 179	T	89	12 Nov 43	7 Jul 44	Lost in action
FR 180	H	41-30720	30 Oct43	18 Mar 44	Ditched
FR 181	K,R	21	9 Nov 43	13 Jan 45	Lost in action
FR 182	R	24	9 Nov 43	8 Jun 44	Mid air/FR150
FR 183*	E	25	21 Sep 43	15 Aug 43	To RAF
			6 Mar 47	16 Jan 48	
FR 184	U	41-30804	9 Nov 43	4 May 44	Ditched
FR 185	Z	41-30812	13 Nov 43	25 Jul 44	Lost in action
FR 186	B	42-87132	22 Mar 44	19 Dec 44	Write off
FR 187			Unassgnd		
FR 188*#	H	42-87262	19 Mar 44	15 Aug 45	To RAF
			6 Mar 47	30 Sep 49	Scrapped
FR 189*^	F	63	29 May 44	25 Dec 44	Damgd, Rpaird
			6 Mar 47	30 Sep 49	Scrapped
FR 190	E	64	16 Mar 44	31 Aug 44	Write Off
FR 191	Y,A	65	23 Nov 43	12 Jun 44	Ditched

APPENDIX J (Cont.)

MLD No	Code Letter	U.S. No	Taken on Charge	Struck Off Charge	Disposition
FR 192*	M	41-30791	7 Jun 44	15 Aug 45	To RAF
			6 Mar 47	11 Feb 48	Scrapped
FR 193*	L	92	23 Mar 44	15 Aug 45	To RAF
			6 Mar 47	29 Mar 53	To Museum
FR 194*		94		15 Aug 45	To RAF
			6 Mar 47	15 Aug 51	Write off
FR 195*	R	95	12 Jun 44	11 Sep 44	Damgd, Reprd
			6 Mar 47	1 May 52	Write off
FR 196*	T	96	13 Jun 44	25 Aug 45	Damgd, Reprd
			6 Mar 47	21 Jul 48	Crashed
FR 197*#		99		15 Aug 45	To RAF
			6 Mar 47	30 Sep 49	Scrapped
FR 198*	C	41-30838	23 Jun 44	16 May 45	Damgd, Reprd.
			6 Mar 47	16 Jan 48	
FR 199*	N,M	42-87261	16 Jun 44	14 Jun 45	Damgd, reprd
			6 Mar 47	4 May 54	Write Off
FR 200*^	Q,F	42-87137	23 Mar 44	15 Aug 45	To RAF
			6 Mar 47	30 Sep 49	Crashed
FR 201*	Z	42-87322	27 Jul 44	9 Aug 44	Damgd, reprd.
			6 Mar 47	11 Feb 48	Scrapped
FR 202	G	23	3 Mar 44	23 Apr 45	Write Off
FR 203				10 Nov 43	Crshd in Ferry
FR 204	S	58	6 Mar 44	24 Jan 44	Lost in action
FR 205	O	81	13 Dec 43	13 Jun 44	Lost in action
FR 206*	J	42-87405	25 Mar 44	15 Apr 44	Damgd, reprd
			6 Mar 47	29 Aug 53	Write Off
FR 207	U	08	9 May 44	14 Jun 45	Write Off

* Airplanes remaining from Lend Lease assignment at Kirkbride in 1945
^ Airplanes cannibalized in UK to keep others serviceable
# Scrapped for parts in Holland

(Opposite) Royal Netherlands Air Service, 320 Sq. Borrowed these Mitchell II airplanes from the RAF

** MLD   Marine Luchtvaart Dienst (Naval Avn. Svc)

RAF Number	Code Letter	US Number	Taken on Charge	Struck Off Charge
FL 168	H		9 Apr 43	5 Aug 43
194				15 Feb 44
202	T		9 Apr 43	5 Aug 43
679	U		14 Apr 43	4 Aug 43
686	M		14 Apr 43	17 Aug 43
FV 928				29 Jan 44
969			11 Jun 44	13 Jun 44
970	K	41-30832	16 Jun 44	22 Jan 45
FW 164			10 Jun 44	13 Jun 44
178	S	43-3287	11 Aug 44	15 Aug 45
187	W	-3393	4 Aug 44	15 Sep 44
193	X	-3459	18 Aug 44	25 Dec 44
197	A	-3482	15 Jun 44	19 Nov 44
212	J	-3478	30 Oct 44	9 Feb 45
219	J	-3539	15 Aug 44	18 Oct 44
227	P	-3547	29 Oct 44	13 Jan 45
229		--3549	Aug 45	15 Aug 45
258	W	-3693	11 Aug 44	19 Aug 44
HD 305		-3759	Aug 45	15 Aug 45
306	N	-3760	6 Nov 44	1 Apr 45
346	V	43-3874	3 Dec 44	15 Aug 45
349	T	43-27755	1 Feb 45	5 Mar 45
358	J	-27764	19 Feb 45	15 Aug 45
364	X,H	-27992	30 Dec 44	15 Aug 45
367	G	-27995	23 Apr 45	15 Aug 45
392	A	44-28734	27 Nov 44	15 Aug 45
393	K	-28735	19 Feb 45	5 Mar 45
KJ 579	W	-28770	29 Apr 45	15 Aug 45
587	F	-28953	4 Jan 45	24 Feb 45
593	T	-28959	26 Apr 45	15 Aug 45
596	Z	-28965	11 Feb 45	15 Aug 45
603	Y	-28972	24 Apr 45	15 Aug 45
629	T	-29158	6 Mar 45	25 Apr 45
678	K	-29636	6 Mar 45	30 Mar 45
700	U	-29686	16 Jun 45	14 Aug 45
701	C	-29687	17 May 45	18 Aug 45
746	K	-29979	16 Jun 45	18 Aug 45

APPENDIX K

B-25 ALLOCATIONS TO NETHERLANDS EAST INDIES AIR FORCE AND ROYAL AUSTRALIAN AIR FORCE

NEIAF No.	RAAF No.	U.S. No	Date Recd	Squadron	Disposition
N5-128		41-12935	24 Aug 42	18	18 Sq 45/46, OOS 46 Take Off Crsh 20 Jan 45 SOC Feb 45
-129		41-12916	24 Aug 42		NEI Pool, RAPWI Detach. 45/46, TB-25 49 DVM
-130		41-12914	24 Aug 42	18	Crash at Cressy 30 July 45; Scrapped 14 Aug 45
-131		41-12936	24 Aug 42		NEI Pool, 18 Sq 45, OOS 47, 20 Sq 47/48 C to C TB-25 Apr 48
-132		41-12919	24 Aug 42	18	Crashed McDonald Field, Aus. Totaled 5 Feb 43
-133		41-12924	24 Aug 42	18	LIA Ditched near Melville Is. 2 Apr 43
-134		41-12885	28 Sep 42	18	No. 1 Engr. School 20 July 45; TB-25 49
-135		41-12912	28 Sep 42	18	LIA 28 April 43
-136		41-12933	14 Sep 42	18	Missing after enemy action 9 Oct 43
-137		41-29735	17 Sep 42	18	Missing after enemy action 5 Jan 44
-138		41-12934	14 Sep 42		NEI Pool, 20 Sq 47/48; 18 Sq 48 TB-25
-139		41-12913	10 Sep 42	18	Crashed, Port Keats, total loss 13 Feb 43
-140		41-29723	14 Sep 42	18	Ditched, Darwin Sea, Enemy Action 6 April 43
-141		41-29725	22 Sep 42	18	Crashed at Mascot 7 Nov 44, C-C
-142		41-29716	28 Sep 42	18	NEI Pool 6 Mar 44; OOS 47; 20 Sq TB-25 47
-143		41-29722	28 Sep 42	18	Probably RAPWI 45/46.SOC at PEP as TB-25 NEITS 1 May 44
-144		41-29717	28 Sep 42	18	Ditched, enemy action 19 Feb 43
-145		41-12798	17 Sep 42	18	Crashed at Batchelor 18 Oct 43 C-C 21 Feb 44
-146		42-32512	1 Apr 43		18 Sq 45 20 Sq 47 (TB-25)
-147		42-32484	1 Apr 43	18	LIA 23 May 43
-148		42-32338	3 Apr 43	18	PVA 47/48 (FB-25)
-149		42-32511	3 Apr 43	18	20 Sq 47 (TB-25)
-150		42-32337	7 Apr 43	18	LIA 2 Jun 43
-151		42-32485	7 Apr 43	18	PVA 47/48 (FB-25)
-152		42-32483	12 Apr 43	18	Crashed on Takeoff, total loss 23 May 43

NEIAF No.	RAF No.	U.S. No	Date Recd	Squadron	Disposition
N5-153		42-32339	4 May 43	18	Crash lnd, Batchelor aftr enmy actn 10 Sep 43 SOC 28 Feb 44
-154		41-30584	25 Sep 43	18	PEP 4 Jun 45 PVA 48 (FB-25)
-155		41-30586	28 Sep 43	18	Crashed at Bankstown, spares 28 Sep 44
-156		41-30587	28 Sep 43	18	Write off 28 Sep 43
-157		41-30588	24 Sep 43	18	Crash landing 8 Aug 44, C-C 18 Sep 44
-158		41-30589	28 Sep 43		To Holland, 1946
-159		41-30682	28 Sep 43		Missing in Action 22 Dec 43
-160		41-30713	28 Sep 43		PEP 46, 20 Sq 47/48, 18 Sq 49(TB-25)
-161		41-30816	24 Sep 43	18	Accident, Drysdale River Mission, Scrap 14 Jan 44
-162		42-87349	1 Oct 44	18	Departed U.S. 4 Dec 42; MIA 26 Jun 44
-163		42-87350	11 Jan 44		Lft US 6 Dec 43; 18 Sq 8 Feb 45, OOS 1947, Spares Oct 48 (TB-25)
-164		42-87305	8 Jan 44		Lft U.S. 6 Dec 43; 18 Sq 26 Jul 44, OOS 47; 20 Sq 47; PVA 49 (FB-25)
-165		42-87595	4 Feb 44		18 Sq 17 Mar 45; PVA 47 (FB-25)
-166		42-87398	27 Jan 44	18	PVA 48/49 (FB-25 or TB-25)
-167		41-30414	27 Jan 44	18	Left U.S. 20 Dec 43; Dest. by fire and bomb expl. 19 Dec 44
-168	A47-35	41-30416	27 Jan 44	2RAAF	Left US 20 Dec 43, RAAF, Sold 10 Mar 50
-169		41-30321	31 Jan 44	18	Left US 27 Dec 43, Missing in Action 25 Aug 44
-170		42-87254	25 Feb 44	18	PEP 3 Aug 45
-171	A47-36	42-87255	25 Feb 44	2RAAF	2 Sq 28 Aug 44; Sold 10 Mar 50
-172		42-87256	10 Feb 44	18	PEP 30 Nov 44; OOS 46/47; PVA 48/49(FB-25 or TB-25)
-173		42-87257	24 Feb 44	18	PEP 3 Jul 44; 20 Sq 47/48; PVA 49 (FB-25 or TB-25)
-174	A47-37	42-87258	13 Feb 44	18	Lost, ferry to Biak 14 Aug 45
-175	A47-33	42-87259	24 Feb 44	2RAAF	2 Sq 9 Aug 44; LIA;SOC 20 Dec 44
-176		42-87313	13 Feb 44	18	Crashed in sea, Grove Is. Tng Flt. 30 May 44
-177		42-87311	10 Feb 44	18	Missing on Operations 21 May 44
-178		42-87312	24 Feb 44	18	PVA 48/49; 18 Sq until Mar 50 (FB-25) PEP 15 Mar 45
-179		42-87307	12 Feb 44	18	Missing in Action SOC 7 Mar 44
-180		42-87321	25 Feb 44	18	History Uncertain
-181	A47-3	43-3423	30 Mar 44	2RAAF	LIA North Coast Timor 22 Sep 44
-182		42-87597	18 Feb 44		Crashed near Swan Hill 29 Mar 44 C-C 31 Jul 44
-183	A47-1	42-87607	24 Feb 44	2RAAF	Sold through disposals 10 Mar 50
-184		43-3282	15 Feb 44	18	PEP 14 Jun 45; OOS 47; SOC Oct 48 (TB-25)
-185		43-3421	10 Feb 44		Recd 18 Sq 13 Jun 45; history uncertain
-186	A47-34	42-87608	14 Feb 44	2RAAF	Sold 20 Mar 50
-187	A47-2	43-3422	24 Feb 44	2RAAF	Crash landed Hughes Strip 26 Dec 44; Scrapped 6 Feb 45
-188		42-87260	29 Feb 44		19 Sq 45; PEP 14 May 45/46 SOC April 48 (TB-25)
-189	A47-4	43-3434	27 Mar 44	2RAAF	2 Sq 22 Apr 44; Scrapped 2 Dec 46
-190	A47-22	43-3830	29 Apr 44	2RAAF	2 Sq 13 Jun 44; Sold 10 Mar 50
-191		43-3425(?)			Lost near Hawaii on ferry (may be 43-3435)
-192	A47-5	43-3436	27 Mar 44	2RAAF	2 Sq 22 Apr 44; Sold 10 Mar 50
-193	A47-6	43-3427	30 Mar 44	2RAAF	Crshd, srch for N5-199 near Perron Is. SOC 9 Feb 44; 2 Sq 22 Apr 44
-194	A47-7	43-3607	30 Mar 44	2RAAF	2 Sq 22 Apr 44; Sold 10 Mar 50
-195	A47-8	43-3613	30 Mar 44	2RAAF	2 Sq 22 Apr 44; LIA, SOC 4 Nov 44
-196	A47-9	43-3621	30 Mar 44	2RAAF	2 Sq 22 Apr 44; Takeoff crsh & fire, Hughes Strip 26 Dec 44; SOC 11 Jan 45
-197	A47-10	43-3623	30 Mar 44	2RAAF	2 Sq 22 Apr 44 Sold 10 Mar 50
-198	A47-11	43-3624	30 Mar 44	2RAAF	2 Sq 22 Apr 44; Crshed at Bathurst with cmbat dmg 5 Dec 44; SOC 23 Jan 45
-199	A47-12	43-3625	30 Mar 44	2RAAF	2 Sq 22 Apr 44; Ditched near Perron Is fuel shortage SOC Sep 44
-200	A47-13	43-3626	30 Mar 44	2RAAF	2 Sq 22 Apr 44; Training crash 6 Aug 44 Scrapped 12 Aug 44
-201	A47-14	43-3766	30 Mar 44	2RAAF	2 Sq 22 Apr 44; Sold 10 Mar 50
-202	A47-15	43-3767	13 Apr 44	2RAAF	2 Sq 22 Apr 44; Sold 10 Mar 50
-203	A47-16	43-3768	13 Apr 44	2RAAF	2 Sq 21 Apr 44; Sold 10 Mar 50
-204	A47-17	43-3769	13 Apr 44	2RAAF	2 Sq 21 Apr 44; Sold 10 Mar 50
-205	A47-18	43-3770	13 Apr 44	2RAAF	2 Sq 21 Apr 44; Sold 10 Mar 50
-206	A47-19	43-3790	13 Apr 44	2RAAF	2 Sq 21 Apr 44; Crshd escorting PBY from Balikpapan. SOC 16 Sep 45
-207	A47-20	43-3791	13 Apr 44	2RAAF	2 Sq 21 Apr 44; lost frm brake failure at repair depot 1 June 44; SOC 27 Nov 44
-208		43-3833	14 Apr 44		PEP 19 Sep 44; 19 Sq 45; OOS 47; PVA 1948/49 (FB-25)
-209		43-3835	25 Apr 44		PEP 25 Jun 45; 19 Sq 45; PVA 1948; 18 Sq 1949; crashed 14 May 1949 SOC
-210		43-3834	25 Apr 44	18	Shot down at Langgorkai by enemy AA fire 19 Aug 44
-211		43-3836	29 Apr 44	18	Crashed on takeoff at Batchelor 8 Jan 45 SOC 15 Jan 45
-212	A47-23	43-3823	10 May 44	2RAAF	Lost on rescue 9 Oct 45; Scrapped 13 Dec 45
-213	A47-21	43-3789	29 Apr 44		2 Sq 9 Jun 44 Sold 10 Mar 50
-214			11 May 44		Written off 1 Sep 44
-215	A47-25	43-3869	11 May 44	2RAAF	2 Sq 9 Jun 44 Sold 10 Mar 50
-216	A47-24	43-3867	11 May 44	2RAAF	2 Sq 10 Jun 44; Crashed Torquay Firing Range SOC 12 Dec 44
-217			19 May 44		Belly landing 10 Feb 45; Scrapped 14 May 45
-218		43-27692	22 May 44		PEP 26 Dec 44; 16 Sq 1948; 18 Sq 1949 (SB-25)

APPENDIX K(Cont.)

NEIAF No.	RAF No.	U.S. No	Date Recd	Squadron	Disposition
-219	A47-27	43-27691	9 Jun 44	2 RAAF	2 Sq 9 Jun 44 Sold 10 Mar 50
-220	A47-26	43-27689	9 Jun 44	2 RAAF	2 Sq 9 Jun 44 Sold 10 Mar 50
-221		43-27688	5 Jun 44		16 Sq 1947/48; 18 Sq 1949 (SB-25)
-222			21 Jun 44		Possibly 43-27690 damaged in ferry in Hawaii
-223		43-27926	29 Jun 44		18 Sq 1946; 16 Sq 1947; 20 Sq 1947/48 18 Sq 1948/49 (SB-25)
-224	A47-28	43-27927	11 Jul 44	2 RAAF	2 Sq 11 Jul 44 Sold 10 Mar 50
-225	A47-29	43-27928	11 Jul 44	2 RAAF	2 Sq 11 Jul 44 Sold 10 Mar 50
-226		43-27929	14 Aug 44		PEP 26 Nov 45; 16 Sq 1948; 18 Sq 1949 (SB-25)
-227	A47-32	43-28181	31 Jul 44	2 RAAF	2 Sq 5 Aug 44 Sold 10 Mar 50
-228		43-28182	1 Aug 44		PEP 5 Jul 45; 18 Sq 1946; 16 Sq 1948 18 Sq 1948/49 (SB-25)
-229	A47-30	43-28185	27 Jul 44	2 RAAF	2 Sq 27 Jul 44 Sold 10 Mar 50
-230		43-28184	27 Jul 44		PEP 10 Jul 45;18Sq 46; downed by Indonesians at Kalibanteng 4 Aug 46
-231	A47-31	43-28183	27 Jul 44	2 RAAF	2 Sq 27 Jul 44 Sold 10 Mar 50
-232	A47-38	44-29021	13 Jul 44	2 RAAF	2 Sq 13 Jul 44 Sold 10 Mar 50
-233		44-29022	15 Sep 44		PEP 2 Feb 45; 16 Sq 1948;18 Sq 1949/50 (SB-25)
-234		44-29023	19 Sep 44		PEP 25 Jul 45;16 Sq 1948;18 Sq 1948/50 (SB-25)
-235	A47-39	44-29024	19 Sep 44	2 RAAF	19 Sep 44 Sold 10 Mar 50
-236		44-29029	19 Sep 44		Crashed at Merauke, N.G. 29 Mar 45
-237		44-29030	19 Sep 44		PEP 24 Jul 45; 20 Sq 1947; 18 Sq 1948/49 (SB-25)
-238		44-29031	25 Sep 44		PEP 25 Jun 45; 18 Sq 1946; SOC aftr emgncy lndg at Pakan Barde 7 Feb 46
-239		44-29032	19 Sep 44		PEP 2 Aug 45; 20 Sq 1947; 16 Sq 1948; 18 Sq 1948/49 (SB-25)
-240		44-29033	25 Sep 44		PEP 6 Aug 45; 16 Sq 1947; 20 Sq 1947/48; 18 Sq 1948/49 (SB-25)
-241		44-29034	21 Sep 44		Crash landed Canberra 14 Nov 44; SOC 19 Dec 44
-242		44-29260	25 Nov 44		PEP 4 Aug 45; 18 Sq 1949 (BB-25)
-243		44-29261	12 Dec 44		18 Sq 27 Jun 45/49 (BB-25)
-244		44-29262	25 Nov 44		PEP 20 Sep 45; 18 Sq 1945; 20 Sq 1947 18 Sq 1949 (TB-25)
-245		44-29263	14 Dec 44		18 Sq 27 Jun 45; crashed Andir due to exploded bomb 17 Sep 47 (BB-25)
-246		44-29514	10 Dec 44		PEP 6 Aug 45; 18 Sq 1945 DVM 1949 18 Sq 1950 (BB-25)
-247		44-29515	28 Nov 44		PEP 20 Sep 45; OOS 1947; 18 Sq 1950 (TB-25)
-248		44-29516	27 Nov 44		18 Sq 17 Dec 45; 20 Sq 1947/48; 18 Sq 1948 (TB-25)
-249		44-29517	3 Dec 44		PEP 17 Mar 45; 18 Sq 1945/49 (BB-25)
-250		44-30504	27 Mar 45		18 Sq 14 May 1945; 20 Sq 1947; 18 Sq 1949 (TB-25)
-251		44-30506	27 Mar 45		PEP 11 Oct 1945; 18 Sq 1945/49 (BB-25)
-252		44-30507	27 Mar 45		PEP 11 Oct 1945; 18 Sq 1945; 16 Sq 1947 Shot dwn Palembang 21 Jul 1947
-253		44-30508	27 Mar 45		Burned at Archerfield 9 Jun 45; SOC 24 Jul 45
-254		44-30900	19 Apr 45		PEP 1945; SOC after ditching off Northern Territory 21 Nov 45
-255		44-30903	17 Apr 45		18 Sq 1945; crashed at Malino 4 Sep 45
-256		44-30505	11 May 45		18 Sq 26 Jul 1945; 16 Sq 1947; 18 Sq 1947/48 DVM 1949 (BB-25)
-257		44-30391	23 May 45		18 Sq 26 Jul 1945/46; 16 Sq 1947; SOC Jun 1947
-258		44-30399	30 May 45		18 Sq 8 Aug 1945;16 Sq 1947;18 Sq 1948/49 (BB-25)
-259		44-31201	8 Jun 45		18 Sq 22 Jun 1945; 16 Sq 1947; 18 Sq 1948/49 (BB-25)
-260		44-31202	8 Jun 45		18 Sq 28 Jun 1945; 16 Sq 1947 18 Sq 1949 (BB-25)
-261		44-31203	7 Jun 45		18 Sq 28 Jun 45; 20 Sq 47; 18 Sq 49 (TB-25) Ditched 22 Dec 49 at Makassar
-262		44-31204	10 Jun 45		18 Sq 5 Jul 1945/46; SOC 1946
-263		44-31256	12 Jun 45		18 Sq 22 Jun 1945/46 (TB-25) Pers. a/c of Gen. Kengen; SOC Feb 1947
-264*		44-31258	18 Jun 45		18 Sq 3 Aug 1945; 16 Sq 1947; 18 Sq 1948/49 (BB-25)
-265		44-31259	25 Jun 45		18 Sq 7 Aug 1945/46; SOC after ditching Ambon-Biak 15 Apr 1947
-266		44-30902	20 Jul 45		18 Sq 23 Aug 1945/46; SOC 1946
	A47-40	44-30888	12 Apr 45		Crash lnd after TO from Laverton; C/C 3 Dec 1945
	A47-41	44-30889	13 Apr 45	2 RAAF	Sold 10 Mar 50
	A47-42	44-30890	13 Apr 45		Sold 10 Mar 50
	A47-43	44-30895	24 Apr 45	2 RAAF	Sold 10 Mar 50
	A47-44	44-30896	28 Apr 45		Sold 10 Mar 50
	A47-45	44-30897	1 May 45		Sold 10 Mar 50
	A47-46	44-31255	26 May 45		Sold 10 May 50
	A47-47	44-31254	28 May 45		Sold 10 May 50
	A47-48	44-31253	3 Jun 45		Sold 10 May 50
	A47-49	44-86859	19 Aug 45		Sold 10 May 50
	A47-50	44-86855	27 Aug 45		Sold 10 May 50

* See Chapter 26

APPENDIX L
Dutch Glossary

OOS	Conversion Training School, Biak, 1945-1947
RAPWI	Rescue Allied Prisoners of War
DVM	Depot, Aircraft Materiel
PEP	Personnel & Equipment Pool; Canberra, Biak, Andir
PVA	Photo Recon Squadron
NEITS	NEI Transport Squadron (Australia, 1944-1945)
16 Sqn	B-25 Strafer Squadron, post war
19 Sqn	NEI Transport Squadron, post war
20 Sqn	Transport Squadron
TB-25	B-25 converted to transport
FB-25	B-25 Photo aircraft
BB-25	Standard Medium Bomber
SB-25	Strafer with factory 8 gun nose or with bombardier's nose section and forward fuselage blister guns.
LIA	Lost in Action
C-C	Converted to Components
SOC	Struck Off Charge

APPENDIX M
B-25s IN TOKYO RAIDS AND CREWS

The B-25s participating in the Tokyo raid are listed in order by airplane number with respective crews listed in order by pilot, co-pilot, navigator, bombardier, engineer/gunner and gunner.

* - Navigator Bombardier

(1) 40-2242
Capt. Edward J. York
Lt. Robert G. Emmens
Lt. Nolan A. Herndon *
S/Sgt. T.H. Laban
Sgt. David W. Pohl

(2) 40-2247
Lt. Edgar E. McElroy
Lt. Richard A. Knobloch
Lt. Clayton J. Campbell
Sgt. Robert C. Bourgeois
Sgt. Adam R. Williams

(3) 40-2249
Capt. C. Ross Greening
Lt. Ken E. Reddy
Lt. Frank J. Kappeler
S./Sgt. William L. Birch
Sgt. Melvin J. Gardner

(4) 40-2250
Lt. Richard O. Joyce
Lt. J. Royden Stork
Lt. Horace E. Crouch
Sgt. George E. Larkin Jr.
S/Sgt. Edwin W. Horton

(5) 40-2261
Lt. Ted W. Lawson
Lt. Dean Davenport
Lt. Charles L. McClure
Lt. Robert S. Clever
Sgt. David J. Thatcher

(6) 40-2267
Lt. Donald G. Smith
Lt. Griffith T. Williams
Lt. Howard A. Sessler*
Sgt. Edward J. Saylor
Lt. Thomas R. White (M.D.)

(7) 40-2268
Lt. William G. Farrow
Lt. Robert L. Hite

40-2268 (cont.)
Lt. George Barr
Cpl. Jacob deShazer
Sgt. Harold A. Spatz

(8) 40-2270
Lt. Robert M. Gray
Lt. Jacob E. Manch
Lt. Charles J. Ozuk
Sgt. Aden E. Jones
Cpl Leland D. Factor

(9) 40-2278
Lt. William M. Bower
Lt. Thadd H. Blanton
Lt. William R. Pound
T/Sgt. Waldo J. Bither
S/Sgt. Omer H. Duquette

(10) 40-2282
Lt. Everett W. Holstrom
Lt. Lucien N. Youngblood
Lt. Harry C. McCool
Sgt. Robert J. Stevens
Cpl. Bert M. Jordan

(11) 40-2283
Capt. David M. Jones
Lt. Rodney R. Wilder
Lt. Eugene F. McGurl
Lt. Denver V. Truelove
Sgt. Joseph W. Manske

(12) 40-2292
Lt. Travis Hoover
Lt. William N. Fitzhugh
Lt. Carl N. Wildner
Lt. Richard E. Miller
Sgt. Douglas V. Radney

(13) 40-2297
Major John A. Hilger
Lt. Jack A. Sims
Lt. James H. Macia*
S/Sgt. Jacob Eierman
S/Sgt. Edwin V. Bain

APPENDIX M (cont.)

(14) 40-2298
Lt. Dean E. Hallmark
Lt. Robert J. Meder
Lt. Chase J. Nielsen
Sgt. William J. Dieter
Sgt. Donald E. Fitzmaurice

(15) 40-2303
Lt. Harold F. Watson
Lt. James M. Parker
Lt. Tom C. Griffin
Sgt. Wayne M. Bissel
T/Sgt. Eldred V. Scott

(16) 40-2344
Lt. Col James H. Doolittle
Lt. Richard E. Cole
Lt. Henry A. Potter
S/Sgt. Fred A. Braemer
S/Sgt. Paul J. Leonard

The following airplane numbers are listed in order of takeoff from _Hornet_.

1. 40-2344
2. 40-2292
3. 40-2270
4. 40-2282
5. 40-2283
6. 40-2298
7. 40-2261
8. 40-2242
9. 40-2303
10. 40-2250
11. 40-2249
12. 40-2278
13. 40-2247
14. 40-2297
15. 40-2267
16. 40-2268

APPENDIX N
FOREIGN ALLOCATIONS

ARGENTINA
Three B-25Js were sold to Argentine buyers from US surplus sales. The first, 44-31498, went on the Argentine civil register as LV-GJX on 27 June 1960. It was seen in 1964 in derelict condition and its ultimate fate remains unknown.
The second Argentine B-25J, LV-GXH, formerly TB-25N 44-31172 was first registered in June, 1961. It was thereafter acquired by a provincial government airline and when retired from use put on static display at del Estro Airport at Santiago.
Seen in August 1960 a third B-25J carried provisional registration LV-PWE, US number unknown - as is the ultimate fate of the airplane.
All three airplanes had been retrofitted with semi collector exhaust rings on the top cylinders and on the first two airplanes listed the Holley carburetors were replaced by Bendix.

BOLIVIA (Fuerza Aerea Boliviana)
At least six B-25Js have been reported used by Bolivia in 1947-1948 but this information has never been confirmed.

BRAZIL (Forca Aerea Brazileira)
Brazil took delivery of 80 B-25s the first 29 under Lend Lease during WW II. Seven B-25Bs were delivered prior to December, 1941: 40-2245; 2255; 2263; 2306; 2309; 2310; and 2316.
B-25C, 41-12558 was delivered 10 July for use in mechanic's training school.
The remaining 21 Lend Lease aircraft were all B-25J-NTs delivered between August and November, 1944: 44-29007/29011; 29015/29020; 29493/29502/ All were serialed in the FAB 5000s and 5100s.
Between 11 July 1946 and 2 October 1947 Brazil received at least 64 additional B-25s under the American Republics Projects and subsequent military assistance programs:

43-27491	27605	27610	27626	27775	27847	27864	
27865	27869	27876	27878	27880	27881	28033	28046
28196	28210	28720	28721	35967	36083	36087	36093
36096	36097	36132	36141	36147	36154	36167	36224
3915							
44-28717	28913	28928	28929	28930	28939	28940	28948
28949	29056	29891	29905	30069	30095	30137	30139
30142	30225	30242	30245	30246	30248	30311	30326
30350	30351	30406	30783	30784	30787	30911	

Between 30 September 1957 and 30 June 1958 the FAB had 32 B-25s and possibly more on strength supported by the US Military Assistance Program

CHILE(Fuerza Aerea de Chile)
Under American Republics Project #94525-S twelve B-25Js were delivered to Chile officially on 13 October 1947 but were actually on FAC strength in early January. Eleven are accountable indicating that one may have crashed during delivery. The numbers are 44-30252; 30272/30274;

APPENDIX N (Cont.)

CHILE (Cont.)
30392; 30401; 30412; 30413; 30416; 30445; 30465.
Serials were originally FAC 801/811 but were later reserialed in 900 sequence. As of 30 June 1954 eight are known to have been on strength.

CHINA
Well over 100 B-25 C&D models were supplied the Nationalist Chinese. A considerable number of late model B-25s went to the Chinese Air Force. Those known are listed as follows: B-25H-1 43 - 4113; 4114; 4116; 4124 ; 4146; 4183; 4184; 4186; 4188; 4189; 4193; 4199; 4201; 4478; 4481; 4483; 4587; 4588; 4589; 4590; 4662; 4663; 4668; 4674; 4678; 4679; 4680; 4681
B-25J-1 43-3869; 3894; 3896; 3897
B-25J-30 44-31387; 31388
An unknown number of B-25s were abandoned to the People's Republic after Nationalist Forces withdrew to Formosa

COLOMBIA (Fuerza aerea Colombiana)
Under American Republics Project #491 Colombia received 3 B-25Js on 21 July 1947 numberes 44-30358;30397; 30408 and were assigned FAC serials 657; 658; and 659 of unknown sequence. All were on strength as of 5 May 1948. by 30 June 1954 two remained in doubtful combat condition.

CUBA (Fuerza Aerea Ejercito de Cuba)
Four B-25s were purchased by Cuba from a US source in 1947. Two more were confiscated following the aborted Dominican invasion from Cayo Confites in 1947. By December, 1955 four remained on strength and were presumed combat ready. Serial numbers unknown.

DOMINICAN REPUBLIC (Cuerpo de Aviacion Dominicana)
In 1951 one B-25 was privately purchased for revision to a VIP aircraft. It is believed to have been derelict in 1965.

GREAT BRITAIN
Nine hundred and ten B-25s went to Britain under Lend Lease and many were returned to the US. A few of those known are listed here but the RAF cross referenced numbers are not available. Many to RCAF.
B-25D-15 41- 30476; 30477; 30478
B-25D-30 43- 3387 3395 3398 3458 3478 3531 3536 3569
3647 3683 3686 3701 3703 3704 3705 3707
3708 3710 3714 3718 3720 3723 3750 3753
3756 3764 3779 3788 3792 3801 3844 3858

MEXICO (Fuerza Aerea Mexicana)
On 12 March 1945 Mexico received three B-25Js under a late combination Lend Lease/ARP arrangement: 44-86712;86717 and 86718 but the paperwork did not make the arrangement official until December. The only known serial is FAM3503 and it is assumed to have been preceded by 3501 and 3502. By 30 June 1954 only one remained on strength.

PERU (Fuerza Aerea del Peru)
Under ARP #94493 eight B-25Js were received by Peru on 21 July 1947 numbers 44-29912; 30296; 30360; 30361; 30384; 30398; 30403 and 30418. All were assigned to Grupo 21 with all airplanes believed combat ready. By June 1954 six were carried on strength and five were believed combat ready when assigned to the 21 Bomb Squadron at Chiclayo.

SOVIET UNION
Eight hundred and seventy B-25B,C, D, H and J models were delivered to the USSR under Lend Lease. Serial numbers not known.

URUGUAY (Fuerza Aerea Uruguaya)
The exact total of B-25s received by Uruguay is not confirmed. It is known that ten were delivered in 1950 under the American Republics Projects: 44-30269; 30273; 30641; 30593; 30604; 30723; 30729; 30735; 30878; 31190. Twelve FAU serials are known, FAU 150, 152, 153, 155, 156, 157, 158, 161, 162, 163, and 164 showing two unexplained gaps. As of September 1957 the FAU had 8 on strength supported by the Military Assistance Program and this number had increased by 31 December 1957 to twelve airplanes of which ten remained active until 30 June 1958. Four additional B-25s were received under MAP grant aid as of 30 June 1954 which may account for some of the FAU number gaps and as of this date ten were on strength. All are believed to have been scrapped by 1966.

VENEZUELA (Fuerza Aereas Venezolanas)
The possible cumulative total of B-25s operated by the FAV may be as high as 40 airplanes. Fourteen B-25Js were delivered to Venezuela under the American Republic Projects b etween August 1947 and April 1949.

APPENDIX N (Cont.)

These were B-25Js 44-30302; 30411; 30433; 30467; 30614; 30619; 30626; 30627; 30630; 30631; 30638; 30678; 30730 and 31191. Thirteen were on strength, 10 flyable, in 1952 when 10 more were purchased from the US and an additional 9 former RCAF airplanes were bought in December 1963. At least one B-25H was received in 1955 and another five airplanes were delivered under the Reimbursable Aid Program before December 1957. Most were used, when operational, by Escuadron de Bombardeo 40. Serials initially were 1 B 40; 2 B 40 etc. Later serials were 12 B 42 etc. indicating use of some B-25s by Squadron 42. About 1967 or 1968 a new random set of numbers were used for B-25s. Two known numbers are FAV 5851 and 3712.
Nine B-25s were extensively overhauled and modified for Venezuela by the L.B. Smith Aircraft Corp. at Miami in 1957.

APPENDIX O
RCAF MITCHELLS

RCAF No.	USA No.	B-25 Type	Remarks
5200	41-30267	D-10	Trenton, Ret to USA Dec 1953
5201	41-30393	D-15	#2 Air Obs Sch Winnipeg 1958
5202	44-30812	J-25	Trenton
5203	44-86724	J-30	Flight Instructor School
5204	44-86820	J-30	Trenton 1951
5205	44-86879	J-30	Trenton, Ret to USA Dec 1953
5206	44-28847	J-15	Trenton, Ret to USA Dec 1953
5207	44-30391	J-25	Flight Instr School Trenton 1952
5208	44-30304	J-25	Training Command Trenton 1951
5209	44-30402	J-25	Training Command Trenton 1951
5210	44-30953	J-30	North Bay 1951-52
5211	44-30254	J-25	Became CF-MWC
5212	44-30947	J-30	Became CF-NTP
5213	44-30479	J-25	2 Air Obs School, Winnipeg
5214	44-30481	J-25	2 Air Obs School, Winnipeg
5215	44-30485	J-25	Central Exp & Proving Estab
5216	44-86731	J-30	Saskatoon 1951-52
5217	44-30483	J-25	2 Air Obs School 57/58
5218	44-31504	J-30	Adv Flight Sch Saskatoon 1952
5219	44-30478	J-25	Adv Flight Sch Saskatoon 1952
5220	44-86729	J-30	412 Sq 1956

The above 21 aircraft taken on strength latter half of 1951 and struck off strength 1953-1963

5221	44-86728	J-30	Possibly Not Received
5222	44-86733	J-30	"
5223	44-86697	J-30	"
5224	44-86725	J-30	"
5225	Unk		"
5226	Unk		"
5227	44-86735	J-30	Crash, Write off Winnipeg Feb 57

The following aircraft through No. 5248 (excepting 5231) were taken on strength Jan 1952

5228	44-31506	J-30	Saskatoon 1952
5229	44-86738	J-30	Saskatoon 1952
5230	44-86727	J-30	Saskatoon 1952
5231	44-30475	J-25	Saskatoon 1952
5232	44-31494	J-30	Saskatoon 1952
5233	44-86736	J-30	Cent Exp Prov Sta, Ottawa 1957
5234	44-31399	J-30	418 Sq 1953
5235	44-86730	J-30	Saskatoon 1952
5236	44-29128	J-20	Cold Lake 1956
5237	44-86726	J-30	Training Command 1952
5238	Not rec.		
5239	44-86697	J-30	1 Adv Flt School Saskatoon
5240	Not rec		
5241	Not rec		
5242	44-86733	J-30	Crash, Write off, Cold Lake, July 1955
5243	44-86725	J-30	1 Adv Flt School Saskatoon
5244	44-86699	J-30	1 Flt Instr Schl, Trenton Museum Ottawa May 1964

192

APPENDIX O (cont.)

RCAF No.	USA No.	B-25 Type	Remarks
5245	44-31491	J-30	1 Adv Flt School Saskatoon
5246	44-31346	J-30	Lost Feb 1953 Saskatoon
5247	44-86728	J-30	Cent Exp Prov Est Nanimo, BC
5248	44-86698	J-30	412 Sq 1956 Became CF-NWU
5249	44-31493	J-30	Composite Flying Sch, Trenton

The following aircraft through 5258 taken on strength 1952

RCAF No.	USA No.	B-25 Type	Remarks
5250	44-30484	J-25	3 All weath. Opn Tng Unit, North Bay
5251	44-30315	J-25	3 All weath. Opn Tng Unit, North Bay
5252	44-30714	J-25	North Bay 1952
5253	44-30317	J-25	North Bay 1952
5254	44-30812	J-25	Cent Exp Prov Est, Quebec, 1952
5255	44-30128	J-25	North Bay 1952
5256	44-29251	J-20	Crash, Write Off, North Bay Aug 1954
5257	44-30641	J-25	Winnipeg 1958, became CF-NTS
5258	44-30642	J-25	North Bay 1952

The following aircraft through 5283 taken on strength 1953

RCAF No.	USA No.	B-25 Type	Remarks
5259	44-30601	J-25	
5260	44-30828	J-25	
5261	44-30639	J-25	
5262	44-30652	J-25	
5263	44-30615	J-25	Cent Exp Prov Est, Suffield
5264	44-30612	J-25	
5265	44-30629	J-25	
5266	44-30599	J-25	406 Sq 1954
5267	44-30625	J-25	406 Sq 1955
5268	44-30645	J-25	2 Air Nav School 1953
5269	44-30234	J-25	2 Air Nav School 1953
5270	44-30239	J-25	2 Air Nav School 1953
5271	44-30375	J-25	2 Air Nav School 1953
5272	44-30421	J-25	2 Air Nav School 1953
5273	44-30791	J-25	2 Air Nav School 1953
5274	44-29726	J-20	2 Air Nav School 1953
5275	44-30359	J-25	2 Air Nav School 1953
5276	44-30259	J-25	Crash, Write off; Keadingly, Man.
5277	44-29750	J-20	2 Air Nav School, Winnipeg 1953
5278	44-29699	J-20	" "
5279	44-29907	J-20	" "
5280	44-30366	J-25	" "
5281	44-30786	J-25	" "
5282	44-86733	J-30	" "
5283	44-29903	J-20	" "
FW 220	43-3540	D-30	5 Open Training Unit
FW 237	43-3557	D-30	5 Open Training Unit
FW 246	43-3566	D-30	Central Flight School, Trenton
FW 251	43-3686	D-35	406 Sq
FW 259	43-3694	D-35	418 Sq, Crash Write Off, Jan 1955
FW 260	43-3695	D-35	Whitehorse, Yukon
FW 272	43-3710	D-35	418 Sq
FW 273	43-3412	D-30	5 Open Training Unit
FW 274	43-3718	D-35	5 Opn Tng Unit, Boundary Bay Crash, Write off Aug 1944
FW 278	43-3751	D-35	418 Sq
FW 279	43-3752	D-35	418 Sq
FW 280	43-3753	D-35	418 Sq
891	41-29886	D-1	(U.S. F-10)
892	41-29924	D-1	"
893	41-30195	D-10	"
894	41-29877	D-1	"

The following six aircraft were taken on strength Aug 26 1954 and struck off strength June 23 1955. All were assigned to the 3 All Weather Opn. Training Unit, North Bay, Ont.

RCAF No.	USA No.	B-25 Type	Remarks
None	44-30314	J-25	
"	44-30390	J-25	
"	44-30439	J-25	
"	44-30442	J-25	
"	44-30444	J-25	
"	44-30449	J-25	

APPENDIX O (cont.)

RCAF No.	USA No.	B-25 Type	Remarks
HD 310	43-3764	D-35	5 Opn Tng Unit
HD 311	43-3779	"	Minor Accident May 1945
HD 312	43-3780	"	5 Opn Tng Unit minor acc. June 1945
HD 313	43-3781	"	418 Sq 1947
HD 314	43-3782	"	5 Opn Tng Unit, Write off May 1945 Boundary Bay
HD 315	43-3783	"	5 Opn Tng Unit, Boundary Bay Dec 1945
HD 317	43-3785	"	West Air Comd Instructional airframe
HD 318	43-3786	"	West Air Comd Instructional airframe
HD 319	43-3787	"	Missing July 1 1944
HD 320	43-3788	"	406 Sq 1953
HD 322	43-3790	"	Crash, write off, Comox, BC July 1956
HD 323	43-3794	"	418 Sq Crash write off July 1952
HD 324	43-3795	"	Trenton 1950
HD 325	43-3796	"	2 Air Obs School, Crash write off, Dec. 1950
HD 326	43-3797	"	5 Opn Trng Unit
HD 331	43-3844	"	406 Sq Crash write off, Aug 1954
HD 332	43-3845	"	Western Air Command
HD 333	43-3846	"	Vancouver
HD 334	43-3847	"	406 Sq 1949
HD 335	43-3848	"	406 Sq 1952
HD 337	43-3850	"	1 Tng Comd Nov 1944
HD 338	43-3851	"	Air Obs School Trenton
HD 339	43-3852	"	418 Sq 1948
HD 340	43-3853	"	406 Sq 1952
HD 341	43-3854	"	Crash, write off Dec 1949
HD 342	43-3855	"	418 Sq crash, write off Aug 1953
HD 343	43-3856	"	5 Opn Tng Unit, Crash write off Dec 1944
HD 344	43-3857	"	Vancouver
HD 345	43-3858	"	Missing June 1944
KL 133	41-30548	D-20	5 Opn Trng Unit
KL 134	41-30596	D-20	Western Air Command
KL 135	41-30637	D-20	Boundary Bay
KL 136	41-30757	D-20	22 SR Depot
KL 137	41-30758	D-20	5 Opn Trng Unit
KL 138	41-30759	D-20	22 SR Depot
KL 139	41-30760	D-20	Edmonton, Crash write off May 1953
KL 140	41-30814	D-20	5 Opn Trng Unit
KL 141	42-87146	D-25	5 Opn Trng Unit
KL 142	42-87288	D-25	5 Opn Trng Unit
KL 143	42-87290	D-25	
KL 144	42-87352	D-25	5 Opn Trng Unit
KL 145	42-87379	D-25	Central Flying School, Trenton
KL 146	43-3629	D-35	Western Air Command
KL 147	42-87501	D-30	5 Opn Trng Unit May 1945
KL 148	43-3634	D-35	418 Sq
KL 149	43-3647	D-35	5 Opn Trng Unit
KL 150	43-3300	D-30	5 Opn Trng Unit
KL 151	43-3301	"	5 Opn Trng Unit
KL 152	43-3302	"	Gimli, Manitoba
KL 153	43-3303	"	418 Sq
KL 154	43-3304	"	406 Sq
KL 155	43-3307	"	Lachine, P.Q. May 1953
KL 156	43-3308	"	2 Air Obs School, Winnipeg
KL 157	43-3310	"	Vancouver
KL 158	43-3311	"	5 Opn Trng Unit
KL 159	43-3312	"	5 Opn Trng Unit
KL 160	43-3316	"	2 Air Obs School
KL 161	43-3318	"	3 All Weather Open Training Unit; Became CF-OGQ

The nine aircraft listed at the right were on a one month loan from the USA and all assigned to 2 Opn Training Unit. USA numbers for these airplanes are unknown.

RCAF No	B-25 Type	RCAF No	B-25 Type
KJ 641	J	FK 176	B
KJ 764	J	FK 177	B
FK 164	B	FK 178	B
FK 166	B	FK 180	B
FK 171	B		

APPENDIX P
B-25s OF THE ROYAL AIR FORCE

RAF No	MK	B-25 Type	QTY	Remarks
FK 161	I	B	1	
FK 162/183	I	B	22	To 111 Opn Tng Unit, Bahamas
FL 164/218	II	C	55	FL 209 crashed in transit
FL 671/709	II	C	39	Deliv. Jun, Jul 1942
FL 851/874	II	C	24	Deliv. of 859 only confirmed
FR 141/207	II	C,D	67	See MLD Dutch Navy Serials
FR 208/209	II	G	2	
FR 362/384	II	C	23	FR 368 lost in transit
FR 393/397	II	C	5	Deliv 1942-1943
FV 900/939	II	D	40	
FV 940/999	II	C	60	
FW 100/280	II	C,D	181	See RCAF-USA Serials
HD 302/345	II	D	44	See RCAF-USA Serials
HD 346/400	III	J	55	
KJ 561/800	III	J	240	774; 777 thru 783; 785; 787 thru 792; 795 thru 799 diverted to USA. 641 and 764 to RCAF
KL 133/161	II	D	29	All to RCAF. See RCAF-USA Serials
KP 308/328	III	J	21	Lend Lease 1945. All ret. to USA
MA 956	II	C	1	Ex- Dutch Destroyed by fire
MA 957	II	C	1	Crashed at sea, Nov. 1944.

Assignments

Aeroplane and Armament Experimental Establishment, Boscomb Down
FK 161 162 165; FL 189 191 688; FR 208 209 370;
FV 904 906 922 963 984; FW 143 151 266; HD 347 361 373

Bombing Trials Unit
FV 959 963; FW 155 226 266; HD 302

Royal Aircraft Establishment, Farnborough
FV 909; HD 370 373

2 Group Support Unit
FL 169 182 183 202 673 680 684 698 699; FR 208 397; FV 935 962
968 979; FW 106 166 223 242; HD 348 354 359 369 386 394 395 399;
KJ 600 605 615 623 625 626 635 637 660 662 677 679 690 709 715
728 732 754

13 Operational Training Unit
FL 193 194 195 671 687 694 699 703 706; FV 902 916 918 950 955
964 966 969 971 972 981 983 986 991 992 993 995 996 999; FW 103
108 114 117 119 120 133 136 137 139 140 166 172 198 221 231 241
261; KJ 587 590 597 602 604 612 617 619 628 647 673 680 715 732
754 760 763; FR 370 373; HD 381

98 Squadron ID Letters VO*

FL	165F	166Q	167	168H	169	174	176B	178	179	
	181Q	182J	186R	192M	197	201	202T	204C	205	
	206	207	210P	211	213	216	674W	675M	679	682N
	683L	690	693	698K	699	700J	701A	702I	704S	708
FV	913Q	914A	916	921	925	928C	929D	931H	934	
	937	938W	940	944	967	969D	974E	976L	977M	
	981	982D	983B	985S	970					
KJ	564J	569	570W	576P	577E	578	591N	594F	614	
	620	621U	622Q	624Q	627Y	628	632G	633	638	
	643	644B	658H	666A	674Z	701	746			
FW	102M	107X	109D	115K	122R	124J	129	134	142P	
	164G	165B	167E	168U	170	173	182A	184D	188	
	189A	192Y	194	197	198	200	201C	203T	205N	
	208K	211Y	215V	218Q	219P	224V	225	228Q	229R	
	240A	252N	253	254	255	256V	262	263	264	
	275F	277S	368A	371J	372D					
HD	305	308Y	329B	350	351K	363H	365C	368A	371J	
	372D	375	376Z	377	380	390U	396K			

Mitchell II Sep 42 through Nov 45
Mitchell III Sep 44 through Nov 45

APPENDIX P (Cont.)

21 Squadron
FL 169; FV 904 907 912

45 Group (Canada)
FK 168; FV 917 994 998; HD 352; FW 159 165 234 235 243 247 265
267 270; KJ 584 588 695 721 722 735 751

The following B-25s were lost in service with 98 Squadron

FL	167	Lost to flak	10 Jun 1943
	179	Crashed, birds	16 Nov 1942
	197	Lost on raid	13 May 1943
	206	Crashed, training	17 Oct 1942
	207	Raid damage	16 May 1943
	216	Crash, flak	24 Jun 1943
	682N	Crash, mid air	7 Jan 1944
	683L	Shot Down	21 Sep 1943
	693	Crash, flak	22 Jan 1943
	708	Crash	30 Nov 1942
FV	921	Lost to flak	6 Sep 1943
	944	Shot down	21 Sep 1943
FW	109D	Lost to flak	8 May 1944
	167E	Shot down	12 Sep 1944
	173	Crash landing, flak	17 Aug 1944
	188	Crash landing, flak	8 Sep 1944
	218Q	Lost to flak	13 Apr 1944
	224V	Crashed	2 Feb 1945
HD	308Y	Lost to flak	6 Feb 1945
	365C	Lost to flak	10 Feb 1945
	376Z	Shot down	20 Mar 1945
	390U	Shot down	25 Feb 1945

111 Operational Training Unit

FK	163	164	166	167	169	170	171	172	173	174
	175	176	177	178	179	180	181	182	183	
FL	180	187	199	200	208	697	702			
FR	362	363	364	365	366	371	372	374	375	376 377
	378	379	380	381	382	383	384	393	394	396
FV	946	949	951	952	953	954	997			
FW	104	123	132	145	147	148	149	150	154	176 179
HD	308	309	327	330						
KJ	580	581	582	583	601	668	669	670	671	716 717
	718	719								

114 Squadron   FL 169

180 Squadron ID Letters EV*

FL	168	169	170	171	173	175	180	188	190	192
	198P	201	205	211	212A	214	217	218	672B	675
	676	677	678J	681	684	685	686	689	691	
	695B	696	705	707Z	708	709				
FV	902	903	904	912	915	916	928	945	965	967
	975	977	998							
FW	100	101	107	110	113	118	124	125	135	142
	158	161	166	169	170	172	175	185	190	
	191	199	200	202	206	207	208H	209	214	
	221	225	228	232	236	240U	244	248	249	
	250	254	261	263	264	268	269			
FR	396K									
HD	305	307	316	328	355	360	374Q			
	375	379	386	387	388	391	397			
KJ	563	567B	573	574	585	586	589	592		
	595	598	603	610	612	639	649	652		
	653	656A	657	665	681	682W	684J	691		
	694D	700	705T	729	736	755				

226 Squadron ID Letters MQ*

FL	164	196	203	673C	680	691			
FR	397V								
FV	900F	902	905	908	910G	919	920	924H	926A
	927	930	932	934	935	936G	937	940C 943	945
	947	948	950	958	960	966	973	978	989

APPENDIX P (Cont.)
226 Squadron (Cont.)

FW	105C	106	111	112	121	126A	127C	128	130
	131	134	144	146	152	153	160	162	163
	171	174	181	183A	186	195	196	204	205
	210S	213	216S	217	222	230	233C	238	239
	241	242	245	271	276				
HD	303	304	336	348	353	354	355	357	362
	378	381	383	384	389	400	561	571	572
	594	599	608	613	616	626	631	635	667
	672	687							

305 Squadron (Polish) ID Letters SM*

FL	182	192	201	686	691
FV	911	913	923	937	941	948	976

313 Ferry Training Unit   FV 987

320 Squadron Royal Netherlands NAS   ID Letters NO

FR 141 through FR 207 (See MLD/USA Numbers)
Following aircraft (FL through KJ) borrowed from the RAF

FL	686M	168H	194	202T	679U			
FV	928	969	970					
FW	178S	187W	193X	212J	219J	227P	229C	258W	164
HD	305U	306N	346V	349T	358J	364H	367G	392A	393K
KJ	572	579W	587F	593T	596Z	603Y	629T	678K	700J
	701C	746K							

342 Squadron (Lorraine, Free French)

FW	153	174	181W	200	239				
HD	306	368	379	393					
KJ	565A	568	575C	585Q	598	609	618	626	630
	642	645	651	661	666V	678	683	687	729S
FV	916								

1482 Bomber Gunnery Unit

FV	956	957
FW	116	

APPENDIX Q
SERIAL NUMBER BLOCKS

Model	USAAF Number	Mfrs Number	Qty
B-25	40-2165/40-2188	62-2834/62-2857	24
B-25A	40-2189/40-2228	62-2858/62-2897	40
B-25B	40-2229/40-2348	62-2898/62-3017	120
B-25C	41-12434/41-13038	82-5069/82-5673	605
B-25C-1	41-13039/41-13296	82-5674/82-5931	258
B-25C-5	42-53332/42-53493	90-11819/90-11980	162
B-25C-10	42-32233/42-32382	94-12641/94-12790	150
	(42-32281 Modified to XB-25E Heated Wing)		
B-25C-15	42-32383/42-32532	93-12491/93-12640	150
B-25C-20	42-64502/42-64701	96-16381/96-16580	200
B-25C-25	42-64702/42-64801	96-16581/96-16680	100
B-25D	41-29648/41-29847	87-7813/87-8012	200
B-25D-1	41-29848/41-29947	87-8013/87-8112	100
B-25D-5	41-29948/41-30172	87-8113/87-8337	225
B-25D-10	41-30173/41-30352	87-8338/87-8517	180
B-25D-15	41-30353/41-30532	87-8518/87-8698	180
	41-30533/41-30847	87-8698/87-9012	315
B-25D-20	42-87113/42-87137	100-20606/10020630	25
B-25D-25	42-87138/42-87452	100-20631/100-20945	315
B-25D-30	42-87453/42-87612	100-20946/100-21105	160
	43-3280/43-3619	100-23606/100-23945	340
B-25D-35	43-3620/43-3869	100-23946/100-24195	250
B-25G-1	42-32384/42-32388	93-12491/93-12495	
	(Modified B-25C-15)		
B-25G-5	42-64802/42-64901	96-16681/96-16780	100
	42-64902/42-65101	96-20806/96-21005	200
B-25G-10	42-65102/42-65201	96-21006/96-21105	100
B-25H-1	43-4105/43-4404	98-21106/98-21405	300
B-25H-5	43-4405/43-4704	98-21406/98-21705	300
	(43-4406 modified with P&W R-2800 engine)		
B-25H-10	43-4705/43-5104	98-21706/98-22105	400

APPENDIX Q(Cont.)

Model	USAAF Number	Mfrs Number	Qty
B-25J-1	43-3870/43-4104	108-24196/108-22430	235
	43-27473/43-27792	108-34486/108-34805	320
B-25J-5	43-27793/43-28112	108-34806/108-35125	320
B-25J-10	43-28113/43-28222	108-35126/108-35235	110
	43-35946/43-36245	108-35236/108-35535	300
B-25J-15	44-28711/44-29110	108-31986/108-32385	400
B-25J-20	44-29111/44-29910	108-32386/108-33185	800
B-25J-25	44-29911/44-30910	108-33186/108-34185	1000
B-25J-30	44-30911/44-31510	108-36986/108-37585	600
	44-86692/44-86891	108-47446/108-47645	200
B-25J-35	44-86892/44-86897	108-47646/108-47651	6
	45-8801/45-8818	108-47652/108-47669	18
	45-8820/45-8823	108-47671/108-47674	4
	45-8825/45-8828	108-47676/108-47679	4
	45-8832	108-47683	1

The following 72 airplanes were not completed and accepted contractually. They were in flyable condition, however, and were included as part of the contract termination inventory.

45-8819	108-47670	1
45-8824	108-47675	1
45-8829/45-8831	108-47682/108-47682	3
45-8833/45-8899	108-47684/108-47750	67

APPENDIX R
COMPARATIVE BOMBER COSTS

Figures given represent total flyaway costs including both contractor and government furnished equipment. Some averaging was required and numbers rounded to the nearest thousand.

B-25.	A,B	$148,000	B-26A	$212,000	A-20B	$138,000
	B-25C	154,000	B	240,000	C	119,000
	D	172,000	C	306,000	G	112,000
	G	140,000	F	221,000	H	98,000
	H	139,000	G	200,000	K	105,000
	J	150,000			J	119,000
A-26B,C		$235,000	B-17E	$300,000	B-24D	$325,000
	D	181,000	F	261,000	E	360,000
			G	230,000	H	351,000
					J	250,000

Source: Technical Order No. 00-25-30 Unit Costs of Aircraft and Engines Budget and Fiscal Office, Hq. ATSC 1 August 1945

APPENDIX S
Drawing Structure Breakdown

The drawing structure breakdown used by North American was by far the most logical and easiest to use of any in the author's experience. A number was not just a number. The numbers shown on the breakdown were the same for every airplane built by the company. As an example 00003 was <u>THE</u> NAA Inboard Profiile Drawing and the airplane identified by it was defined by a prefix:

82-00003 Inboard Profile B-25C   108-00003 Inboard Profile B-25J
105-00003 Inboard Profile P-51D   192-00003 Inboard Profile F-100A

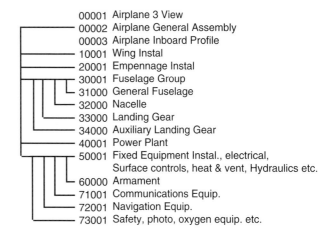

00001 Airplane 3 View
00002 Airplane General Assembly
00003 Airplane Inboard Profile
10001 Wing Instal
20001 Empennage Instal
30001 Fuselage Group
31000 General Fuselage
32000 Nacelle
33000 Landing Gear
34000 Auxiliary Landing Gear
40001 Power Plant
50001 Fixed Equipment Instal., electrical, Surface controls, heat & vent, Hydraulics etc.
60000 Armament
71001 Communications Equip.
72001 Navigation Equip.
73001 Safety, photo, oxygen equip. etc.

APPENDIX T
COMPARATIVE MEDIUM BOMBER DATA

	A-20G-10	A-26B-15	B-25C-10	B-25J-15	B-26B-2	B-26G-5
Span, ft in	61 4	70 0	67 7	67 7	65 0	71 0
Length, ft in	48 0	50 0	52 11	52 11	58 3	56 1
Height, ft in	17 7	18 6	15 9	15 9	19 10	20 4
Wing Area, Sq ft	464	540	610	610	602	658
Empty Weight, lbs	15,984	22,370	20,300	19,500	22,380	23,700
Loaded Weight, lbs	16,990	27,600	26,122	26,122	27,200	31,600
Maximum Weight, lbs	27,200	35,000	34,000	35,000	34,000	38,200
Wing Loading, lbs/hp	36.4	51.1	42.8	42.8	45.2	48.1
Power Loading, lbs/sq. ft.	5.3	6.9	7.7	7.7	6.8	7.9
Maximum Speed mph @ ft	333 @12,400	355 @ 15,000	284 @15,000	272 @13,000	317 @14,500	274 @10,000
Cruising Speed mph @ft	272 @10,000	284 @ 15,000	237 @10,000	230 @10,000	260 @10,000	225 @10,000
Landing Speed, mph	95	100	105	97		120
Climb Rate, ft/ min	10,000/8.0	10,000/8.1	15,000 /16.5	15,000 / 19.0	15,000 / 12.0	15,000 / 24.5
Service Ceiling, ft	25,800	22,100	21,200	24,200	23,500	20,000
Normal Range, miles	1,090	1,400	1,500	1,350	1,150	1,300
Maximum Range, miles	2,100	3,200	2,750	2,700	2,800	2,100

APPENDIX U
SUMMARY OF CONTRACTS

NAA No.	B-25 Type	Contract No.	For	Qty	Orig. Date
NA-62	B-25,A,B	W535-ac-13258	USA	184	9-5-39
NA-82	B-25C	W535-ac-16070	USA	863	10-1-40
NA-90	B-25C	W535-ac-7131L/NA	Netherlands	162	6-30-41
NA-93	B-25C	W535-DA-897	China	150	1-14-42
NA-94	B-25C	W535-DA-896	Britain	150	1-14-42
NA-96	B-25C	W535-ac-27390	USA	300	3-28-42
NA-96	B-25G	W535-ac-27390	USA	400	3-28-42
NA-98	B-25H	W535-ac-30478	USA	1,000	6-20-42
NA-87/100	B-25D	W535-ac-19341	USA	2,290	2-24-41 & 6-26-42
NA-108	B-25J	W535-ac-19341	USA	4,318	4-14-43

APPENDIX V
SCHEDULE OF FIRST FLIGHTS

TYPE	AAF NO.	MFRS NO.	DATE	PILOT
B-25	40-2165	62-2834	8-19-40	Vance Breese
B-25A	40-2189	62-2858	2-25-41	Edw. Virgin
B-25C	41-12434	82-5069	11-9-41	Edw. Virgin
B-25D	41-29648	87-7813	1-3-42	Paul Balfour
XB-25G	41-13296	82-5931	10-22-42	Edw. Virgin
XB-25E	42-32281	94-12838	2-4-44	Joe Barton
XB-25H	42-32372	93-12651	5-15-43	Edw. Virgin
NA-98X	43-4406	98-21407	3-31-44	Joe Barton
B-25H	43-4105	98-21106	7-31-43	Robt. Chilton
B-25J	43-3870	108-24196		Joe Barton

APPENDIX W
PRODUCTION RECORD

TYPE	NAA DIVISION	1941	1942	1943	1944	1945	TOTALS
B-25	California	24					24
B-25A	California	40					40
B-25B	California	107	13				120
B-25C	California	1	1107	517			1625
B-25D	Kansas		435	1699	156		2290
B-25G	California			400			400
B-25H	California			335	665		1000
B-25J	Kansas			2	2856	1460	4318
		172	1555	2953	3677	1460	9817

Quantities exclusive of the final seventy-two B-25Js which were contractually accepted although incomplete but flyable at the time of contract termination at the end of the war.
Source: NAA Publication No. 527-V-2 Deliveries of Completed Aircraft 31 July 1967

APPENDIX X
B-25s PROCESSED THROUGH MODIFICATION CENTERS

CONTRACTOR	FOR	J	F	M	A	M	J	J	A	S	O	N	D
Chicago & So.	Dutch		14										
Mid Con	Britain										6	8	12
NWA	Britain			2	20	21							
NAA (Kansas)	USAF							90	53	77	75	85	88
NAA (Kansas)	Britain					38	36			9	12	3	
NAA (Kansas)	Russia								11	13		12	10
TOTAL FOR 1942		0	14	2	20	59	36	90	64	99	93	108	110
Republic	USAF											53	15
NAA (Kansas)	USAF	41	74	112	171	108	146	33	38	49	67	36	40
NAA (Kansas)	USN					20	19	6		10	14		
NAA (Kansas)	Britain					13	11		21	7	40	44	38
NAA (Kansas)	Russia	13	12	13								25	25
NAA (Kansas)	Dutch	10	16	10					2	2	9	27	2
TWA	USAF		5	29	17								
TWA	Britain					5	28						
TWA	Russia				12	12	12	14	25	36	25		
TWA	Dutch					9	4	8	7	1	4	9	
TWA	China								8	8			
Mid Cont	Britain	2		1									
Martin (Neb)	USAF										47	41	93
Martin (Neb)	China												11
Martin (Neb)	USN									21	3	25	15
NWA	USAF			35	64	13	3						
Douglas (OK)	USAF	77	55	100	1							24	27
Douglas (OK	China											26	5
TOTAL FOR 1943		143	162	300	265	180	223	61	101	134	209	310	271
Republic	USAF	9	3										
NAA (Kansas)	USAF	68	82	182	211	196	312	200	91	64	2		
NAA (Kansas)	Britain	72	33	15		34	4	37	3				
NAA (Kansas)	Dutch	7	9	9	5	5	5						
NAA (Kansas)	Russia	35	31	9	25	29	20	1					
NAA (Kansas)	USN			17	10	7	9	30					
NAA (Kansas)	China			8		4		49	1				
Martin (Neb)	USAF	96	37	78	35								
Martin (Neb)	USN	37	3	8	69	135	12						
Martin (Neb)	China		4		9								
Douglas (OK)	USAF	48	1										
TOTAL FOR 1944		372	203	326	364	410	362	317	95	64	2	0	0
TOTAL FOR YEARS 1942 - 1944		515	379	628	649	649	621	468	260	297	304	418	381

APPENDIX Y
PRINCIPAL UNITS OF B-25 ASSIGNMENT USAAF

Fifth Air Force
  3rd Bomb Group
    Squadrons: 8th 13th 89th 90th
  38th Bomb Group
    Squadrons: 69th 70th 405th 822nd 823rd
  345th Bomb Group
    Squadrons: 498th 499th 500th 501st
  22nd Bomb Group
    Squadrons: 2nd 33rd 408th
Seventh Air Force
  41st Bomb Group
    Squadrons: 47th 48th 396th 820th
Ninth Air Force
  12th Bomb Group (To 12th AF Aug 1943)
    Squadrons: 81st 82nd 83rd 434th
  340th Bomb Group(To 12th AF Aug 1943)
    Squadrons: 486th 487th 488th 489th
Tenth Air Force
  12th Bomb Group (From 12th AF Feb 1944)
  341st Bomb Group (To 11th AF Nov 1943)
    Squadrons: 11th 22nd 490th 491st
  1st Air Commando Group
    (Operated a section of 12 B-25Hs
    for several months in 1944)

Eleventh Air Force
  28th Composite Group
    Squadrons: 73rd 77th 406th
Twelfth Air Force
  12th Bomb Group (From 9th AF Aug 1943)
  310th Bomb Group
    Squadrons: 379th 380th 381st 428th
  321st Bomb Group
    Squadrons: 445th 446th 447th 448th
  340th Bomb Group (From 9th AF Aug 1943)
Thirteenth Air Force
  42nd Bomb Group
    Squadrons: 69th 70th 75th 100th 390th
Fourteenth Air Force
  1st Bomb Group (Chinese American Composite Wing)
    Squadrons: 1st 2nd 3rd 4th
  341st Bomb Group (From 10th AF Nov 1944)
    (Less 490th BS)

APPENDIX Z
EXISTING MITCHELLS

ARGENTINA
44-31172 B-25J-30
Static display at **Santiago del Estero** Airport LV-GXH as of June 1961
AUSTRALIA
41-30222 B-25D-10
Continuing restoration. Darwin Aviation Museum **Northern Territories**. Formerly 345th BG, 500th Sq later 498th BS.
44-86791 B-25J-30
Australian war memorial, Canberra . Airworthy. Restored, Stockton, California as N8196H in 1982/1983 Aero Heritage, two years as VH-XXV 'A47-31' then to Canberra War Memorial
BOLIVIA
FAB542 B-25J
USAF serial unknown static display, **Cochabamba** as of 1983 Possibly ex RCAF
BRAZIL
44-30069 B-25J-25
Static display. Museu Aerospacial (Brazilian Air Force Museum) **Rio de Janeiro** Brazilian Serial 5127
5070 (44-29500) CB-25J
Status unknown. Eduardo Andrea Matarazzo War Museum, **Bebeduoro**, Brazil
5133 B-25J
Static display at **Belem** since 1988. USAF serial unknown
CANADA
44-28866 (TB-25-N) B-25J-15
Currently in use as a borate bomber. Northwestern Air Lease **Fort Smith, Yukon**
44-30641 (44-30791?) B-25J-25
Coutts, Alberta
44-30254 B-25J-25
CF-MWC Ex RCAF 5211
44-86698 B-25J-30
C-GUNO Ex RCAF 5248 Texas to Canada 1983 Ex N543VT
45-8835 B-25J-35
C-FDKU
Formerly Bendix N69345
These three airplanes(listed above) are reported to be in use as fire bombers by G & M Aircraft, **St. Albert, Alberta**
44-86699 B-25J-30
Storage. National Aviation Museum **Ottawa, Ontario** Ex RCAF 5244
44-86726 B-25J-30
Static display. Reynolds Aviation Museum **Wetaskiwin, Alberta** Ex RCAF 5237
44-86724 B-25J-30
Static Display. Air Command Hq. CFB **Winnipeg, Manitoba** Ex RCAF 5203
45-8883 B-25J-35
Airworthy. Canadian Warplane Heritage **Hamilton, Ont.** Former Bendix, C-GCWM Ex N75755.Restored as HD372 of 98Sq RAF
CHINA
43-4120 B-25H-1
43-4329 B-25H-1
ECUADOR
44-86866 (TB-25J) B-25J-30
Static Display. Museo de La FAE **Quito** Airport Ex N 9069Z
FRANCE
45-8811 (TB-25N) B-25J-35
Airworthy. To France in 1990 N9621C "Lady Jane".
French Reg: F-AZID
INDONESIA
44-29023 B-25J-15
Static display. Indonesian Air Force Museum Adisucipto Air Base, **Yogyakarta, Central Java** M-439 Formerly Dutch N5-239
44-30399 (TB-25M) B-25J-25
Static Display. Indonesian Armed Forces Museum, **Jakarta** M-458 Formerly Dutch N5-258

MEXICO
44-29128 B-25J-20
Static Display. pole mounted, Technical Museum, Chapultepec Park, **Mexico City** Ex N92872
NETHERLANDS
41-30792 B-25D-20
Static display. National Orlogs en Verzetsmuseum, **Overloon** Formerly FR 193, 320 Squadron, Royal Netherlands Naval Air Service (MLD)
44-29507 (TB-25N) B-25J-20
Airworthy. Ex N3698G Markings 320 Sq RAF
44-31258 B-25J-30
Static Display. Militaire Luchtvaart Museum **Soesterberg** M-464 Formerly N5-264 Donated by Indonesian Government 1971
PAPUA, NEW GUINEA
41-12442 B-25C
Static Display. **Aitape** Recovered in NG 1974
41-30163 B-25D-5
Static Display. National Museum **Port Moresby**
SPAIN
44-29121 B-25J-20
Static Display. (Restored) Museo del Aire Cuatro Vientos, **Madrid** Ex N86427
UNITED KINGDOM
43-3318 B-25D-30
The Fighter Collection **Duxford**, Airworthy 'Grumpy' Ex N88972, CF-OGQ and RCAF KL161
44-29366 (TB-25N) B-25J-20
Static Display. Bomber Command Museum, **Hendon** Ex N9115Z Catch 22
44-30823 (B-25J-25)
Airworthy Aces High., **North Weald, Essex** Catch 22 camera airplane to North Weald 1988
44-30861 (TB-25N) B-25J-25
Static Display. **North Weald, Essex** Ex N9089Z
44-30925 (TB-25N) B-25J-30
Dismantled. **Coventry** Former Catch 22 N9494Z Pending restoration
44-31171 (JTB-25J) B-25J-30
Restoration to static display. Imperial War Museum, **Duxford** Ex N7614C
UNITED STATES
40-2168 B-25-NA
Airworthy. under further restoration at **Chino, California** Fourth B-25 off production line. N2825B, former Hughes Tool Co. N75831 'The General' (See Transports & Trainers)
40-2347 B-25B-NA
In storage. incomplete Aero Trader, **Chino California**. Full restoration possible.
41-13251 B -25C-1
Static display. Milestones of Flight Museum Fox Field, **Lancaster, California** N3968C Ex Hughes Tool Co.
41-13285, B-25C-1
Static Display, South Carolina State Museum,**Columbia, South Carolina**
41-29784 (TB-25D) B-25D
Static display. Patriots Point Naval and Maritime Museum **Charleston Harbor, South Carolina** N2XD, Ex N2DD, N122B, N5078N
42-32354 B-25C-10
Storage. Major airframe parts only Aero Trader, **Chino, California**
43-3308 B-25D-30
Static display. as PBJ-1D USMC Air-Ground Museum **Quantico, Virginia**. Brought from La Paz, Bolivia
43-3374 (PBJ) B-25D-30
Static display. US Air Force Museum Wright Patterson AFB **Dayton, Ohio** Formerly photo mapping F-10 displayed as 40-2344
43-3634 B-25D-35
Airworthy. Yankee Air Museum Willow Run Airport **Ypsilanti, Michigan** N3774 Ex RCAF KL148, CF-NWV 'Yankee Warrior'

43-4030 (VB-25J) B-25J-1
Static display. South Dakota Air & Space Museum, **Ellsworth AFB South Dakota** since 1984 N3339G (See 'Transports & Trainers')
43-4106 B-25H-1
Airworthy. Weary Warriors Squadron **Rockford, Ilinois** Former Bendix aircraft Restored as 1st Air Commando Gp. N5548N 'Barbie III'
43-4432 B25H-5
Experimental Aircraft Association Museum **Oshkosh, Wisconsin** N10V Ex N90399 Catch 22 Aircraft
43-4899 B-25H-10
Static Display. Kalamazoo Aviation History Museum, **Kalamazoo, Michigan** N37L Ex N1582V
43-4999 B-25H-10
Under restoration. New England Air Museum **Windsor Locks, Connecticut** N3970C
43-5103 B-25H-10
Static display. **Lackland AFB, Texas**
43-28834 B-25J-1
Static display. Grand Forks AFB **Grand Forks, North Dakota**
43-27712 (TB-25N) B-25J-1
Static display. Pima Air Museum **Tucson, Arizona**
43-27868 (TB-25N) B-25J-5
Airworthy.'Yellow Rose' Confederate Air Force Yellow Rose Squadron **San Antonio, Texas** N25YR, Ex N9077Z
43-28059 (TB-25N) B-25J-5
Restoration to airworthy. Weeks Air Museum **Tamiami Airport, Florida** N1943J, Ex N26975, N9857C
43-28204 (TB-25N) B-25J-10
Airworthy. Aero Trader, **Chino, California** 'Pacific Princess; N9856C Catch 22 aircraft
43-28222 (TB-25N) B-25J-10
Static display. Edward F. Beale Museum, **Beale AFB California** N5256V
43-35972 B-25J-10
Under restoration. Confederate Air Force, Arizona Wing, Falcon Field, **Mesa, Arizona** N9552Z
44-28738 (TB-25N)B-25J-15
Strategic Air Command Museum **Offut AFB, Nebraska.** Sectional display N3441G
44-28765 (VB-25N) B-25J-15
Aero Trader, **Chino, California.** In storage, dismantled N9443Z
44-28844 B-25J-15
Static Display. Grand Forks AFB **Grand Forks, North Dakota**
44-28875 (TB-25J) B-25J-15
Goodfellow AFB **San Angelo, Texas.** Not on general display
44-28925 (TB-25N) B-25J-15
Under restoration. **New Smyrna Beach Airport, Florida** N7687C Former Catch 22 aircraft
44-28932 (TB-25N) B-25J-15
Under restoration. Collings Foundation **Stowe, Massachussetts** N3476G
44-28938 (TB-25N) B-25J-15
Under restoration to airworthy. Aero Nostalgia **Stockton, California** Airport N7946C 'Dream Lover'.
44-29035 (TB-25N) B-25J-15
Crated, **Atlanta, Georgia**
44-29127 (TB-25N) B-25J-20
Under restoration to airworthy. Colvin Aircraft **Big Cabin, Oklahoma** N9899C
44-29199 (TB-25N) B-25J-20
Airworthy. **Rialto, California** N9117Z 'In The Mood'
44-29465 (TB-25N) B-25J-20
Airworthy. **Frazer, Michigan** N25GL, Ex N3523G 'Guardian of Freedom'
44-29812 (TB-25N) B-25J-20
Poor condition. City Park, **Brainerd, Minnesota** NN2854G
44-29835 (TB-25N) B-25J-20
Static Display. USAF History & Traditions Museum, **Lackland AFB, Texas** N3676G
44-29869 (TB-25K) B-25J-20
Airworthy. Confederate Air Force, Southern Minnesota Wing, Fleming Field, **So.St. Paul, Minnesota** 'Miss Mitchell' N27493 Ex N3160G

44-29887 (TB-25N) B-25J-20
Storage. National Air & Space Museum **Washington, D.C.** N10564 Catch 22 Aircraft
44-29939(TB-25N) B-25J-25
Airworthy. Mid-Atlantic Air Museum **Reading Municipal Airport Pennsylvania** N9456Z'Briefing Time' Catch 22 aircraft
44-29943 (TB-25N) B-25J-25
Under restoration. **Fairacres, New Mexico** N943 Ex N9444Z
44-30077 (TB-25N) B-25J-25
Dismantled for restoration. **Kissimmee, Florida** N2849C Catch 22
44-30090 (TB-25K) B-25J-25
Dismantled for restoration. Aero Trader, **Chino, California** N9633C
44-30129 (TB-25K) B-25J-25
Atlanta, GA N7947C Being restored to airworthy
44-30203 B-25J-25
From Venezuela. Disassembled, restorable to airworthy. **Santa Rosa, California.**
44-30210 (TB-25J) B-25J-25
Believed static display. March AFB Museum, **Riverside, California** N9455Z 'Big Bad Bonnie'
44-30243 (TB-25N) B-25J-25
Dismantled for restoration. **Kissimmee, Florida** N17666, Ex N9622C
44-30302 B-25J-25
Crated, **Atlanta, Georgia**
44-30324 (TB-25N) B-25J-25
Reported Airworthy. On loan in Massachussetts N3161G
44-30363 (TB-25M) B-25J-25
Static display. Strategic Air Command Museum, **Bellevue, Nebraska**
44-30423 (JB-25J) B-25J-25
Airworthy. Planes of Fame Air Museum **Chino, California** N3675G 'Photo Fanny'
44-30444 (TB-25M) B-25J-25
Static display. General Mitchell Field **Milwaukee, Wisconsin**
44-30456 (TB-25L) B-25J-25
Airworthy. **Breckenridge, Texas** N43BA, Ex C-GTTS, N3512G 'Silver Lady'
44-30493 (TB-25N) B-25J-25
Static display. Malmstrom AFB Museum **Great Falls, Montana.** N9451Z Catch 22 Aircraft
44-30535 (TB-25N) B-25J-25
Static display. Liberal Air Museum **Liberal, Kansas** N9462Z 'Iron Laiden Maiden' Restored as 8 gun nose strafer of 498 BS,345 BG
44-30606 (TB-25N) B-25J-25
Airworthy. **Carson City, Nevada** N201L, Ex N5249V 'Tootsie'
44-30627 B-25J-25
Crated, Restorable, **Atlanta, Georgia**
44-30635 (TB-25L) B-25J-25
Chanute AFB Tech. Tng. Center **Rantoul, Illinois** Static display as 40-2270 of the Doolittle Raiders.
44-30649 (TB-25N) B-25J-25
Static display. Maxwell AFB Museum **Montgomery, Alabama.** Ex 9452Z Catch 22 Aircraft
44-30734 (TB -25J) B-25J-25
Airworthy. **Niagara Falls, New York**, N9079Z 'Panchito'
44-30748 (TB-25N) B-25J-25
Under restoration. **San Fernando, California** N8195H, Ex N3447G 'Heavenly Body' Marked as 390 BS, 42 BG Catch 22 Aircraft.
44-30756 (TB-25N) B-25J-25
In storage. Aero Trader, **Chino, California** N9936Z Basic airframe complete
44-30801 (TB-25N) B-25J-25
Airworthy. **Van Nuys, California** N30801, Ex N3699G 'Executive Sweet' Ex Catch 22 Aircraft
44-30832 (TB-25N) B-25J-25
Airworthy. **Arvada, Colorado** N3155G, 'Can Do'
44-30854 (TB-25N) B-25J-25
Static display. USAF Armament Museum Eglin AFB **Valparaiso, Florida**
44-30988 B-25J-30
Airworthy. Confederate Air Force **Harlingen, Texas** N5865V 'Big Ole Brew 'N Little Ole You'. Reported for sale.

44-31004 (TB-25J) B-25J-30
Under restoration. USS Alabama **Mobile, Alabama** N9463Z
44-31032 (TB-25J) B-25J-30
Static Display. March AFB Museum **Riverside California** N3174G, Ex
Catch 22 Aircraft
44-31121 B-25J-30
Restorable, **Atlanta, Georgia**
44-31385 (TB-25J) B-25J-30
Airworthy. Confederate Air Force, Missouri Wing, **St. Louis, Missouri**
N3481G Restored as 345 BG 'Show Me'
44-31504 B-25J-30
Static Display. Hickam AFB Collection, **Hawaii** N9753Z, Ex RCAF
5218
44-31508 (TB-25K) B-25J-30
Airworthy. **Ocala, Florida** Battle of Britain camera aircraft in the UK &
Spain, 1968-1969, N6578D 'Chapter XI'
44-86697 B-25J-30
Crated, **Atlanta, Georgia**
44-86715 (TB-25N) B-25J-30
Under restoration to airworthy. **Rialto, California** N3442G
44-86725 B-25J-30
Under restoration. **New Smyrna Beach, Florida** N25NA, Ex Bolivia
FAV 5880 and Venezuela FAB 541, both unconfirmed. RCAF 5243
N25NA in 1985
44-86727 B-25J-30
Static display. El Toro Marine Corps Air Station, **Santa Ana, California**
N92875 Ex RCAF 5230
44-86734 (TB-25N) B-25J-30
Airworthy. Lone Star Flight Museum Hobby Field, **Houston, Texas**
N333RW , ExN600DM N9090Z 'Special Delivery'
44-86747 (TB-25N) B-25J-30
Airworthy. Planes of Fame East, Flying Cloud Airport **Eden Prairie,
Minnesota** N8163H 'Mitch The Witch'
44-86758 (TB-25K) B-25J-30
Airworthy. Confederate Air Force **Harlingen, Texas** Restored with 8
gun nose shell and markings of USMC VMB-612 N9643C

44-86772 (TB-25N) B-25J-30
N9333Z, disassembled, **Ft. Lauderdale, Florida**
44-86777 (TB-25J) B-25J-30
Airworthy. **Cincinnati, Ohio** N9176Z 'Man of War', 345 BG colors.
44-86785 (TB-25K) B-25J-30
Airworthy. **Troy, Alabama** N5262V 'Georgia Mae'
44-86797 (TB-25J) B-25J-30
Airworthy. **Troy, Alabama** N3438G 'The Old Gray Mare'
44-86843 (TB-25J) B-25J-30
Static display. **Grissom AFB Heritage Museum, Indiana** N3507G
Catch 22 aircraft 'Passionate Paulette'
44-86872 (TB-25J) B-25J-30
Static display.**Robins AFB Museum, Georgia** N2888G
44-86880 (TB-25L) B-25J-30
Static display. Reese AFB collection **Lubbock, Texas**
44-86891 (JB-25J) B-25J-30
Static display. Castle Air Museum, **Atwater, California** Restored as
40-2344 Ex N3337G
44-86893 (TB-25K) B-25J-35
Airworthy. Kansas City Warbirds, Richards Gebaur AFB, Missouri
Combat Air Museum, Forbes Field, **Topeka, Kansas** (For sale early
1992) N6123C 'Fairfax Ghost'
45-8882 B-25J-35
Aero Traders **Chino, California** N32T, Ex N75754 Forward Section
Only Remainder in New Smyrna, Florida
45-8884 (TB-25J) B-25J-35
Airworthy. **Alpharetta, Georgia** N5833B, Ex C-GCWJ, Ex N3156G
'Georgia Girl'
45-8887 (TB-25N) B-25J-35
Dismantled, stored Aero Trader, **Chino, California** N3680G
45-8898 (TB-25N) B-25J-35
Airworthy. **Scottsdale, Arizona** RAF Color Scheme N898BW
VENEZUELA
44-30369 B-25J-25
Static display, FAV 5-B-40 Museo Aeronautico, **Maracay**.
US Serial unknown:
FAV 4-B-40 static display at entrance to **Teniente Vincente Landaeta
Gil Base** at **Barquisimeto**

**Not a World War II flight line, but Holman Field, St. Paul, August 1992. For the Confederate Air Force, Southern Minnesota Wing, Air Show
four B-25 survivors muster: (left to right: MITCH THE BITCH, HOT GEN., MISS MITCHELL, and YANKEE WARRIOR.**